# SIX QUESTIONS OF SOCRATES

Also by Christopher Phillips

*Socrates Café*

*The Philosophers' Club* (children's book)

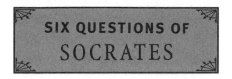

**SIX QUESTIONS OF**
# SOCRATES

A Modern-Day Journey of Discovery
through World Philosophy

## CHRISTOPHER PHILLIPS

W. W. Norton & Company
New York  London

Copyright © 2004 by Christopher Phillips

Manufacturing by the Haddon Craftsmen, Inc.
Book design by Blue Shoe Studio
Production manager: Julia Druskin

Library of Congress Cataloging-in-Publication Data

Phillips, Christopher, 1959 July 15–
  Six questions of Socrates : a modern-day journey of discovery through world philosophy / Christopher Phillips.
    p. cm.
Includes bibliographical references and index.
  **ISBN 0-393-05157-9**
  1. Virtues. I. Title.
  BJ1521.P45 2004
  179'.9—dc22

                                                    2003018200

W. W. Norton & Company, Inc.
500 Fifth Avenue, New York, N.Y. 10110
www.wwnorton.com

W. W. Norton & Company Ltd.
Castle House, 75/76 Wells Street, London W1T 3QT

3 4 5 6 7 8 9 0

For Cecilia,
*luz de mi vida*

# CONTENTS

WHAT IS

VIRTUE?

# *ARETE* INTERRUPTED

"I don't think that virtue—what we call *arete*—exists anymore." No such thing as virtue? How can that be, in this of all places?

I'm in the ancient *agora* of Athens, Greece, and I have just posed the question "What is virtue?" About twenty of us are huddled together in a tranquil spot amid the relentless bustle of this sprawling city of four million, which is readying to host the 2004 Summer Olympics. *Agora* typically is translated as "marketplace," but I think a more appropriate translation is "gathering place" (in fact, the noun *agora* comes from the Greek verb *ageiro*, which means "to gather"). Those who converged centuries ago in this center of commercial and civic life didn't just come to barter and sell a wide range of merchandise, but also to exchange and examine ideas and ideals. The *agora* was situated in the heart of the Athenian *polis*, or city-state, the cradle of the first genuine democracy, which Pulitzer Prize–winning historian Daniel Boorstin said was responsible for the "grand concepts that for the Western world would define morals, create communities, cement nations, and build empires." That so many lasting and noble achievements, says Boorstin, "should have come from so few"—its population was a mere eighty thousand—"is another miracle of classic Greece."

Most tourists milling about the area pay us no mind as we sit in the shade among the ruins of the stoa of the Greek god *Zeus Eleutherios*— or Zeus "the Deliverer"—which was erected here to commemorate those who'd fought to win freedom for the Greek city-states, and to honor Zeus, who Greeks at the time believed delivered them to freedom. Where we're sitting, on pieces of marble that were once pillars of the stoa, is almost precisely where in the fifth century B.C. Socrates gathered with friends and acquaintances and antagonists to engage in philosophical dialogue.

—

All our eyes are now fixed on Maria, the woman who has just spoken. I don't seem to be the only one taken aback by this first response out of the starting gate. Before I can ask her why she believes there's no longer such a thing as virtue, or *arete*, another participant looks at her and says, "Was there ever such a thing as virtue?"

"Oh yes," Maria says. "Most definitely."

"How so?" I ask.

She does not respond right away. Maria, an artist, is a distant cousin of mine whom I met for the first time the previous day. She moved a decade ago to Athens from the volcanic island of Nissyros, part of the country's Dodecanese Islands, from which my father's parents immigrated to the United States in 1922. At a time when Greece, ruled by the constitutional monarchy of George II, was mired in miserable economic straits, made worse by an ongoing war with Turkey, my grandparents entered through Ellis Island, where their last name was summarily changed from Philipou to Phillips.

"Look around you," Maria says now. "What do you see? Magnificent ruins. You see the remains of a society that was steeped in virtue. Where we're sitting now, where Socrates held court, is the most virtuous place of all—an oasis of virtue."

She makes a sweeping gesture toward the breathtaking and largely intact Parthenon temple perched in the distance on the Acropolis Hill, which the Athenian ruler Pericles had ordered built as a monument to the cultural and political achievements over which he'd presided. Maria says, "The Parthenon, and all these ruins around us, are the product of virtue, of great minds and souls, free from illusions, soaring to heights never before or since attained." Her voice full of passion, she goes on: "They make your spirit soar. They inspire you to imagine new possibilities of what it is to be a human."

Then she says, "When I say that I'm not sure there's such a thing as virtue anymore, I mean that if we're no longer creating the *products* of virtue, then it seems to me that virtue itself can no longer exist. We can't boast anymore that we're creating great works of art and architecture. We can't boast anymore of having a democracy that's the envy of the world. We can't boast of having great playwrights and great public intellectuals, like Socrates and his peers Aeschylus and Sophocles, who didn't just create products of virtue, but *were* products of virtue. We haven't had any of these products of virtue for centuries. So how can we have virtue itself?"

A man named Giorgos, who'd strolled by as we were getting under way, and was intrigued enough to join in, now says, "This *agora* was just excavated and rediscovered several decades ago. Soon after Socrates' death, it was abandoned, and the public life was abandoned along with it. Without a public life, where everyone feels like they're reaching toward greater heights than they can reach alone, there can't be virtue."

He falls silent, his long beard blowing one way and then the next, at the whim of the ever-changing direction of the wind blowing in from the Aegean Sea. Then he says, "This is the place where Socrates asked: What is justice, *dikeosyni*? What is virtue, *arete*? What is moderation, *sophrosune*? What is courage, *andreia*? What is good, *agathos*? What is piety, *eusebeia*? He didn't just want to gain a better understanding of the nature of virtue and its qualities, by asking these questions. He wanted to apply his discoveries, so he and others could realize their nobler potentials. Who does this anymore?"

Renet, the woman seated beside him, says, "I think people were scared to do it after what happened to Socrates. They convicted him on trumped-up charges of being a heretic and traitor, as a message to all the others who inquired with him that they'd better quit their critiques of the corrupt rulers." She points to a nearby field, where wild-flowers are growing. "That's where he's said to have drunk the small cup of hemlock, and died. He hoped that others would be inspired by his example, and would continue questioning more than ever. But when he died, virtue died too."

Eleftheria, a librarian and a friend of Maria, now says, "We declared the year two thousand and one the 'Year of Socrates' in Greece. There were all these conferences and readings. We did reenactments of Plato's Socratic dialogues. We had more Socrates impersonators than you have Elvis impersonators in your country. But we didn't hold one dialogue as we're doing now. It wouldn't have occurred to us, we're so far removed from the type of questioning Socrates practiced. We treat Socrates like a musty museum piece. So we no longer live the examined life that he modeled."

"So," I say, aiming to steer her heartfelt response so it connects with the question we're examining, "virtue is . . ."

"Virtue," Eleftheria says, "is questioning convictions, with the intent of discovering a higher purpose in life, and then pursuing that purpose, so you can become more excellent, and in the process, inspire your society to become more excellent."

"What do you mean by 'higher purpose'?" I ask.

"Something that's greater than yourself," says Patti, a high school student who, we'd discovered earlier in the day, is also a distant relative of mine. "The Athenian civilization that existed back before Socrates' adulthood is the best example. They worked together to create an open society where everyone could develop their talents to the fullest. They had a perfect combination of selfishness and selflessness, because they knew you couldn't reach higher ground without helping your society reach it too."

Then Nikos, a junior-high-school student, says, "Virtue isn't something to be defined, really. It's something to be lived. Like, when Socrates was having dialogues here, his society was no longer living the virtuous life. Socrates and company began asking, 'What is virtue?' because they'd quit living virtue. When you have to start asking what virtue is, that's a sure sign that you've stopped being virtuous."

"Is that always true?" I query. "Can it really hurt, while you're living the virtuous life, to ask what virtue is from time to time? Just to be on the safe side? Or maybe to see if your idea of virtue agrees with others'?"

His girlfriend, Zoe, says, "Maybe that was the problem in the first place. The Athenians didn't step back and ask themselves what exactly it was they were doing, until it was too late. What we're doing now, exploring what virtue is and isn't, can be an example of virtue in action, because we have a chance to learn more about virtue, and how to act on what we learn. Like, this dialogue has me thinking that the road to virtue is one you create for yourself. It seems like no two people, and no two societies, take the same road to become more virtuous. But I think they all have the same starting place. They all start by asking, 'What is virtue?' because only by answering that question can you then answer, 'How can we become more virtuous?' "

Antonis, a retired history professor, says, "Socrates never arrived at a final answer to any of the questions he posed about virtue. I don't think he expected to. He left it up to generations to come to discover a more final answer. But if we no longer ask the questions he asked, we'll never learn more about virtue, never become more virtuous, because we won't have new answers to experiment with."

"What do you mean by experiment?" I ask.

"Socrates asked certain questions about virtue to discover how to heal his ailing society. The more he examined these questions, the more he was able to discover and experiment with possible 'cures.' "

We fall silent until Maria says, "I think the way Socrates chose to die is what virtue is all about. He chose to die with *aksyoprepya*, dignity, and *akereotyta*, integrity, because that was the way he lived."

After a moment further to collect her thoughts, she goes on, "Virtue is choosing a way of life that's so excellent, you'd rather sacrifice your life than sacrifice your way of life."

"Do you really have to be willing to sacrifice your life?" I ask.

"I think you have to be willing to sacrifice who you are at any given moment," she says. "Socrates experienced continual death and rebirth, in his quest to become more virtuous. In the dialogues he held here, he had the courage to open himself up to others' views, and to do justice to them, by carefully considering and weighing them against his own. He was this way because of his piety to the pursuit of virtue. He never emerged unchanged from a dialogue."

She pauses before then saying, "Socrates never showed his essential goodness more than in the moment he drank the hemlock. I disagree that when he died, virtue died too. He died so that virtue would live on."

## ALL THE WORLD'S AN *AGORA*

In *Essays*, the French Renaissance intellectual Michel Montaigne (1533–92), who devoted himself to the study of human nature, wrote: "Someone asked Socrates what country he was from. His reply wasn't 'I'm from Athens.' Instead, Socrates replied, 'I'm of the world.'" Montaigne goes on to say that Socrates "embraced the whole world as his city. . . ." Though Socrates may have claimed to be a citizen of the world, he pretty much stayed put in Athens. He wouldn't even leave when he was told that if he didn't go into exile, he would be put to death. He apparently felt he could best set an example of a person imbued with universal and timeless virtues if he put them into practice at home, at a time when the Greek city-state was unraveling, and when leading the virtuous life was no longer held in high esteem.

I'm not sure if I think of myself as a citizen of the world, but more and more of the world has served as my *agora*. Over the last several years, I've traveled to a number of far-flung places to hold philosophical dialogues. In doing so, I have been following in Socrates' footsteps at least in this respect: Wherever I go, I've been asking six questions asked by the historical Socrates, and about which Plato wrote in his early dialogues.[1] By doing so, I've taken for my own his quest to discover more about the nature and potential of human excellence, and the type of virtue, or set of virtues, a person or a society needs in order to become more excellent. These six questions are: What is virtue? What is moderation? What is courage? What is justice? What is piety? What is good?[2]

———

My travels have taken me to places like Greece and Spain in Europe, and Japan and Korea in Asia. I've ventured throughout Mexico—from Mexico City, the largest city in the world, to the remote outpost of Chiapas, where the region's indigenous people still struggle for fundamental human rights. I have traveled extensively throughout the United States, from New York City to the Navajo Nation. I've taken part in dialogues in the United States with immigrants from Islamic nations, and with university students who have come here from Israel and the Palestinian territory and other Middle Eastern nations. Besides holding dialogues with people of all walks of life in such places as cafés and community centers and plazas—including a plaza

---

1. As Terry Penner, professor of philosophy at the University of Wisconsin at Madison, writes in *The Cambridge Companion to Plato*, "the character Socrates" in Plato's early dialogues "speaks more or less for the historical Socrates," whereas in the middle and later dialogues, "the main character (now not always Socrates) speaks rather for Plato."

2. These English translations of the original Greek words of course can be translated otherwise, though I think these words in most contexts do the Greek originals adequate justice.

where one of the most tragic human-rights protests in modern history took place—I've also been to places such as a public-housing project, a homeless shelter, a maximum-security prison, a mental-health institute. In all these dialogues, I hoped to gain a greater understanding, from a multicultural and multiexperiential standpoint, of virtue and its role in human excellence.

These experiences also inspired me to delve into the philosophical and religious and cultural traditions of the people with whom I engaged in dialogue. Along the way, I discovered numerous philosophical thinkers who were kindred spirits of Socrates. In many ways, these individuals were paradigms of virtue and autonomy who, in challenging the received "wisdom" of their day, and quite often risking their lives in the process, engaged in a lifelong pursuit of a rare type of excellence. Each believed that an individual's most creative and liberating potentials could not be reached unless society as a whole also strove for such ends. Many of them, particularly non-Western philosophers, remain unheralded or altogether overlooked in even the most comprehensive encyclopedias and dictionaries of philosophy. Those that are included tend to be noted for their technical works, with little or no mention of their active and outspoken involvement in public affairs—as if this involvement did not have philosophical intent or content, and did not matter or count in terms of their philosophical contribution. Yet in most instances their public outreach represents their most significant and lasting contribution to philosophy, and humanity. Their refusal to play it safe, as they immersed themselves in the most vexing issues of their day, was based on a philosophical code that would have made it unconscionable *not* to play a vital role in public life, when their societies were at critical crossroads. To them, as with Socrates, casting one's lot with the rest of humanity was the paramount duty of a philosopher.

—

Why did I ask just these particular six questions? Was Socrates saying that if one delved into these six specific questions, using a certain method of inquiry that he originated, then all the answers at which one could ever hope to arrive about the nature and potential of human excellence were there for the taking? I don't think so. I'm sure Socrates explored many other questions besides these six, and that the extant dialogues of Plato's that feature the historical Socrates and that have been passed down to us represent just a fraction of Socrates' curiosity on the subject. Still, I'd be hard-pressed to imagine a philosophical investigation into human excellence that *didn't* include these six questions, so they seem an ideal springboard to launch into a modern inquiry into the subject.

The Socrates scholar Laszlo Versenyi writes in *Socratic Humanism* that these questions were "merely different ways of asking the same fundamental question, "What is man?" and that Socrates was asking "not only the same" question, "but the same about the same . . . circling around the same center, approaching the same thing from seemingly different directions." While I agree that each of the six questions is, in a sense, asking "the same about the same," I don't think Socrates was primarily asking "What is man?" Rather, he was asking, "What is humankind capable of?" and "How can we become more excellent?"

—

My own pursuit, to discover an array of timely answers to these timeless questions about the virtuous life, is not in any way meant to be the end point of inquiry. My hope is that it might serve as a launching pad to inspire readers, as they immerse themselves in these dialogues, to come up with their own answers, then to put them into effect, experiment with them. In fact, as some participants at the Athens *agora* suggested, engaging in dialogue about these questions can be one way of putting them into practice.

I was also prompted to ask these six questions at this particular juncture in human history, at the beginning of the twenty-first century, for much the same reason that Socrates asked them in fifth century B.C. Athens: A number of patterns seem to be recurring today, in most of the places I've traveled, that mirror the travails that beset Athens in its days of decline, when Socrates was philosophizing. Like then, many people in the places I visited worry that their societies are becoming morally rudderless, in some cases to such an extreme that the fabric of society threatens to unravel. Just as in Athens, many with whom I engaged in dialogue are concerned about growing corruption in the political and economic spheres, and the increasing cynicism and alienation that this has fomented among ordinary citizens. Athens of the Golden Age had seemed above and even immune to such failings, much less to suffering them to such a remarkable degree—making its precipitous decline all the more stunning. But many today wonder whether such a downward spiral in their own societies is inevitable, or if it can be stemmed and reversed.

This seemed to me a critical moment to hold dialogues around the globe on these foundational questions about human excellence. And it seemed that the answers we discovered together might help all of us better understand how we got ourselves into this predicament, how we might learn from mistakes and successes of the past and present, and how we might get out of it. My efforts in this regard make no pretense of exhaustiveness in scope. I do try, though, to present a careful look at the value systems of the cultures and societies of those with whom I engage in dialogue, and hope this might inspire readers to delve even deeper into these and many other cultures besides. Learning about the unique ways of world-viewing and world-making of people around the globe and across the ages can serve as one valuable way of helping and informing those today and in the future who embark on their own quest to lead a more excellent life.

—

Like Plato, I use some license in fashioning the dialogues adapted here from the actual dialogues in which I took part, in order to reflect *more* faithfully the tone and tenor and substance of what took place. To this end, the actual dialogues best serve as a template from which to cull and structure and compose. However, I suspect that Plato often culled and refined too much. The participants in his written dialogues on the six questions do not often mention concrete examples to support their abstract thinking. More rarely still do they make specific reference to the many salient and pressing social issues of their times, in which they were embroiled, even though these issues relate directly to the six questions, and are surely the inspiration for them. This silence of Plato's has led to a great deal of guesswork by scholars, whose efforts at filling in these gaps, and setting the contextual stage for these dialogues in the political and social turmoil of ancient Athens, have met with mixed results at best.

There is a widespread misperception that framing philosophical questions within timely contexts somehow dates and diminishes them. Just the opposite is true. By looking at how these questions are conducive to examining particular issues in specific places and times, we can better see how certain universal patterns emerge, and we can better apply them as we grapple with the pressing problems of today and tomorrow.

## A PATCHWORK HARMONY

"What is virtue?" I ask the gathering of about eighteen members of the Navajo Nation with whom I am gathered, sitting in a circle, at a community center in a remote outpost on the reservation.

The seventeen-million-acre reservation is the largest in the United States, and covers parts of Arizona, New Mexico, Colorado, and Utah, where about 160,000 of the 200,000 members of the Navajo Nation dwell. Although originally a nomadic tribe, the Navajo—who call themselves *Dineh*, 'the People'—are one of the few tribes, of more than five hundred federally recognized tribes, whose reservation is on the same land they once roamed.

"Virtue is that which brings everything into harmony," says eighteen-year-old Jimmy. "Our word for this 'bringing into harmony' is *hozho*."

His girlfriend, Maria, adds, "The closer you come to *hozho*, the closer you come to a type of beauty and order and harmony that makes you and everyone around you ... happy."

"Are beauty and harmony and order virtues themselves, or are they qualities that make up virtue?" I ask.

Jimmy's father replies, "They're parts of virtue. But they're not all of it. If you still practice traditional Navajo ways, then you believe that every move you make must be done with the idea of bringing yourself into harmony with your total environment, or *ho*, which is made up of things like nature, family, tribe, society, country, planet, universe."

He reflects further and then says, "Even that doesn't really cover it. Because all types of harmony—spiritual, mental, physical—must be '*in* harmony' with one another for there to be *hozho*. You can always be in a more perfect state of *hozho*."

"Even the way we herd our sheep between summer and winter camp is a part of *hozho*," his wife says. "The sheep care for us, provide for us, and we do the same for them. This contributes to *hozho*. Before I tend my sheep each day, I pray to the Holy People, and give thanks to them for the sheep and how they help make my life more harmonious."

Her elderly mother then says, "The most important thing, in order to have *hozho*, is that you must 'walk in Beauty.' Every morning, before sunrise, you must run toward the sun to greet the day. This is the Beauty Way."

She goes on: "Every dawn is a new day. If you run toward the sacred sun, if you greet and embrace it as it rises, you are blessed with a new beginning, a new chance for *hozho*."

One of the older adolescents taking part in our dialogue now says, "Even if you failed miserably the previous day—like, even if you couldn't quit using drugs or alcohol—you have a new chance with the rising sun to walk in beauty. When you walk in beauty, you don't dwell on yesterday and how you failed. You focus on today, and on how you can overcome those things within you that kept you from *hozho*."

Jimmy's grandfather, Hosteen, says to me, "To get back in harmony, traditionally a medicine man would perform a healing ceremony of chanting and dancing and singing, and he would create sand paintings, using sand from our sacred places inhabited by our gods. The sand painting helps restore *hozho* to someone who has fallen off the path."

"It's not just the sand painting itself that must be harmonious, but the way it is made," he continues. "How you go about making any work of art is just as important as the finished product. The artist must have *hozho* in order for his work to have beauty and order and harmony—and, I would add, balance—and to transmit it to the person who looks at it."

According to scholar David Maybury-Lewis, the Navajo conception of *hozho* "requires the individual not merely to create beauty sporadically, but to think it, act it, and live in it constantly." It "requires a determination that the aesthetic not be reduced to a commodity and ourselves passive consumers of it." He says *hozho* is imbued with the "conviction that creativity and imagination are essential to our lives. It requires us to break the vicious cycle of compartmentalization that obliges us to live and work in a functional world that leaves little room for aesthetic response."

Twenty-year-old Michael then says, "After September eleventh, my friend's grandfather made a sand painting as a way of helping restore *hozho* to the world. He thinks people everywhere are hurting worse than ever. These paintings usually are made to heal just one person who is hurting. But he looks at the universe itself as one being, and he made this painting to heal the hurting universe."

Like Navajo medicine men, Tibetan monks revere nature itself as sacred, and they also traditionally have created an intricate type of sand painting, which they call *mandala*, of colored sand, taken from sacred places, to bring about healing that restores harmony. Also like the Navajo, the sand painting to them represents the cosmos in a state of perfect harmony, and they share the Navajo belief that the person making the sand painting must himself be in harmony.

Michael pauses before adding, "My friend's grandfather says we have to start realizing that we're all connected, or we're going to destroy what little harmony there is left."

Scholar Gary Witherspoon says in *Language and Art in the Navajo Universe* that the Navajo process of creating a more harmonious universe is through "prayer, ritual, ceremony, myth, song, and art," which heals the "sickness-illness in both the mind and in the body, fragmentation in the environment and in the universe, disharmony in customary relationships and holistic schemes," created by *hochxo*, or evil. Because of their holistic way of looking at the world, good and evil are not opposites to the Navajo, but rather parts of the same whole—and so out of evil, good can be created. Anthropologist Gladys A. Reichard writes in *Navajo Religion* that the Navajo "is concerned with maintaining harmony with all things, with subsistence and the orderly replenishment of his own kind." She says they believe they must play an active role in accomplishing this, since in the natural state of the universe, "dangers, evils, and mistakes . . . exist."

There is a long silence that is finally broken when Elizabeth says to me, "*Hozho* is what has given us the ability to adapt and endure, no matter the hardships."

This leads me to ask, "Can you adapt too much? Can you 'adjust' so much that you lose the essence of who you are?"

"It depends on what you mean by adapt," she replies. "You can adapt in ways that aren't, like, selling out. What I'm talking about isn't the kind of adapting where you're like a chameleon, where you'll be anyone or anything that anybody wants you to be. When you adapt within, when you accept the way things are outside you, those things you can't control, then you change how things are within *and* without. Because you look at the outside world differently when you bring your inside world into harmony with the outside world. Like, I can live in resentment about all the bad things that have been done to our people. Or I can accept the past as the past and make the most of the way things are now."

"That's not the same thing as resignation?" I ask.

"No, because to be resigned would be to be passive. To be resigned would be not to change. But adapting means change. And change, the way I'm talking about it, means growing as a human being, bringing yourself more in harmony with the universe, and so becoming more virtuous."

Says an elderly man, "Change is constant. Even if outsiders hadn't come to our part of the world and tried to destroy us, to steal our land from us and destroy our culture, there would have been other tragedies, other catastrophes. For instance, lately we've had a bad drought. Most people in the rest of the world would try to 'fight' the drought, and make a bad situation worse. But we look for its beauty— how it fits in the grand scheme of things—so we can live in harmony with it."

Tony Hillerman, the popular New Mexico writer whose novels of the Navajos are as known for their comprehensive grasp of Navajo

ways as they are for the gripping tales themselves, gives this example
of *hozho* in his book *Sacred Clowns*:

> Terrible drought, crops dead, sheep dying. Spring dried out. No water.
> The Hopi, or the Christian, maybe the Moslem, they pray for rain.
> The Navajo has the proper ceremony done to restore himself to har-
> mony with the drought. . . . The system is designed to recognize what's
> beyond human power to change, and then to change the human's atti-
> tude to be content with the inevitable.

I ask now, "So beauty, in relation to *hozho*, is just seeing 'the grand
scheme of things'?"

Sixteen-year-old Sara responds, "Sort of, but not completely. Like,
we hold beauty pageants on the rez, just like people do everywhere.
Only, our standards of beauty aren't based on what's on the surface,
on outward beauty, but the type of beauty that comes from *hozho*.
This type of beauty is shown by the way you carry yourself, the way
you deal with the grand scheme of things. It doesn't matter whether
you're skinny or fat. Beauty comes from within, from your spirit,
your outlook. A person who has this beauty is the most virtuous
person."

"If you *really* want to see beauty, come to one of our high-school
basketball games," boasts David, a high-school student. "You've never
seen such beautiful teamwork as on our team. Man, we flow. We are a
well-oiled harmonious machine."

His mom says just as proudly, "The reason our kids' teams excel in
basketball is because they all play in harmony with each other. None
tries to stand out. The team members don't care about individual
glory, only team glory."

Scholars Clyde Kluckhohn and Dorothea Leighton write that while
personal excellence is a key Navajo value, "personal 'success' is not.

The only success that matters is that of the tribe as a whole, and that demands excellence among all members."

Says another, somewhat hesitantly, "But I think it's also a reason why, even though we often have exceptional high-school teams, few of our players get college scholarships." He turns to me and says, "A key Navajo virtue is humility, not standing out or sticking out—because when you stand out, we believe that it creates discord, and destroys *hozho*. But if one member of our tribe excels in college, it casts a good light on all of us."

Writing in the *New York Times*, Selena Roberts says that in many Native American communities, "humility is celebrated and individuality is suppressed." According to Roberts, "(t)he difficulties American Indians have encountered in trying to reach the elite levels of sport reflect some of the larger social forces that have hampered their achievement in other realms of American life," ranging from "the prejudice of some outsiders, to what many American Indians say is an ambivalence within their communal culture toward individuals who seek to stand out." One of the results, she reports, is that even though "American Indians make up about 1 percent of the country's population . . . , they account for only four-tenths of a percent of the scholarship athletes at the major college level."

No one seems inclined to dispute what has just been said. There is an extended silence, until Beth, who is studying to become a teacher, changes course and says to me, "The Dineh concept of *hozho* is based on what we call *Sa'ah Naaghai Bik'eh Hozhoon*. This is a philosophy that all human life must be in harmony with the rest of the universe. Those who practice this will attain *t-aa ho ajit-eego*, a greater spirituality and happiness that comes from acting correctly in the world."

"What to you mean by 'acting correctly'?" I ask.

"Acting in ways that make the world more harmonious. Acting with a sense of responsibility for yourself and your tribe, confronting evils great and small every day, and trying to turn them into good is virtue itself."

Scholar Gary Witherspoon writes that "*(h)ozho* is not the natural state of the universe, but one the Navajo strive to create out of its opposite, *hochxo*," or evil. *Hozho*, then, is "the positive or ideal environment. It is beauty, harmony, good, happiness, and everything that is positive, and it refers to an environment that is all-inclusive." This outcome of *hozho* is almost identical to the type of happiness Socrates says one will achieve when one is virtuous—a type of holistic happiness made up of such qualities as beauty, harmony, good, and "everything positive."

Beth then says, "I agree that *hozho* is the road to good and to happiness. But to learn how to get on that road, and move forward on it, takes hard-earned knowledge."

"Knowledge in general, or specific types of knowledge?" I ask.

"Specific types that are all connected and make up part of a whole, and that lead to harmony within yourself, and harmony between yourself and the world around you, the world of your friends, and the world of nature."

Again, this is remarkably similar to the view of Socrates. Contrary to what some scholars have set forth, Socrates didn't say simply that "knowledge is virtue," but rather that certain types of knowledge can put one on a path to becoming more virtuous.

Janice, a volunteer educator, says, "I think a big reason why there's no longer so much *hozho* on the rez is that we're not able to educate our children in a way that incorporates traditional forms of Navajo knowledge."

Navajo scholar Herbert John Benally writes that "the present Western organization of knowledge" in schools, "with its fragmentation, ill-defined goals and lack of connectedness, does not promote *hozho*." Learning among Navajo youth, he contends, must be completely reoriented in ways that take Western knowledge into account, but that "place it in a native framework, so that it works for our benefit . . . the traditional native philosophy must become the main stalk of the educational system." He maintains that all knowledge that is imparted to young Navajos "must be weighed in terms of its value in promoting and drawing one closer to *hozho*," so it must "show the student that all things are interconnected and interdependent."

Janice continues, "If we were able to give our children a modern education, but one that's based on our traditional beliefs, I think many problems we are experiencing—from alcoholism to delinquency to growing cases of criminal violence—would begin to resolve themselves."

Violence on the Navajo reservation appears to be escalating dramatically. After the first nine months of October 2002, there were thirty-four murders on the Arizona section of the Navajo Nation—nearly double the number that occurred in year 2000. While in 1998 there were 1,775 calls to police to report incidents of domestic violence, in the year 2000 (the last year in which statistics are available) there were 2,816 such calls. A report in the Flagstaff, Arizona, *Daily Sun* says that perhaps all "serious crimes on the reservation . . . are alcohol-related." An Associated Press article about increasing problems of violence among Native American youth and crime points to a number of root causes: "Isolated, impoverished, dispirited—disconnected both from their traditional culture and Western society—American Indian youth have grown increasingly violent, drug-dependent and depressed."

"All of us have a role to play, a responsibility, in helping our tribe become more harmonious," says soft-spoken Debbie, seated at my side. "I think a lot of the problems we're having now on our reservation show that we're having trouble living in harmony with the modern world. On the one hand, many of our people cling to the traditional ways, and on the other, there's those who want to let go of them. What we need is sort of a harmonious middle ground, if we're to bring back Navajo virtue."

The man on the other side of Debbie says, "*Hozho* itself recognizes that the world is ever-changing. But what is happening right now, on the rez and in the outside world, is that more and more people are choosing to live out of touch with nature. So harmony itself is unraveling."

"It's because of the money disease," says an elderly woman. "It's the reason we sold out on Peabody Coal, which destroyed nature on our reservation."

In *The Ecological Indian: Myth and History*, Shepard Krech III, a professor of anthropology at Brown University, writes that in the 1960s, the Navajo and Hopi agreed ". . . to allow Peabody Coal Company to strip-mine coal from their lands, with which utility companies generated approximately 2 percent of the nation's electricity—for American cities, not native people." The result was an ecological disaster. "Pollution cut sunlight 15 percent downwind in Flagstaff, Arizona. At the source—the arid reservations—deeply scarred, stripped lands will take centuries to recover. Uranium mining simultaneously affected the Navajo with active tailings, one large spill, ground and animal contamination, and irradiated workers." It also has created deep tribal rifts—the type of discord that is the antithesis of *hozho*—that are "exacerbating splits between antidevelopment traditionalists . . . and prodevelopment progressives; they also led to demands for indigenous control over—if not a halt to—the extraction of resources."

This prompts Jimmy to say, "But now many tribespeople are trying to remedy our mistake in leasing the land to Peabody. Traditionals *and* progressives are trying to get the lease agreement changed, and they're trying to restore the damage done to the land. We made a mistake with what happened there, but we're learning from it, and trying to heal the environment and restore *hozho*."

Debbie now says, "*Hozho*, Navajo virtue, is all about healing and restoration, creating good out of bad—between people in conflict with themselves or with one another, or between people and the universe. If each of us aims for *hozho*, not just here on the rez but everywhere, then the world we will live in will become more good than bad, and so it will have more virtue than vice."

## *ARETE* AND *HOZHO*

The Navajo conception of harmony is very similar to the classical Greek conception. Scholar Paul Cartledge writes that the Greek word *kosmos* was a "universal Greek term" that means "order," which the Greeks equated with "beautiful" and which is manifested in a variety of ways. He notes that the Athenian philosopher Gorgias said that "(f)or a city, the finest *kosmos* [both order and adornment] is a good citizenry, for a body it is beauty, for a soul it is wisdom, for action it is *arete*," or excellence.

The classic Greek scholar H. D. F. Kitto writes in *The Greeks* that we "miss all the flavor" of the Hellenic Greek word *arete* when it is translated only as virtue, which "at least in modern English, is almost entirely a moral word." *Arete*, he says, "simply means excellence. Thus the hero of the *Odyssey* is a great fighter, a wily schemer, a ready speaker, a man of stout heart and broad wisdom . . . an excellent all-rounder." A person with *arete* has "a respect for the wholeness or oneness of life . . ." and an understanding that achieving harmony "exists not in one department of life but in life itself."

This "wholeness" and "oneness" are equivalent to the holistic "balance" and "order" and "harmony" of the Navajo philosophy of *hozho*.

Kitto also writes, "What moves the Greek warrior to deeds of heroism is not a sense of duty as we understand it—duty towards others: it is rather duty towards himself." In *Zen and the Art of Motorcycle Maintenance: An Inquiry Into Values,* Robert M. Pirsig, commenting on Kitto's book, concludes that this "motive of 'duty toward self' . . . is an almost exact translation of the Sanskrit word *dharma,* sometimes described as the 'one' of the Hindus." Pirsig asks, "Can the *dharma* of the Hindus and the 'virtue' of the ancient Greeks be identical?"

Pirsig clearly thinks they are one and the same. But what both Kitto and Pirsig fail to grasp is that for the ancient Greeks, there was no distinction of any sort between duty toward others and duty toward self. Every act, every deed in ancient Greece was committed by a member of its citizenry with a keen mindfulness of its impact on everyone else. Each recognized that one could not attain personal excellence at the expense of others, but only by paving the way for them to attain it as well. There was no private self as there is today, only a self that was part of a whole, part of an excellent citizenry and society. In that respect, *arete* is indeed like the Hindu conception of *dharma:* both concepts encompass an individual's duty not just to himself, but also to his religion, his society, his nation.

This sense of duty toward others and oneself is equivalent to *hozho's* underpinning philosophy of *t-aa ho ajit-eego,* in which the Navajo are inculcated from a young age to believe that there are no divisions between duty to themselves, to their tribe, and to the universe as a whole. They have the same respect and sense of duty for "the wholeness or oneness of life" that Kitto ascribes to the ancient Greeks. In striving further to develop this individual wholeness, in becoming an "excellent all-rounder," one is at the same time furthering one's duty to one's community, contributing to greater social harmony.

# TOWARD A MORE HARMONIOUS HARMONY

In *The Ecological Indian: Myth and History*, Shepard Krech III appears to go a long way toward debunking the image of Native Americans as noble environmentalists who lived in idyllic harmony with their natural surroundings. Rather, like all human groups, he shows that they have a decidedly mixed environmental record. This would seem to indicate that *hozho*, the type of harmony many Navajo strive for, and they claim is equivalent to virtue itself, is elusive, and maybe illusive.

In supporting his argument, Krech asserts that indigenous groups such as the Navajo have "often been at loggerheads with environmentalists, whose pursuit of preservation in the spirit of John Muir has pitted them on innumerable occasions against Indians whose everyday realities do not afford them the same luxuries." But what should also be pointed out is that environmentalists themselves often are at odds with one another. Many, for instance, believe that land does *not* have to be preserved in its original pristine state—and in fact can be used for many purposes, such as stock grazing—and still be of perfectly sound environmental use, while others believe that such a view is blasphemy. Ultimately, though, it doesn't seem that Native American ways of living fit any Western-prescribed conceptions of environmentalism.

I think that if the Navajo, and other indigenous groups on our continent with a similar worldview, were compelled to use a word from the English lexicon to describe their environmental and ecological outlook, most would use the word *naturalist*. Their most common outlook is kin to the views of prominent American naturalist and conservationist John Muir (1838–1914). As scholars Kluckhohn and Leighton point out, the Navajo form of naturalism is one in which they "try to utilize what nature furnishes," all the while recognizing that "no man can master the wind and the weather." Contrary to the operating "premise" of most Westerners toward nature—namely, that "nature will destroy them unless they prevent it," because to them nature is "a malignant force with useful aspects that must be harnessed"—the Navajo and other indigenous tribes believe that "nature will take care of them if they behave as they should and do as she directs." As Herbert John Benally writes, to the Navajo, "(e)stablishing an intimate relationship with nature begins with the acceptance that all creation is intelligent and beneficial in and of itself." While a naturalist strives to use carefully "what nature furnishes," he still can make mistakes, even unwittingly disastrous ones, in this regard. But he learns from mistakes, and potentially comes away with a much keener grasp of how in the future to live in a more sustainable way with the environment.[3]

Few recognized and appreciated Native Americans' applied naturalism as did the philosopher and naturalist Henry David Thoreau, who more than anyone influenced John Muir. Thoreau devoted twenty

---

3. For instance, in past decades there have been a number of developmental projects, with damaging environmental ramifications, on Native American reservations, but decision making by Native Americans on such matters is no longer done in traditional indigenous ways. Rather, an alien Western model of government has been foisted on them. Moreover, quite often a prodevelopment federal Bureau of Indian Affairs can have inordinate sway on decisions that are supposed to be made autonomously by individual tribes. For instance, the negotiations that led to the Navajo decision to lease land to Peabody Coal, according to scholar Alvin Josephy in a newspaper interview, "were carried out so quietly" behind the scenes that they represent a textbook case "of how serious has become the lack of accountability by government agencies working hand-in-glove with industry in the United States today." What's more, even prodevelopment Native Americans entering into such agreements often have no idea of their potentially detrimental impact. For instance, notes Raymond Locke, when the Navajos leased uranium mines in the 1950s, "(n)o one told the Navajos that the sand and rock were dangerous." The tragic outcome is that the "open pits and tunnels, and millions of tons of radioactive sand and rock" that still are there seem to be the cause of "an appalling link in cancer and birth defects" in the area. Consequently, the Peabody Coal dilemma, rather than serving as a compelling example that the indigenous aren't environmentalists, can serve as a cautionary tale of how the poor typically are the most exploited. For the Navajo, what is of long-term importance is that they learned from this debacle, and are striving to undo the environmental damage and restore *hozho*.

years of his life to "learning all that he could about the Indian," writes Richard F. Fleck in *Henry Thoreau and John Muir Among the Indians*, in order "to foster his own harmonious and natural pattern of living." Thoreau believed the Indians, "in their humanity and their thought, in their harmony and their wholeness, might guide men into the happiness proper to civilization." Fleck notes that for Thoreau, "no other human being so effectively integrated himself with his natural environment" as the Indians with whom he came in contact. Thoreau held this view at a time—the 1840s and 1850s—when white civilization was "in the process of destroying the . . . woods for . . . short-term gain."

To Thoreau, "(t)here can be no better teacher" to reverse this trend of the white settlers' wanton destruction of nature "than the Indian," whose mythology and religion emanate from "the sacred source" of nature itself. Fleck writes that "(t)he Indian's essentially harmonious relationship to his natural environment and his original self-reliance not only gained Thoreau's deep respect but also inspired him to lead a similar life. To be close to nature was to be close to the creation and generative forces of life." Thoreau wrote in his *Journal*, "How much more conversant was the Indian with any wild animal or plant than we are, and in his language is implied all that intimacy . . . The Indian. . . . preserves his intercourse with his native gods, and is admitted from time to time to a rare and peculiar society with nature." The way the American Indian lived was, to Thoreau, "a confirmation, a paradigm of his own philosophy of living simply and harmoniously in a natural environment," which to him was tantamount to the most virtuous way of life.

———

What about *hozho* in the *human* environment? Native Americans do not subscribe to the Western notion of "man versus the environment," because to them man is an integral part of the natural world; and yet the discord within many reservation tribes, evidenced by the rampant delinquency among their youth and the increasing judicial conflicts among tribe members, might seem to suggest that whatever Native Americans believe about *hozho* has yet to find its way into practice.

Nevertheless, concerted efforts are being made. In a pioneering program, the Navajo Nation justice system now has charged "Peacemakers" with the task of restoring *hozho* between victims and perpetrators of crimes. According to an essay written by Robert Yazzie, chief justice of the Navajo Nation, this experiment with peace-making was started out of necessity. "The Navajo Nation courts get close to 28,000 criminal cases each year. The largest categories of crimes are assaults and batteries (most often among family members), other crimes against family members, driving while intoxicated and other alcohol-related crimes, and disorderly conduct." But because there is only jail space for about 220 people at any given time, "the judges found themselves with "few sentencing options." Turning a negative into a potential positive—building *hozho* out of *hochxo*—the Navajo justice system began appointing respected leaders of the community, called peacemakers, to meet with the person who committed the offense and those who were affected by his actions. The peace-maker, according to Yazzie, brings about healing by using the Navajo process of *nalyeeh*, in which the person who committed the hurt has to talk about why he did what he did and, ultimately, come to terms with the hurt it brought to others, with the end of finding a way to restore and heal. The entire family of the accused takes part in this process, because in the traditional Navajo value system, it shares some of the responsibility for the actions of any family member, and so shares in the task of restoring *hozho*. So all family members share the goal of coming up with an agreeable form of restitution to those harmed, and are equally devoted to helping the person in their family who committed the infraction to overcome the evil within him that brought him to do it in the first place.

Tony Hillerman describes it this way in *Sacred Clowns*:

> If you damage somebody, you sit down with their family and figure out how much damage and make it good. That way you restore *hozho*. You've got harmony again between two families. . . . If somebody harms you out of meanness . . . then he's the one who's out of *hozho*. You aren't taught he should be punished. He should be cured. Gotten back in balance with what's around him. Made beautiful again.

For the Navajo, this "making beautiful again" is virtue at work.

Chief Justice Yazzie says the aim of the peacemaker approach is restoration, restitution, and reconciliation—of making beautiful again. Where the "Western criminal-justice system assumes that the problem" is solely "the actor," which justifies its sole "solution" of imprisoning the offender, Yazzie says the Navajo system "deals with people's actions." While "Western adjudication is a search for what happened and who did it, Navajo peacemaking is about the effects of what happened. Who got hurt? What do they feel about it? What can be done to repair the harm?" How can *hozho* be restored?

The Navajo way of restoring social harmony, Yazzie asserts, deals "with actions, not actors, allowing people to face and solve their own problems." He says that peacemaking is fast proving to be of immense benefit "for crime prevention." Its positive ramifications also seem to be spilling over into the entire reservation, restoring harmony between clans and neighbors, and so stemming any further unraveling of Navajo society. "By getting at the *nayee* [the "monsters" or "antisocial" elements within] early on," Yazzie says, peacemaking is "rewriting old scripts." It is making beautiful again.

# HONESTLY!

"I think dishonesty is virtue in Japan."

The remark by Hitomi, a first-year political science student at a university in Tokyo, seems to stun everyone.

I'm holding a Socrates Café—a type of philosophical inquiry that features the Socratic method—in Tokyo, the principal city of this island nation of 127 million, which has been mired in a decade-long recession, with record bankruptcies and unemployment. We're in a large *tatami* room that serves as a community room for the six-floor apartment complex where some of the people live who are taking part in the dialogue. There are eighteen participants in all, and several have come from a relatively long distance. We're arranged in a circle, and are kneeling on a *tatami*, or floor mat, made of tightly woven straw. I'm seated the farthest away from the entrance to the room; this is considered the place of honor. Before I sat down, everyone gave me a low and deep bow. I bowed in turn, albeit awkwardly.

A friend who'd spent some time with my wife and me in the United States had arranged this gathering. He'd forewarned me that he didn't know whether the participants would be receptive to the dialogue— none had ever taken part in anything like this—but said he'd gladly host it, come what may.

I've just asked the question "What is virtue?"

With Hitomi's candid opening salvo, I no longer wonder or worry whether they will be open with me, a *gaijin*, or foreigner.

"What do you mean?" I now ask her.

She has a look on her face that seems to indicate she regrets she'd blurted out loud what she'd been thinking. But now she takes a deep breath and goes on, "To us Japanese, virtue, or *toku*, is that which creates *Wa*, or social harmony. So we've made an art form out of dishonesty, because we think it's usually what best facilitates this harmony. For instance, our government and media try to paint a picture of how safe Japan is compared to other nations—as if the perception of safety will create the reality. But even if Japan is safer than other places, it still is a very dangerous place."

A November 19, 2002, Associated Press article says that crime in Japan has risen to "a post–World War II high," while "the arrest rate fell to a record low," serving to "undercut its reputation as one of the industrialized world's safest societies."

"They try to say what a cohesive and harmonious place we are," Hitomi goes on. "But the truth is, our society is coming apart at the seams. Our businesses are failing, our families are separating, our government is corrupt. This picture of harmony is false and dishonest, and so it is the opposite of genuine *Wa*. Dishonesty has kept us from addressing and confronting our problems, so they only worsen. So really, it's a great vice, though many in our society consider it virtue."

In *The Japanese Social Crisis*, Jon Woronoff writes that in the 1980s, everyone who wrote about Japan described it as "one of the most harmonious, dynamic and in many ways admirable societies that ever existed." He said they turned a blind eye to the "true crisis" in Japan, in which "virtually all social institutions" in the nation "are being undermined in one way or another and they could easily collapse."

Hitomi falls silent, and I think she has finished. But then, without looking directly at any of us, she goes on: "In the Western world, you claim to place a premium upon *makoto*, which means truthfulness and honesty combined. You say you want 'the truth, the whole truth, and nothing but the truth.' But in Japan today, we never say what we really think or feel. It's too risky. Our policy is, *nami kaze wo tatenai*. It means, 'don't make waves.' We go about fulfilling *nami kaze wo tatenai* by practicing *honne tatemae*. *Honne* is our private side, and means 'genuine feelings' and *tatemae*, our public side, means 'masking yourself.' Today, we think masking our genuine feelings *is* virtue, because it enables us to avoid confrontation and create a surface harmony in all our relationships."

In his book, *You Gotta Have Wa*, Robert Whiting says that the Japanese place such a high premium on maintaining *Wa*, or group harmony, that "they have refined the suppression of their *honne* in favor of *tatemae*, to a high art," keeping "their mouths shut, their feelings to themselves."

I expect the other participants, judging by their deep frowns, to disagree wholeheartedly with Hitomi. Instead, they nod almost uniformly and say, "*Hai*," or Yes, to indicate that they are absorbing all that she has said.

Finally, my host, Matsui, responds, "What Hitomi says is quite true, in the sense that we Japanese will go to great lengths to avoid confrontation, and we achieve this by *honne tatemae*.' "

"But *honne tatemae* shouldn't be seen as dishonest," he insists. "Ideally, it helps create a more genuine *Wa*. *Honne tatemae* is just our way of adjusting and reconciling our personal thoughts and feelings with society's norms. I think everyone in *every* society has a public and a private side. It means we're not completely 'I's,' but that we're also 'we's,' part of a group. Besides that, we all wear masks."

"Yes, but we take it to an extreme," replies Hitomi. "I traveled to the United States last year in an exchange program, and the people I met there who'd been to Japan say they always wonder what the Japanese are really thinking, because it's so obvious we hide our real thoughts. This creates tension and distrust over the long term, and so, as I said, it's the opposite of virtue, which creates a more lasting harmony."

Writer Kyoko Mori, who was born and raised in Japan but now lives in the United States, writes in her book *Polite Lies* that she "did not value" *honne tatemae* as a young person. While Mori says it is a misconception that she and her Japanese friends were "brought up to lie on all occasions," they did receive "a very mixed message: Lying is all right under certain circumstances," but "honesty is also very important," particularly when "linked with the idea of respect." Whether one tells the truth, or a partial truth, or a lie apparently depends on which will best contribute to creating or preserving harmony. Then the question is, What type of harmony does it lead to, an artificial and deceptive type, or one that leads to the type of lasting harmony, based on trust and openness, that Hitomi favors?

"I only talk in complete *honne* when I trust someone, and feel that what I say will not create discord," Aiko, a social worker, says to me. "Like, I feel very angry still about what your country did to Hiroshima and Nagasaki. And I'm angry that I have relatives in the United States who were interned in World War Two, just because they were of Japanese descent. But I only vent these feelings fully to those I know will understand, or try to understand, where I'm coming from. Because understanding leads to genuine *Wa*, which is Japanese virtue. But if I'm in a situation where those I'm speaking to don't have any clue where I'm coming from, and don't care to, then speaking my mind will only make a bad situation worse."

"The key to having genuine *Wa* is to find the right balance between fulfilling the needs of the individual and of the group," says Shuichi, who as an international business consultant travels back and forth between the United States and Japan. "But I think there has to be more *tatemae* than *honne*, because the individual's needs can only be met after those of the group are met. *Honne tatemae*, if used rightly, will lead to *Wa*, which is the opposite of self-centered 'virtue' based on extreme individualism. In the United States, individual accomplishments are admired most. Here, it's about 'team, team, team.' We don't seek to stand out individually, not in sports, not in business. Collective accomplishment, not individual accomplishment, is what matters; we aim to stand out as a group."

"True enough," says Kenichi, an executive at a department store chain, "but while *Wa* has always been a consensus-seeking type of harmony based on satisfying the needs of the group, too often today we reach consensus in artificial ways, which only creates an illusory surface harmony, which is the opposite of virtue. I think it's why so many Japanese corporations are failing. The shared code of the group is to portray a bad situation in a good light. This is what's happening to my company, which is near bankruptcy. This betrays the essence of *Wa*, because we don't allow ourselves to go through the process of honest and open dialogue in which we confront our problems, so we can remedy them. If you're honest and open, with the intent of creating greater harmony, there will be some rough waves at first, but ultimately you'll achieve Japanese virtue."

"What other qualities must each individual in a group possess to create 'Japanese virtue'?" I ask.

"Each must have a cooperative spirit, and must care for the excellence of the group more than individual excellence," he replies. "Each must have qualities like *nintai*, which means your ability to persevere toward a goal in the face of hardship. Each must know that to attain *subarashi*—to become excellent as a team player—he not only has to endure individual trials and tribulations, and to overcome them, but also has to have the ability to help others do the same. And each must have *omoiyari*, empathy, the ability to take into account the feelings of others who are part of his group."

Shuntaro, who works for an insurance company, now chimes in: "If an employee who works under me makes a mistake, I don't confront him and criticize him bluntly in front of everyone else. What good purpose would that serve? It would only make him feel shame. I try to put myself in his shoes and understand why he messed up."

Then he says to me, "It's like when you forgot to take your shoes off before entering this room. I said to you in private, 'There're slippers for you at the door.' I accomplished what needed to be accomplished, and preserved harmony. If I hadn't said anything to you, if I'd masked my thoughts, some of us would be upset right now, because wearing shoes in this setting disrupts harmony. On the other hand, imagine how you'd have felt if I'd yelled at you from across the room, 'Hey, you idiot, don't you know to take your shoes off before entering a room!' "

"I'd have felt like an even bigger schmuck," I say, "and I'd have been miserable."

John C. Condon writes in *With Respect to the Japanese* that "(f)rom the Japanese perspective . . . being direct and to the point can mean being insensitive to the other's feelings as well as lacking in aesthetic subtlety." Cultural anthropologist Ruth Benedict says in *The Chrysanthemum and the Sword* that Japanese society is largely a "shame culture," and that the Japanese derive, or lose, their esteem based on their treatment by others in their social network. Because shame "is a reaction to other people's criticism," and so "a potent sanction," those who criticize are keenly aware of how the way they do so has the potential to do great good, or harm. If their conduct serves to help a person grow and develop, at the same time as they help the group become more excellent, then to the Japanese this is tantamount to virtue in action.

Eventually I ask, "The group *always* comes before the individual, if *Wa* is to be achieved?"

"Yes," replies Naohiko, who is the cousin of my host and is visiting from Okinawa, "though, of course, sometimes an individual has to act against the group over the short term, because she may have a better notion of what's good for the group over the long term than the group itself. I think Martin Luther King, Jr., challenging the racist laws in your country, is an example of that."

"Or," she continues, "sometimes a small group of individuals has to act against the wishes of the larger group of which it is a part, because the smaller group has a different idea about what's best for society's long-term harmony and preservation."

"I was part of the protest in Okinawa against the U.S. military," she then tells us. "Our government was against our action, but there was no way we could stay silent while the soldiers who hurt that girl looked like they were going to get away with just a slap on the wrist."

In 1995, about 80,000 Okinawans, who are among the poorest people in this prosperous nation, formed a human chain around the U.S. base there, where nearly 30,000 of the 48,000 U.S. troops in Japan are stationed.[4] They protested vehemently after three American soldiers were accused of kidnapping and raping a twelve-year-old girl, and the U.S. military refused to let the soldiers be tried in civilian court. In part because of the protest, the U.S. military relented and handed the soldiers over to a Japanese court, where in 1996 they were tried and convicted, and now are serving sentences of up to seven years apiece.

Naohiko continues: "I have a tavern near the military base, and one day soon after our protest a U.S. soldier came in, and he said he was bewildered by our actions. He said to me, 'You Japanese always acted like you loved us. But this protest shows that you really hate us.'

"Does this mean we were dishonest about our true feelings all along? I honestly don't know; I think others are the best judge of this. It does mean we were guarded, out of the reality of our situation. The U.S. military is more powerful than we are, and also we depend on them for our economic livelihood. But when it counted, we did make waves. We protested loud and long, and risked our well-being—and

4. The week our dialogue took place marked the thirtieth anniversary of the return of the island to Japanese control, a full twenty years after U.S. occupation of the rest of Japan had come to an end. But Okinawa continues to be a major U.S. military base in the Pacific, and the Japanese government wants this arrangement to stay intact.

the wrath of your country, and disapproval by our government—because we believed our protest would create the best type of harmony over the long term."

"I wish this were always the way we acted," says Matsuo, after a lull. "But I think too often, the way we strive for *Wa* is exemplified by how our government handled the situation at our consulate general office in Shenyang, China."

Shortly before our dialogue took place in late spring 2001, five North Koreans had entered the Japanese consulate in Shenyang, seeking asylum. After a fierce struggle with the Chinese police, they were dragged out of the compound and taken into custody.

"At first, our government stayed silent about the incident," Matsuo continues. "But when the Western world expressed outrage over the treatment of the asylum seekers, it suddenly joined them in crying foul. Our government accused the Chinese of unlawfully entering our compound, and it demanded that they return the North Koreans. Our government didn't care about the North Koreans, only about its image."

Then he says, "But even after coming out against the Chinese action, our government still wasn't completely honest. A videotape of the incident showed that after the Chinese police subdued the asylum seekers, our vice consul picked up the police officers' caps, carefully brushed them off, and handed them back with a bow. He acted as if the North Korean asylum seekers weren't even there!

"And our government had said that the five had been taken into custody outside the compound. It didn't tell the truth until after the video footage was aired around the world. Only then did our ministry acknowledge that the North Koreans were 'seized by the Chinese police' inside the consulate. They would have continued to cover up the truth without the video. They didn't want to offend the Chinese, and they didn't want to offend the West, for the sake of surface harmony. So we say one thing, mean another, end up offending everyone, and disgracing ourselves. This is vice, not virtue, because it creates discord rather than *Wa*."

"It's the same with our school history textbooks," says Suori, a seventeen-year-old budding artist. "Our government still lies about our role in World War Two, and about the atrocities committed by our military. My parents had to buy me books from a bookstore so I could learn the truth about what happened, because we don't learn about it in school. It's important that I know the truth, so I can work toward making sure we never again make the mistakes that created the destructive and pretend harmony we had during that era."

"This type of social illness, this deception among politicians and military leaders and businessmen, is everywhere today," says Aiko, who came a long distance by train, from the city of Kyoto, which was the imperial capital of Japan for nearly one thousand years, to take part in this gathering. "We Japanese don't have a monopoly on dishonesty and lying. For instance, the Bush administration recently pulled out of the Kyoto Treaty for global warming. Nations from all over the world negotiated in good faith for years to reach an international agreement on standards for industrial emissions. The United States had already committed to it. Then your president bails out at the eleventh hour, claiming that there aren't any definitive studies that prove that toxic industrial emissions cause global warming. Anyone with knowledge about this matter knows that this is a lie. And again, this is vice, because this decision puts the natural universe in peril, while the treaty would have helped restore its harmonic balance."

We fall silent, until Seigo says, "I think there are *good* lies, lies that can preserve harmony in a good way."

"My brother was killed in a traffic accident two years ago," he tells us. "I've never told my mother. Whenever she asks about my brother, I say he's fine but very busy, and so hasn't had time to visit. She's in a nursing home because of her poor health. The news would kill her, so I decided to keep this from her, for her own good."

"I agree that was a good lie," says Aiko. "Sometimes, of course, you do have to pass on bad news to loved ones. I had to tell my father that he'd been diagnosed with inoperable cancer. I felt he had a right to know, so he could decide how he wanted to spend the time he still had. But in each one of these types of situations, it's a judgment call, and you make the judgment by deciding what's best for the well-being of your loved one."

"I still practice some Buddhist and Shinto rituals, even though I don't completely believe in them," Shuichi says eventually. "For instance, on New Year's, I go to a Buddhist shrine and pray for the wellness and harmony of my family. And a month after my baby girl was born, my wife and I visited a Shinto shrine, and we gave an offering to the Shinto god, so the god would bestow harmony upon us. This is called *kashiwade*. We do these things, out of custom, even though we're no longer devout believers in Shinto. We figure, it can't do any harm, and, who knows, it just may help bring about greater harmony in our lives."[5]

Shuichi asks us, "If I still practice these religious rituals, but I don't sincerely believe in the religions, am I lying to myself and to others?"

No one answers at first. Then someone says, "I think you are being honestly dishonest—but perhaps in a good way, because your intentions are honorable." To our surprise, it is Hitomi, who'd railed against dishonesty when our dialogue got under way.

"After considering what some others here have said," she contin-

---

5. In *A Year in the Life of a Shinto Shrine*, John K. Nelson writes that "(w)hat is so fascinating in Japanese culture and society is that . . . many of its important ritual practices [still] resemble in structure and expression those dating to the Heian period (794 to 1192 C.E., or A.D.)." Nelson concludes that "whatever changes are occurring in Japanese society do not replace the old models of ethic or moral standards as much as they supplement them with new combinations of Japanese and Western perspectives."

ues," I think that on rare occasions, you can be slightly dishonest—
and that it's okay, as long as you're honest about it, and your goals are
worthy. I still feel strongly that in Japanese society today, too often
we're not as honest as we should be, and for the wrong reasons. We use
too much *tatemae*, and not enough *honne*, for motives that prop up a
superficial harmony. But I've been moved by how everyone here so
honestly has looked at both the bad and good in Japanese society, and
wants to achieve genuine *Wa*."

"But these last examples seem to deal only with individual well-being,
rather than group harmony," I say. "How do they serve to create *Wa*?"

"I've been thinking," Hitomi replies, "that a person is a type of
group, made up of lots of different sides—not just masks, and not just
public and private sides, but different personas, with different
thoughts and feelings and beliefs and emotions that all make up who
she is. And likewise, I think that society is a type of person.

"For each member of society to have well-being and harmony
inside herself, she has to live in a healthy society—one that is open
and honest about its strengths and its failings—that wants the same,
for the long-term good of everyone. To achieve this, both have to honestly confront their shortcomings and contradictions, and try to
resolve them (or at least recognize them), for the long-term good of
everyone. Virtue, I think, lies in this confrontation."

## CAN WE TALK?

In *Confucius Lives Next Door*, T. R. Reid, who for five years was the
*Washington Post*'s Tokyo bureau chief, calls Japan "the native home of
the euphemism." He says there is "something mechanical—in fact,
there's something arguably phony—about all the flowery verbiage"
and "linguistic rigmarole" that "mark normal discourse in Japan." I

think Reid's comments reveal more about himself than about Japan. Their way of conversing certainly may be phony and mechanical and convoluted for him, particularly if he's used to the very discursive and abrupt style of communication used in the United States. But it's not phony or mechanical for the Japanese. For them, it *is* normal discourse, at least in certain situations. It is every bit as innate in them to talk this way as it is for Reid not to—though the truth is that in the United States, as anyone knows who has ever listened to a government press conference, we can be as adept at "linguistic rigmarole" as anyone anywhere.[6]

For Reid to characterize pejoratively the way Japanese communicate is, I think, to reveal his lack of understanding and appreciation for a culture that communicates in ways that are different from his own. Reid also does not take note of the fact that Japanese are much less prone to talk in this manner in settings that they consider private, such as the one in which the dialogue I held with them took place.

His rather one-dimensional take on Japanese ways of communicating would have one think that *tatemae* is tantamount to what one says, and *honne* to what one means. But it would be much more accurate to portray them as distinct but in no way contradictory ways of saying what one means—one of them, to be sure, couched in florid social conventions, and the other more direct, but usually no less gentle and empathetic, at its best.

John Condon is more on the mark in his succinct observation that "each way of communicating, the Japanese and American, must be viewed on its own terms, and not on the expectations of the other." But it must also be viewed in terms of its ends. What *should* be critiqued is not how the Japanese communicate, but what ends their

6. American directness has its downside, too, as evidenced by the tell-all, naked confessionals on our TV talk shows, and the reality shows that thrive on participants gladly humiliating themselves.

form of communication serves. One should examine, for instance, whether their way of communicating leads to a more open society that serves to address its serious social dilemmas, or whether it only serves to mask entrenched social problems that eventually exacerbate to the point that society can unravel.

## THE TRUTH ABOUT LYING

In her book *Polite Lies*, Kyoko Mori, although at one point acknowledging the drawbacks of certain types of lying, nonetheless writes that "(l)ies are fascinating because there are so many possibilities for invention and embellishment. In a liar's mouth, facts are no longer boring and predictable, but interesting and surprising." Such lies, I would add, often are all too believable, and are all too capable of being used for the most pernicious ends. Anyone subjected in any way to the heinous lies of the Nazi propagandists, or of the Jim Crow racists, surely would much prefer the "boring and predictable" truth to the "fascinating, interesting, and surprising" lies that led to their subjugation, torture, and much worse.

Surely lies are vital, even virtuous, if one's ends are to advance humanity. A German gentile hiding a Jew during the era of the Holocaust might well lie to Gestapo agents searching her home, just as an abolitionist might have lied to a slave hunter about whether he was harboring a runaway slave. Such lies are not made for the purpose of invention and embellishment, much less to be interesting or surprising, but instead are made to protect the lives of fellow human beings who otherwise would have suffered what to those sheltering them would have been an unconscionable fate.

The inordinately influential German philosopher Immanuel Kant (1724–1804)—founder of the so-called "critical philosophy" movement—said that one should decide whether to tell the truth, or to lie, based on this "categorical imperative": "Your actions should be based only on maxims that you would like to see become universal laws." In other words, if you want to know whether it's better to tell the truth or lie on any particular occasion, first try to imagine what it would be like if everyone lied. Kant believed that all "rational beings" would prefer a world where everyone told the truth to one in which lying was all-pervasive. He reasoned that no one would or could ever trust anyone else in a society of liars. But I don't think there's much difference between the two. If you knew people always lied, you could easily discern the truth from their lies.

It certainly would be nice if such formulaic imperatives could be applied to every circumstance, as Kant felt they could. But for anyone striving to cultivate a type of virtue in which, at minimum, no harm comes to the innocent or oppressed, there are rare times when dishonesty, even downright lies, might be called for. There's just no way to skirt the hard work of determining what to say, and how to say what one needs to say, in every unique situation.

## NOBLE TRUTHS AND IGNOBLE LIES

In the latter part of the *Republic*, written after abandoning any pretense of faithfulness to the type of forthright inquiry practiced by Socrates, Plato endorsed the telling of lies by rulers, if lies served to forge stronger bonds of identity and unity among members of a society. Plato contended that such lies are not only acceptable, but can also be considered "noble."

While such a lie may serve benign ends in the type of purely imaginary utopia that Plato fashioned, I think historical experience bears out that whenever such "noble lies" are employed in the real world, they oppress some groups of people at the expense of others. Such lies have justified slavery and, as was the case in the World War II era in Japan, legitimized acts of extreme aggression and other forms of human subjugation.

Much better than Plato's version of the noble lie is the type illustrated by Mark Twain's Tom Sawyer. Tom gets a terrible licking after taking the blame, and the beating, for tearing out the picture plate in his teacher's textbook, even though his girlfriend, Becky Thatcher, really did it, to protect someone weaker from a sadistic teacher. When Becky told her dad, Judge Thatcher, what Tom did for her, the ebullient Judge declared that Tom's "was a noble, a generous, a magnanimous lie—a lie worthy to hold up its head and march down through history breast to breast with George Washington's lauded truth about the hatchet."

Thus in Japan, as everywhere else, sometimes the unvarnished truth is called for, but sometimes, an out-and-out lie, depending on the circumstances, in order to advance humanitarian ends.

In Kyoto, Japan, there is a famous nature trail known as the Philosophers' Walk, or *Tetsugaku no Michi*. It features a meandering cherry-tree-lined path that runs along the canal in the city, which in many ways is a throwback to a more traditional Japan. Along the way, there are a number of beautiful temples, and bridges shaped like half-moons, where you can look out over the canal and feel as if you are far removed from the city. It's called the Philosophers' Walk because Japan's revered philosopher Nishida Kitaro (1870–1945) took daily sojourns there.

Kitaro's scholarly passion was to "synthesize" the best of Eastern and Western philosophical thinking, with the aim of revealing hidden likenesses and building bridges of understanding between the two. He pursued this at a time when the divisions between East and West were nearing their most extreme, and when fanatical nationalism held sway in Japan. Kitaro risked his career and perhaps his life in asserting with characteristic honesty—with the end of replacing the crazed climate that pervaded his society with a more rational and humble outlook—that all cultures can have great merit, and have much to teach us. He wrote that "cultural differences make the world rich," and that "the world will have no rest until it finds a way to global cooperation."

Soon after the outset of World War II in the Pacific, Kitaro wrote in an essay, "Principles of a New World Order," that "peace that embraces all of humankind is possible only if . . . a global world comes into being." This view was considered heretical, and was scathingly lambasted by the expansionist zealots in Japan who had convinced their people to go to war, duping them into believing that the "Japanese spirit" made them superior and would overrun everything that stood in its way to worldwide domination.

As Yusa Michiko of the Center for East Asian Studies at Western Washington University notes, Kitaro's philosophical perspective represented a "note of conscience and rationality amidst the tumultuous fanaticism all around him," and it was "far too universal in scope"—and far too honest, for humanitarian ends—"to submit to the petty racial egoism, cultural chauvinism, and pseudo-religious belief in the superiority of the Japanese people that was the hallmark of the . . . ultranationalism . . . prevalent at the time."

Nishida Kitaro felt it incumbent to speak the painful truth, for noble ends—for the long-term good and harmony of humankind—such was his deep "concern for the future of Japan . . . not [as] a matter of abstract philosophical categories, but of living realities of very concrete consequence."

# HARMONY

People of many worldviews associate virtue with harmony.

But what is harmony?

In terms of the ecology, Shepard Krech III notes that until recently, most scientists still subscribed to the view held by nineteenth-century ecologist George Perkins, who described "nature in the absence of man" as "self-regulating, in balance, or in equilibrium." In the last quarter century, Krech says that ecologists discovered that "natural systems are not inherently . . . harmonious," and consequently "abandoned these long-held assumptions in favor of chaotic dynamics in systems, and long-term disequilibrium and flux." Modern biologist Daniel Botkin's view, that "(c)hange . . . appears to be intrinsic and natural at many scales of time and place in the biosphere," has won the day. But this view is also inaccurate. While the previous notion of what constituted harmony was errant, the notion of nature as a harmonious system wasn't. A "chaotic dynamics" and "long-term disequilibrium and flux" are what create harmony in nature.

If we take the Navajo view, and make humans an integral part of the ecological system, then it likely will turn out to be the case that the most harmonious human civilizations will be those with a "chaotic dynamics" and a "long-term disequilibrium and flux." To be in such a state, a society would have to be experimental in bent. It would have to be an open society that thrived on a spirited exchange of ideas that in turn inspired ever more creativity and discovery.

Ancient Athens in its heydey, writes Paul Cartledge, was a place of unrivaled "creative political and social adaptation," and, I would add, aesthetic and philosophical experimentation. This enabled it to attain a "dynamic social equilibrium" that allowed it to be "remarkably stable," a paradigm of harmony, albeit a chaotically dynamic type.

When Athens ceased to be creative and experimental (it didn't just rest on its laurels; it discarded them), when it closed in on itself and no longer cared to grow and change, it attained a static type of stability. Athens, in the end, became a society at rest, a society extinguished.

## HOW SOCRATES SAW VIRTUE

In Plato's dialogue *Protagoras*, Socrates asks, "Is virtue one entity, made up of justice and moderation and piety, or are these all names for a single thing?" In other words, are justice and moderation and piety nothing more than different names for virtue itself, or are they qualities that make up virtue?

Socrates believed that while each quality is unique, each is not virtue itself, but rather a vital ingredient of virtue, and that each quality, in making up virtue, is of equal importance. While Protagoras believed that you can possess one of these qualities without having the others, and still be virtuous, Socrates maintained that a person can't be virtuous without possessing *all* these qualities—not just piety and moderation and justice, but courage and good.

But this still begs certain questions: Do you need an equal amount of each quality in all situations? Or are there situations in which, for instance, you can be extremely courageous, and have just a smidgen of moderation, and middling piety, and still be virtuous? And how would you "weigh" how much of each you have?

Though he may never have come up with precise answers to such questions, Socrates did make advances in discovering what type of moral code is, as philosophy professor Terry Penner writes, "objectively best for humans"—not for just one individual, but for humankind as a whole. In this effort, Penner says Socrates opposed the "sophists and rhetoricians" of his day, who maintained that "what the individual thinks good is what *is* good 'for' the individual," and whose only goal was "to put persuasive *means* in their students' hands to achieve whatever goals 'seem best' to them."

Socrates railed against their "relativism," and sought to create an objective "science of virtue." In this regard, he might usefully have tried to define virtue in a more dynamic way, more in terms of its function, particularly in terms of the ends it serves, rather than dwelling so much on discovering the qualities it is made of. In this way, whether or not a person or a society is virtuous would be determined both by the concrete strides made in advancing humanitarian ends *and* by the humanitarian means employed to achieve these ends. The eminent Socrates scholar Gregory Vlastos writes in *Studies in Greek Philosophy* that to Socrates, you can only "improve your soul" by a combination of "right thinking" and "right action," and that you "can't have one without the other." But right thinking is a form of right action, not something separate and distinct. What I think is much more correct is that you become more excellent by using a combination of "right means" and "right ends," in which the means employed in acting in the world complement and justify the ends, and vice versa, to as great a degree as possible—though recognizing that there're no absolutes, and that there are virtually always exceptions to any normative moral code.

Can questioning itself be considered a virtue?

Political scientist Richard Dagger seems to think so. He contends in *Civic Virtues* that Socrates "persuaded many people to believe that questioning and challenging the prevailing views are among the highest forms of virtue," and that "(i)n making this case," Socrates relies "on the claim that the social gadfly and the unorthodox thinker are really promoting the long-term interests of society and thereby performing a social role of exceptional value."

But I don't think Socrates believed that the mere act of "questioning and challenging the prevailing views" was "among the highest forms of virtue." There are constructive gadflies, who question with the end of realizing a more excellent life for one and all; and there are destructive gadflies, whose aim is to browbeat and intimidate and deconstruct, with no thought whatsoever of attaining any sort of greater good. Socrates of course was of the former variety, though his persecutors tried to paint him as the latter. Perhaps the Japanese and the Navajo, with their emphasis on greater "harmony" as the embodiment of virtue, can help to steer all those striving to live the virtuous life in the right direction.

# What Is Moderation?

# MODERATION UNVEILED

I'm in a cozy sun-drenched room in a community center perched on a cliff overlooking the Pacific Ocean. The center is situated in a medium-sized city with a sizeable population of immigrants from Islamic countries. I'm perched on the edge of a deep-cushioned chair and am in a circle with about twenty Muslim women, most of whom have immigrated to the United States with their families over the last few years. Several are dressed in pastel-colored *burqas*, a type of robe, usually made of silk or cotton, that covers them from head to foot. Many have on *hijabs*, or veils, but none cover their faces entirely, and most do not cover them at all, and the veils seem to serve more as scarves. Some of the *burqas* and *hijabs* are of bright and intricate multicolored patterns, while others are at the other extreme, very plain and simple. A number of participants, particularly younger ones, are dressed in typical American clothing.

The question we choose to explore is "What is moderation?"

"Moderation, to Muslims, means to follow the straight or the middle path," says Suah, a university student who immigrated with her family from Qatar five years ago, and who, after reading my book *Socrates Café*, invited me to facilitate a dialogue. "It's at the core of the Islamic faith. The prophet Muhammad says in a *sura*, or verse, of the Quran that people of the Islamic faith must aim 'to be a community of the middle way.' And in chapter twenty-five, verse sixty-seven of the Quran, the prophet says that we should always seek a 'just mean' or 'balance between extremes.' The prophet believed the middle way was the way to all forms of harmony—spiritual, mental, social, physical."

She then says, "The word for the Islamic virtue *taqwa* usually is translated as 'righteousness' or 'right conduct.' But it also means 'self-control' or 'self-restraint.' The prophet lived his own life with great self-control. He lived very simply. After his minimal needs were met each day, he gave all the rest to the poor, believing that Allah would provide for his future needs. In chapter five, verse eighty-seven of the Quran, the prophet commanded, 'Commit no excess. For Allah does not love those given to excess.'"

The prophet Muhammad (570–630 A.D.), born in Mecca on the Arabian peninsula, is the founder of the Islamic faith. "His well-attested way of behavior," writes Annemarie Schimmel in *And Muhammad Is His Messenger*, "attained a normative value for subsequent generations"—in other words, served as a model to be emulated by the Islamic faithful who came after him—"from at least as early as the second century of Islam." Like Muhammad, Socrates also modeled a life of Spartan simplicity, and was said to have exhorted others to "take everything in moderation; nothing to excess."

A woman beside Suah now says, "Ours is very much a faith of moderation, even if some fanatics today would try to make it otherwise. The prophet says in the Quran chapter five, verse seventy-seven, 'Make no excess in your religion.' This is a message of moderation."

She goes on, "The prophet was a role model for people of all faiths, not just Muslims, for how to have a balanced approach to life. He was moderate not just in his needs, but in his entire nature. He was a model of tolerance and reasonableness. And he was very modest about his role as Allah's messenger."

Annemarie Schimmel writes that Muhammad "knew . . . that he was only a human being . . . whose only prerogative was that he was granted a revelatory experience," and that he "felt that whatever happened to him was nothing but God's inexplicable grace."

"Modesty, or *iffah*, is inseparable from moderation," says Jamileh, who immigrated to the United States from Iran, and now goes to college part-time and works part-time as a graphics designer. "You can't be moderate in the way the prophet has in mind if you are not modest. To be modest is to be humble—not in a meek way, but neither in a way that's overly boastful. It's to be proud of your talents, but in a way that shows that you are grateful and humble to God for being blessed with them. In chapter thirty-one of the Quran, verses eighteen and nineteen, we are told by the prophet: 'Do not swell with pride . . . or walk in insolence as you traverse the earth, for Allah does not love the arrogant boaster. Rather, be moderate in your pace.' "

She continues, "Moderation is living with grace. It means to talk gracefully, neither too loud nor too soft. The prophet says in the Quran, chapter seventeen, verse eleven, 'Do not speak your prayer loud, nor speak it in a low tone, but seek a middle course.' This middle course is the key to a virtuous life. If you sleep too much, you become lazy. If you eat too much, you become overweight. If you talk too much, you don't hear what others have to say, and you become intolerant. If you have too many, or too few, material things, you are preoccupied with them and don't focus on the needs of others. So moderation is all about modesty—in speech, in bearing, in way of life, in dress."

This notion of modesty is very similar to that of the classical Greek concept of *sophrosune* examined by Socrates. He concluded that *sophrosune* was a combination of temperance and modesty and self-restraint—a moderate middle way—that would lead a person to become well-balanced, or harmonious, which in turn would lead to greater wisdom and so greater happiness.

"Do you consider the way you dress to be modest in the way the prophet had in mind?" I now ask Jamileh, who is dressed in a *hijab* and *burqa*.

"Yes I do," she replies without hesitation. "In chapter twenty-four, verses thirty and thirty-one of the Quran, the prophet says: 'And say to the believing women that they should lower their gaze and guard their modesty; and that they should not display their beauty and ornaments except what must ordinarily appear thereof.' And in chapter thirty-three, verse fifty-nine, he says, 'Tell your wives and daughters and the believing women to draw their outer garments around them, when they go out or are among men.' So I'm simply dressed in accordance with what's commanded to us in the Quran, which is the word of Allah."

This inspires Suhaila, from Afghanistan, now a premedical student at a local university, and who is dressed in jeans and a T-shirt, to say, "But nowhere in our holy book does it say that we have to wear a veil or *burqa*. It just says that we should dress in a modest way."

Turning to me, Suhaila says, "To me, what I'm wearing *is* modest. I would never flaunt myself. The Quran doesn't say what we have to wear in covering ourselves, or how much of ourselves we have to cover—only that we shouldn't act in a way that attracts undue attention. You can do that just by lowering your eyes, or by turning away when someone is looking at you in an uncomfortable way."

Similarly, in Plato's Socratic dialogue *Charmides*, the character Charmides, admired for his good looks and grace by the other dialogue participants, agrees that the primary quality of moderation is modesty, and that a person who conducts himself modestly does not do anything purposely to draw attention to himself.

"In Farsi, the word for moderation is *mawazena*," says Suhaila's friend Habiba, also from Afghanistan and also a university student, but dressed in *burqa* and *hajib*. "The word encompasses your total way of presenting yourself to the world in a modest way. What I wear is part of my way of presenting to the world my modest bearing. In somewhat the same way, I think, a woman who is an orthodox Jew dresses so that she's completely covered from head to ankle, to show that she practices *shomer megiah*."

Typically translated as "guardian of purity," *shomer megiah* is the name for the traditional Jewish laws set forth in the Torah for, among other ways of conduct by a single woman, dressing according to the strictures of Jewish modesty. These include dressing in a way in which you are covered from collar to elbow to knees, and conducting yourself in a way in which you do not come in physical contact with any men besides your father and grandfather until you are married.

Habiba's mother, Fatimah, now says, "I was very upset when Laura Bush, the First Lady, went on the airwaves after the U.S. invasion of Afghanistan and said how women there were 'forced' to cover their bodies and wear veils. Most Muslim women dressed this way long before the Taliban came to power. For most of us, a *hijab* is an outward way of saying without words to people we encounter that we have the Muslim virtue of *tahara*, or purity, and of modesty, *iffa*."

Then she says, "Mrs. Bush should have talked instead about the immodest way most American women dress and speak. I walk in the mall, I see how they dress and overhear how they talk, and I'm glad I am wearing a veil so they cannot see me blush. They leave nothing to the imagination. They have no idea what modesty is."

Author Wendy Shalit, for one, advocates a rediscovery and return to "the lost virtue" of modesty in the United States. In *A Return to Modesty*, Shalit writes that it is a "misunderstanding" based on a "cultural myth spun by a society which vastly underrates sexual sublimation" to associate modesty, as she says is commonly done today, "with sexual repression."

A woman seated beside me now says, "I wear *burqa* and *hijab* because I feel it is in line with the Islamic views on modesty, but not because it's required. It does seem that many men treat me more respectfully here in the United States because of what I wear, though they don't necessarily treat me as an equal. But no one should determine whether or not I am modest just by whether I do or don't wear a veil. The *hijab* is only one of many signs of our faith, or *eeman*."

Tahereh, from Iran, who is dressed in a Western skirt and blouse, and who works as a bank loan officer, says, "I just don't think *hijab* has to have anything to do with modesty. I wear modern clothing, but I am an extremely modest woman. And I practice what I feel any Muslim would consider moderate behavior."

Then she says to me, "But I don't believe that it's the clothing—or only the clothing—that shows your moderate values. What's most important is who you are on the inside, and how you behave toward others—whether you share with others once your own needs are met, whether you are tolerant of others, whether you talk softly with others and listen carefully, things like that."

Arizoo, an exchange student from Iran, says, "You can wear traditional clothing, and still be unfaithful to the Quran. You can still be very immodest, and hide this immodesty behind your clothing. You can cheat, be promiscuous, and wear traditional clothes. And even if you're covered so completely that only your eyes are showing, I think you can tell, just by looking into someone's eyes, whether or not they're modest."

Then she says, "I wear modern clothes, yet I don't believe I've ever done anything that has gone against the *Shariah*, Islamic law, as spelled out in the Quran, or anything against the *hadith*, the traditions established by the prophet Muhammad."

"I think *hijab* can make you look *more* appealing, but in a way that accentuates your modesty," says Jamileh. "To me, the veil doesn't conceal who I am. It *reveals* who I am—it reveals my beliefs, my culture, my moderate values."

Marina, who is from Jordan, and now works at a department store, says, "I don't understand why all the focus is on the particular verses of the Quran that Jamileh recited earlier, rather than the one that precedes them, where it says, 'Say to believing men that they should lower their gaze and guard their modesty; that will make for greater purity for them ...'"

She goes on, "No one ever discusses the role of Muslim men when

it comes to moderate behavior and clothing. Muslim men are supposed to 'guard their modesty' and 'lower their gaze,' just like women.
If they do this, why should it matter what women wear?

"The 'five pillars' of the Islamic faith are: to believe that Allah is our
only god and Mohammed his messenger, to give to charity, to pray
five times a day, to fast at Ramadan, and to make the pilgrimage to
Mecca. A lot of extremists would like the wearing of the veil to be the
'sixth pillar.' But, as Suhaila said earlier, there's no place in the Quran
that says a woman must wear a veil, or that says it is a measure of
whether we are moderate in the way commanded by the prophet."

After a pause, Sahar, from Egypt, says, "This virtue of modesty is
supposed to be practiced by *all* devout Muslims, to please God. A person strives to live by modest means, like the prophet. If she has more
than she needs, she is to give it to others in need. She is modest about
her own humanity, humble about her frailty. A modest person knows
that her heart is no greater or smaller, worth no more or less, than that
of any other person."

Then she says, "The problem is, we've allowed extremists to take
over our faith. The Taliban is only one example of this. The rulers of
almost all Arabic nations, who claim to be the most devout of
Muslims, accumulate huge sums of wealth, while the rest of their people live in unimaginable poverty. They don't share. They only dole out
just enough so the poor don't revolt. For the rich in my native country, the goal is endless gain for the few rich at the expense of all the
poor. This is completely counter to how the prophet urged us to live.
Those who lust after power and wealth are not true Muslims.

"My family immigrated here so we'd have the freedom to live in
genuine accordance with the prophet's strictures. To live by this middle way, you first have to be able to have some choice about *how* you
live. In Egypt, we had no choice, we were so poor."

Her friend Mira, who immigrated from Saudi Arabia and now is a student at a local community college, says, "In the creation chapter of the Quran, it's made clear that all men and women are equal, that we are partners in life who share obligations and duties, and that we all must cultivate modesty and moderation. In a true Islamic society, we all would have equal opportunities in education, in careers, in service. But in most Islamic nations, women have almost no rights. We can't work, we can't vote, we're not even allowed to drive. That's why I'd never go back to Saudi Arabia. The Bedouin leaders there practice a form of Islam that's totally opposed to the prophet's moderate ethic."

Suhaila now says, "Before the Taliban, Afghanistan was one of the more progressive Islamic nations. Our constitution gave us equal rights, and banned all forms of discrimination. Before the Taliban, women could be doctors, we could be in parliament, we could be professors. The Taliban did away with all that. They said women couldn't take part in the public life, and that we must live in *purdah*, or seclusion, which they say, wrongly, is based on Islamic law."

Then Suhaila says, "I feel grateful I now have the freedom to choose how I dress, and to choose careers. In Afghanistan, it's still in some ways in the Dark Ages, even with the Taliban gone. Like recently, the Afghan Supreme Court removed a female judge from her job just because she chose not to wear a *burqa* when she visited with President Bush and his wife. They're the opposite of the prophet's moderate voice of reason. The Taliban have only been replaced by other extremist *muhahideen*, so-called holy warriors, who will never allow equal rights for women."

After a pause, Sahar says, "The prophet Muhammad stressed that all *insan*, all human beings, are equal before Allah. Before the prophet became an advocate for women's rights nearly fifteen centuries ago, women were terribly mistreated. He made a lot of inroads in rectifying this. But today, Muslim women face a lot of the same discrimination that the prophet tried to combat."

There is a nice lull as we sip tea and consider all that has been said. Then Suah says, "True Islam is a religion of the middle way. The prophet shunned all forms of extremism. When we recite our prayers at least five times a day, we ask Allah to show us the straight path, the middle path. This is a path between extremes, a path of grace, of tolerance, and reasonableness."

## THE VEIL AND THE MIDDLE COURSE

Faegheh Shirazi of the Islamic Studies Program at the University of Texas at Austin says that the veil is "a simple garment that millions of women deal with in their daily lives as a matter of habit"; but it also is "an enormously important symbol" that "carries thousands of years of religious, sexual, social, and political significance," and is still considered by millions of devout Muslims as "a sign of piety, modesty, or purity."

Fadwa El Guindi, of the University of Southern California, says in *Veil: Modesty, Privacy and Resistance*, that for Muslim women the veil is "situated at the intersection of dress, body and culture." She contends that the notions spread by Western media of the veil as a symbol of oppression, extreme modesty and seclusion "are not an adequate characterization of the phenomenon as it is expressed in the Middle East." Rather, the veil can represent a blend of "nationalism, cultural pride, and Islam."

John L. Esposito, a professor of Middle East studies, writes that for many Muslim women, Islamic dress "is an attempt to combine traditional values and ideals with contemporary levels of education and employment." Suha Sabbagh, who was director of the Institute for Arab Women's Studies in Washington, notes that Muslim women "who hope to leave traditional constraints" are by no means universally opposed to wearing a veil. For instance, for women university students in Algiers, "their protective veiling . . . allowed them to escape the traditional female roles of mother and wife in order to pursue professional, educational, and social lives necessarily conducted in public." While the veil itself may have enabled them to steer a course between adhering to the extremely conservative mores that would keep them at home and participating more fully in a society run by fundamentalists, this kind of compromise is hardly the same as that advocated by the prophet, who never required or espoused veiling of any sort.

Most critically, these scholars seem to overlook what several women stressed in the dialogue—namely, that the veil is not necessarily the principal or the best way, or even *a* way, that a Muslim woman can show her devotion to the moderate ethic espoused by the prophet, no more than it in any way indicates whether she is modest.

## WHAT IS MODESTY?

In her popular book *Return to Modesty*, Wendy Shalit says there are "two very different kinds of modesty": One type is "modesty in the sense of being humble"; and the other is "sexual modesty, the kind we associate with the Medicean Venus." She says that her dictionary "defines the humble kind of modesty as 'having moderate estimation of one's abilities or worth,' and the sexual kind as 'the damping down of one's allure.'"

Shalit says her "inquiry" in her book "is concerned mostly with the latter kind," which she thinks has been the most "seriously misunderstood, even by the experts who write our dictionaries." I think both definitions of the two types of modesty are skewed, and that Shalit has only further muddied our understanding of either one. Shalit says that if you accept the dictionary definition of the latter type of modesty, then you have to adhere to the belief that "for thousands of years women were behaving and dressing in ways that made them unappealing, and they are so dim, they didn't realize it until very recently." This betrays a considerable ignorance of history; many women (and men) of long-ago eras, including adherents of fundamentalist and orthodox faiths, have dressed much more revealingly than most of us do now—consider the fashions on display in the art of ancient Egypt.

The notion of modesty always is relational to the cultural milieu in which one lives. As the French existentialist writer and social critic Simone de Beauvoir (1908–86) notes in *The Second Sex*, "Custom regulates the compromise between exhibitionism and modesty." De Beauvoir also points out insightfully that "decency by no means consists in dressing with strict modesty." She says it can just as well be the case that "a women who appeals too obviously to male desire"—or anyone's desire, for that matter—"is in bad taste," as it can be that "one who seems to reject it is no more commendable."

Similarly, one may "damp down," in the name of modesty, not just one's sexual allure, but, among many other things, one's talents in any area or discipline, for many different reasons. One may do so out of a false or exaggerated humility, or out of a genuine regard for others and a keen desire not to stand out at anyone else's expense, so that others in the process of developing their own "estimate" of their "worth and talents" are not unduly discouraged.

—

In her book, Shalit lambastes feminists' egalitarian perspectives on the concept of modesty. She says "modesty is so threatening to the egalitarians because whenever it emerges it is *evidence* . . . women's experience of love and sex is different from man's, and as such it rebukes the androgynous project." But the truth is that every person on this planet has at least a somewhat, and perhaps dramatically different, experience of love and sex. Shalit's simplistic bifurcation of men's and women's perspectives on this subject is further skewed by her incredibly confused notion of egalitarianism. Egalitarianism does not in any way mean that all males, and all females, respectively, are carbon copies of one another, but that they are all equally, and uniquely, human, that all matter and count, that all think and feel and believe and experience not in terms of black and white, but in a range of dazzling colors. So it is, for instance, that we all likely have differing philosophies of modesty, sexual and otherwise.

A much more insightful perspective on modesty is set forth by the nineteenth-century feminist and novelist Mary Wollstonecraft. In her book *A Vindication of the Rights of Woman*, she asserts that there are "two distinct modes" of modesty. One is "that purity of mind, which is the effect of chastity"—the mode espoused by Shalit and by fundamentalists of various faiths. The other is "a simplicity of character that leads us to form a just opinion of ourselves, equally distant from vanity or presumption"—and so representing a reasonable middle way—which at the same time is "by no means incompatible with a lofty consciousness of our own dignity." Implicit in this latter, and compelling, definition of modesty is "that soberness of mind which teaches" a person "not to think more highly of himself than he ought to think."

Wollstonecraft believed that the cultivation and possession of genuine modesty "is incompatible with ignorance and vanity." While "the downcast eye, the rosy blush, the retiring grace are all proper in their season," genuine modesty, "being the child of reason, cannot long exist with the sensibility that is not tempered by reflection." She goes on to write: "Let women only acquire knowledge and humanity, and love will teach them modesty."

# MODERATION CORRUPTED

"Moderation—what we call *In*—is a Confucian virtue," says Jung, a political science student at Seoul National University. "If you adhere to the ideals of Confucius, as most Koreans do, you believe that to be moderate is to discover the ideal mean in guiding your actions. In *Analects*, the recorded sayings of Confucius, Confucius said to one of his disciples in chapter eight 'that going too far is as bad as not going far enough.'"

Jung is one of about twenty young people, mostly students, with whom I am gathered in the outskirts of Seoul, South Korea, as we seek answers to "What is moderation?" We're on the third floor of the first multistory doughnut shop I've ever been in. It's surrounded by cement-block skyscrapers that accommodate the burgeoning city population of over ten million. These are economic boom times— *BusinessWeek* magazine calls this country of forty-eight million the economic "model for Asia"—and with property scarce, the only option is to build upward.

Says another student, "In his writing of *Jung-yung*, or *Doctrine of the Mean*, Confucius urged his followers to 'strive to bring about inner harmony' in their lives. This inner harmony is an ideal mean, or balance, between too much and too little. When you have this balance, you are moderate. But it takes great self-discipline and self-regulation to achieve it."

"How does one go about discovering this 'ideal mean'?" I ask.

"Mostly, your conscience is your guide," says Hong, a graduate student in engineering. "For instance, some of us here with you are involved in prodemocracy protests. We think this country still has a long way to go in discovering the ideal mean between social harmony and individual freedom. Right now, even though we're supposedly a democracy, we still have a repressive form of social harmony, which comes at the price of individual liberty. We don't think this is the mean that Confucius had in mind."

While many scholars have argued that Confucianism is antidemocratic, or at least is not prodemocratic, Joseph Chan writes in *The East Asian Challenge for Human Rights* that the "central elements in Confucianism," such as its "emphasis on role-based ethics, the Confucian ideal of community . . . and the preference for harmony . . . are all compatible with the idea of human rights," and so "would justify . . . civil liberties," which are at the core of a genuine democracy.

"The Korean word for moderation, *In*, actually has two meanings: One is 'to endure'; and the other is 'to regulate and filter one's desires,'" says Jae, a political science student. "But there're good and bad ways of enduring and filtering. Our government often 'regulates' the people and 'filters' what we can and cannot say and do, so that their corrupt system can 'endure.' On the other hand, we activists endure their criticism and we place our desire for a real democracy over all our other desires, because we care about the future of our people."

She then says, "When our president, Kim Dae Jung, was a student, he was a master practitioner of the genuine form of Confucian moderation. He's from Kwangju, as many of us are, and he was deeply involved in the Kwangju Uprising of 1980. In fact, today is the eve of the twenty-second anniversary of the Kwangju Uprising of May 18, 1980."

The *pan'gol*, or antiauthoritarian protest, was spearheaded by students in the insular city of Kwangju, which is several hours southeast of Seoul. Even before the 1980 protest, Kwangju long had been a hotbed of activism against oppression. A 1929 student demonstration there protested the Japanese occupation of Korea. The Japanese army brutally put down the uprising, but not before it inspired people across the country to stand up to the invading troops and eventually oust them from the country. In the 1980 student revolt against authoritarian rule, it was the Korean military, rather than a force from an occupying nation, that this time intervened brutally to quell the protest. Officially, at least two hundred students died (the actual number is believed to be many times this figure), with over a thousand wounded, and thousands arrested. The military's handling of the protest triggered an even more widespread revolt among prodemocracy groups throughout the nation. It culminated eight years later in a student- and worker-led mass movement that precipitated sweeping democratic reforms.

"Kim Dae Jung was tried and sentenced to death for the key role he played in the Kwangju revolt," Hae, also a political science student, says next. "Fortunately for all of us, his sentence was commuted by the dictator Chun Doo Hwan. Kim lived to see our country become a democracy. He even went on to become president, and to win the Nobel Peace Prize for his efforts at democratic reform and to reunify the Koreas. All those years he spent in exile and in prison, he developed more and more Confucian moderation. He controlled and regulated his passions in a noble way, rather than allowing himself to be controlled by them. He didn't permit himself to be consumed by hate, or resentment, or revenge. He 'endured' and 'filtered his desires' in the way Jae spoke of, for the greater good of humanity. His concern was for creating a real democracy and positive social change."

"But that was then," a student named Chey says sardonically. "In some ways, President Kim has become as controlling, in a destructive way, as his predecessors. In his first year in office, he arrested nearly four hundred people—more than three times that of his predecessor. He said before he was elected that he'd do away with authoritarian rule. But now, when it suits him, sometimes he embraces it. He did give amnesty to many prisoners who'd been jailed for protesting authoritarian rule. But there are still many more kept incarcerated, because they support unpopular causes that he considers a danger to the type of society that he now wants—the type that attracts foreign investment and keeps the economy thriving. President Kim is striking a mean between an oppressive type of stability and a very limited kind of freedom. I think this type of mean is more vice than virtue, and goes against Confucianism."

Says Jong, the woman beside him, "We still have the same National Security Law that was in effect in the time of the dictators, and it's still used immoderately to abuse our freedoms. President Kim has used it to arrest and imprison antiestablishment protesters, and to conduct clandestine surveillance of ex-prisoners of conscience whom the government considers a threat to stability."

The National Security Law, enacted more than fifty years ago, enables South Korea's leaders to clamp down at will on prodemocracy activists who they claim threaten to undermine the Republic of Korea's national security. When President Kim was an opposition leader, he'd indicated he would do away with the law if elected president; but he has kept it intact. Amnesty International's 2001 report on the Republic of Korea says that President Kim's "promises of domestic political and judicial reforms, including a review of the National Security Law and the enactment of a Human Rights Law, were not realized." It goes on to say that "(m)ost political prisoners continued to be detained under the vaguely worded provisions of the National Security Law. Excessive force to quell trade union protests continued, and many trade unionists were arrested." The report also says that, to this day, the government continues to use its Security Surveillance Law "to control and supervise the activities of former political prisoners, including prisoners of conscience. Under the law, former prisoners have to report regularly to the nearest police station, face restrictions on their freedom of movement, and are banned from meeting former political prisoners and participating in demonstrations, especially political demonstrations."

"The government has tried to get students to quit joining the trade union protests," Jong now tells me. "Our economy, after being in the dregs for years, is now the premier economy in Asia. Our government doesn't want anything to upset this. But our unions are protesting because their members have to work six-day workweeks, many in sweatshop conditions, and we support them. We're the only developed nation where all offices and factories are open Saturdays. Our workers want to have free time to enjoy the fruits of their work, rather than just 'endure,' like a slave, in a way that life isn't worth living. But the government would like to 'regulate' them like they're automatons. There has to be a mean or middle ground in society between contributing to your nation's economy, and having time to devote to your own pursuits and interests. We're still far from achieving it."

There is a pause before Jung says, "The problem is that, since we were children, all of us have had drilled into us, by our teachers and parents, that Confucian moderation, Korean style, is to allow yourself to be regulated by adult authority figures. Unquestioning obedience is very much stressed in our society, where you filter all your desires to the will of those above you. Corporal punishment is a longtime tradition in our schools, so teachers can enforce unquestioning obedience. So we learn very young to filter out any desires to think independently, and do whatever authority figures say, or face severe physical punishment. Most parents *want* children to be punished in the classroom. They say that if teachers can't discipline children, they can't learn moderate conduct."

"There's a movement now to ban corporal punishment in South Korea," says Chey. "But the Constitutional Court, the highest court in our land, recently ruled that corporal punishment is appropriate, and the federal government endorsed its ruling. It's pitiful, because it promotes a type of moderate behavior based on fear and intimidation of the young, who are the most vulnerable, by the people with power over them, rather than promote the empowering self-regulation that real Confucianism espouses."

David I. Steinberg, director of Asian Studies at Georgetown University, writes that "(v)iolence is endemic in Korean society, although most of it is submerged under a Confucian façade of proper and formal relationships and behavior. And it is not just students or men. There is an overwhelming pattern of physical abuse against women . . ." To Steinberg, who has taught in Korea, this pervasive abuse stems from the long tradition of corporal punishment in schools: "If students have been physically abused, even for causes that the authorities consider righteous, the pattern becomes ingrained." Moreover, if teachers instill in students that the most "effective method of problem solving is through physical punishment," then the vicious cycle continues. Steinberg believes that just as teachers are now part of the problem, they have a key role to play in remedying this, by being "instruments of change, acting as true leaders." In a student-teacher relationship, Steinberg says that "no one claims that a student and a teacher are always equal, but there is a mutuality of respect that is required if education is to accomplish its goals. There is, or should be, equality of human beings." But when students constantly fear punishment, the atmosphere of "(r)espect for knowledge, for free inquiry, for the spirit of civility to which these concepts are related is lost."

Says Park, another participant in our discussion, "There're other hypocrisies in my country that run counter to genuine Confucian moderation. Like, Confucius tells us to be moderate in our vices, like alcohol consumption, because it weakens society. But we have a soaring rate of alcoholism here, especially among men."

The medical journal *American Psychiatry* reports, in an article comparing alcohol consumption in Asian nations, that "alcoholism in Korea is three times higher than in Taiwan," though both nations still subscribe to "the Confucian moral ethic of moderation and temperance." The dominant male culture in Korea "not only tolerates but encourages alcohol consumption" as a symbol of "male mastery, strength and domination," while in Taiwan, in keeping with its Confucian value system, "not only is drunkenness disapproved of . . . , it denotes degeneration and personal weakness."

Hee, a philosophy student who has taken part in prodemocracy protests, now says, "Until very recently, we were a poor society. We lived with extreme frugality. Now we're a wealthy society, and we're grasping for more and more material things. We want all the creature comforts, like you have in the U.S., and like they have in Japan. We've gone from one extreme to another, and missed the mean completely. Yet we claim that we're a Confucian nation, even though these extremes go against the essence of Confucianism."

"But sometimes the student and trade union protests are quite violent, quite extreme," I say, referring to the fact that in recent years, student protests have included violent clashes with South Korea government security forces, in which some students have used Molotov cocktails, steel pipes, and gasoline bombs. "How does this jibe with Confucian moderation?"

"I don't think the protests are extreme," he says, "though the government paints them that way. We are no more extreme, certainly, than President Kim was when he was our age, leading the same type of protests. You have to be extremely disciplined—self-disciplined, and disciplined as a group—for these protests to make a difference."

He frowns, as if unsatisfied with his response, and then says, "Well, I guess the protests are extreme, in a sense. I think, if we're to have the type of open society we envision, one that is respectful of all humans' rights, one has to take extreme measures at times. In that sense, maybe I'm not in agreement with Confucius. I don't think you can always be in the middle. I think such a view—that you always have to go the middle course, and never deviate from it—is itself an extremist view. I think you have to know when it is called for to go to extremes, and when not to."

After a considerable pause, a student named Anh says, "I agree with what he says. But I think there is another type of middle way that we should strive for."

She goes on: "Several of us here are Buddhists, and the Korean term *chun yo* relates to our Buddhist beliefs. *Chun yo* means 'to take the middle.' To a Buddhist, the 'Middle Way' is about avoiding very specific extremes, rather than all extremes. For instance, we avoid the extremes of asceticism and covetous desire, and we try to find a middle ground between flourishing as an individual, and helping your society flourish."

"I think this middle way is a higher way," she says, "because it leads to greater happiness and fulfillment for everybody in a society."

## MEANS AND MIDDLE GROUNDS

As a young man at the vortex of the prodemocracy movement in his country, Kim Dae Jung was considered such a threat to the authoritarian regime in power that he was arrested and spent fourteen years in exile, house arrest, and imprisonment, including many months in solitary confinement. While in isolation, he was allowed to write one letter per day to his family, and it was in these "prison writings" that Kim first philosophized that "(t)oday's humanity, which tries to attain happiness by maximizing consumption and possessions," ultimately "will only taste defeat and alienation." Kim envisioned a type of society that aspired to make sure everyone had their essential needs met, so they could then have the opportunity to achieve the types of happiness and fulfillment that money can't buy. Yet Korea today, with Kim as president, is in the throes of unprecedented economic prosperity, and now is lurching toward the very extreme of "maximizing consumption and possessions" that Kim once condemned. It has lost sight of the ideal mean, which strikes a balance between material and nonmaterial satisfactions, that Kim aspired to realize when he was an activist, and that many who took part in the dialogue are committed to realizing today.[1]

While in prison, Kim wrote that the "real purpose of politics is to guarantee the rights and life of the oppressed and the poor and help them to become the principals of politics." Yet shortly after becoming president, Kim granted amnesty to those who preceded him in power and had wreaked so much havoc on the ability of the oppressed and poor to live with any semblance of dignity. Kim said in his prison writings that "even those who used to oppress, and those who used to take things by force, must be freed from their sins and allowed to participate." Since Kim went to extremes in reconciling with his erstwhile enemies, it seems he should have gone to equal or even greater lengths to show leniency toward—to "free from their sins" and "allow to participate"—his kindred spirits, today's political and trade union and student activists. Maybe if he'd gone to extremes in both cases, instead of only on behalf of those who least deserved it, he might have forged a creative middle course that furthered the admirable ideals and ends he articulated when he was in prison.

———

Namhee Lee, a professor of history at the University of Utah, notes that the student movement in South Korea was "one of the most important political actors in Korean society," and a "force of con-

---

1. President Kim's term ended in January 2003, when he was replaced by Roh Moo-hyun, who was a human-rights lawyer and activist.

science," or *yangsim seryok*. He writes that "much like former East European dissidents," Korea's student activists "were 'morally superior' because they spoke what was in everybody's mind, without considering the consequences." I would go further and say that their courageous actions inspired a change of mind and heart in everyone else—even an *awakening* of mind and heart. These prodemocracy activists very carefully considered the consequences of their actions; they put their lives on the line, willingly and deliberately, thinking only of their nation's long-term good. What's more, these students, in "(c)laiming themselves to be a voice of conscience and the true representative of the *minjung* (common people)," were not, as Lee insists, claiming moral superiority. Rather, in taking the moral high ground, they aspired to create a more egalitarian society, with no one inherently "superior" to anyone else.

---

Robert Myers notes in *Korea in the Cross-Currents* that Confucius himself "promoted a series of virtues," one of which was the "principal of *jen*," which he defines as "fellow feeling . . . a notion of the personal and societal bond between individuals, and by extension, between groups." But the Chinese word *jen*—which in Korean is *ren*—I think is better translated as "human goodness," a supreme virtue in which all humans regard one another as equally human, as equally deserving of living a life of dignity and promise, and are treated accordingly.[2]

---

2. Throughout human history, many in positions of power and privilege have, as a matter of course, treated their fellow humans in a less equal way. They've treated them as if they should not be able to live in the dignity that they enjoy themselves, and in fact do everything they can to thwart such ends. If and when the situation is reversed, and they find themselves in the more vulnerable position, some may well undergo an epiphany in social conscience, by being treated in a much more magnanimous way than those they'd oppressed. Though this is by no means always or even often the case, this was among the expectations of Nelson Mandela and Kim Dae Jung when they made forgiveness and recon-

Myers points out that Confucius says that *jen* requires "(u)nyielding fortitude and simple modesty." It would seem that this blend of fortitude and modesty is the Confucian ideal of moderation in action. Those who strive for human goodness would seem to have discovered a type of middle way in which, by seeking to liberate others, they at the same time further liberate themselves.

## WHICH WAY IS THE MIDDLE WAY?

Like Socrates, Buddha (circa 563–483 B.C.) left no written works, but instead left it up to his followers and admirers to record faithfully his sayings. According to these sayings, Buddha exhorted people to avoid extremes, and to follow the middle way. In the *Dhamma-Kakka-Ppavattana-Sutta*, or *Discourse on the Turning Wheel*, Buddha exhorted five monks to avoid the two extremes of "a life . . . devoted to pleasures and lusts" and "a life given to mortifications." Avoiding these two extremes, Buddha said, is to discover "the knowledge of the middle path." To Buddha, this middle path is one and the same as the "eightfold path," in which one cultivates certain "noble virtues": right understanding, right aspiration, right speech, right conduct, right means of livelihood, right endeavor, right-mindfulness or -mindedness, and right contemplation or concentration. Following this middle path, Buddha said, "leads to insight, which leads to wisdom, which in turn leads to calm, to knowledge, to supreme enlightenment, to nirvana." When one has reached nirvana, or enlightment, Buddha says that one comes to know four "noble truths": that life is *dukkha*, or suf-

---

ciliation paramount over punishment of their former oppressors. I wonder, though, if creative forms of rehabilitation-oriented penalties—such as, at the very least, "sentencing" a nation's oppressors to a life of community service on behalf of those they'd oppressed—may be a better means of achieving this end, rather than just letting them go scot-free.

fering; that all suffering springs from an ignorance of the true nature of reality, which creates needless cravings; that the only way to overcome the chain of human suffering is to transcend these cravings, by seeing the true nature of reality; and that the way to do this is to pursue the middle way of the noble eightfold path.

Thich Nhat Hanh, a Vietnamese Buddhist monk whose tireless efforts to reconcile North and South Vietnam inspired Dr. Martin Luther King, Jr., to nominate him in 1967 for the Nobel Peace Prize, notes that in *Discourse on the Turning Wheel*, Buddha sought to dissuade the five monks, all ascetics, "from the idea that austerity is the only correct practice." The Buddha "had learned firsthand that if you destroy your health, you have no energy left to realize the path" of the Middle Way. For Buddha, one should no more practice extreme asceticism and spiritualism than gross self-indulgence; rather, one should strive for a middle way that requires development and then disciplining of one's spiritual and intellectual and moral and physical capacities.

Thich Nhat Hanh, who since age forty has lived in exile from Vietnam, after being denounced in 1966 by both the communist and noncommunist governments for trying to build a lasting peace between the two sides, urges people to shun the accumulation of wealth "while millions are hungry," and not to "take as the aim of your life fame, profit, wealth, and sensual pleasure." His ideal in life, to "(l)ive simply, and share time, energy, and material resources with those who are in need," touches a chord with people of conscience everywhere who belong to a variety of religious and cultural traditions.

But then he goes on to say that we must learn to "know our physical and psychological limits . . ." if we are to follow the Middle Way. I wonder, though: How do we know what these limits are, if we don't put them to the test? Not that it's virtuous to test limits of any sort— but what about the limits of our intellect, of our creative capacity for "doing good"? I started out my university studies as an electrical engineering student, simply because it was what I was good at. But at the eleventh hour, I changed direction to study liberal arts, because I felt I wanted to find out what else I might be good at, and to fill in yawning gaps in my mediocre public school education. This decision to set sail in unknown academic waters set me on the course that today has led me to a career pursuit, and a social mission, that otherwise would never have entered my mind.

If we don't to some degree test our capacities, it seems that we run the danger of setting overly constricting limits for ourselves, and our society. It seems that one of the core underpinnings of an open society is that it sets no preconceived parameters on our ability to enhance and expand and cultivate our most humane aspirations. Many throughout history whom I most admire took extreme measures, often risking their lives, as they tested themselves to the limit. Kim Dae Jung, for one. Thich Nhat Hanh for another.

Or is it that they weren't taking extreme action at all? Is it instead the case that their efforts to build a lasting peace through nonviolent means were not extreme measures?

—

In an essay published in *Time* magazine, Ma Kwang Soon, a novelist and professor of Korean literature at Yonsei University in Seoul, writes that "authoritarian culture remains dominant" in Korea, and that the "ultimate solution" for overcoming this "is for Korean society to embrace pluralism and tolerate freedom of expression." He says this is an uphill task, because Koreans still are "caught up in the Confucian mentality of the nineteenth century . . . , which favored . . . authoritarianism and a closed door to cultural influences from abroad."

While some Koreans in positions of authority clearly are "caught up" in an authoritarian, and perverted, form of Confucianism, I don't think this is true of most young people—certainly none I came in contact with—who are trying to resurrect a more genuine form of Confucianism. And young Koreans most definitely are not in any way closed to cultural influences from abroad—just the opposite, in fact.

More critically, Soon fails to mention another still-strong Korean tradition, that of Mahayana Buddhism, which may contain the virtues needed to overcome those forces that he says are impeding Korean progress. The Buddhist virtues of love and compassion, plus the equal role it traditionally gives to women, have the potential to bring about an ideal Buddhist society.

In an essay entitled "Buddhism, Asian Values and Democracy" included in *The Democratic Invention*, the Dalai Lama, recipient of the Nobel Peace Prize, says that "at the heart of Buddhism lies the idea that the potential for awakening and perfection is present in every human being, and that realizing this potential is a matter of personal effort." But I don't think it's just "a matter of personal effort," and I feel sure that the Dalai Lama—who fled Chinese-occupied Tibet in 1959 and went into exile along with over eighty thousand other Tibetans— doesn't either. Rather, one must first live in a type of society that allows and encourages this kind of personal effort, and that strives simultaneously to further its own "awakening and perfection"—its own excellence. To do so would seem to require a type of middle ground between the personal and the political. This middle ground, as one student in the dialogue in which I took part suggested, would also seem to be a higher ground.

## OBESE NATION

"Isn't moderation all about self-control?" a young woman student asks me.

"What makes you think it is?" I ask, as about thirteen other students and seven or so residents of the area look on. Tempe, Arizona, is a medium-sized city, parts of which have been developed in relative conformity with its desert environment, in contrast with the endless sprawl of adjacent Phoenix, where my wife and I lived for a year, and of neighboring cities. Anchored by Arizona State University, Tempe is proudly referred to by some here as the "People's Republic of Tempe," to distinguish their city as an oasis of progressivism in a desert of conservative politics. We're in a café that is as gorgeous inside—with its vaulted ceilings, walls of paneled oak, and stained-glass windows—as it is ugly outside, where the bland architecture of its former occupant, a chain drugstore, has not been altered.

The student now says to me, "Six days out of seven, I watch carefully everything I eat. I obsessively count every calorie. Nothing unhealthy goes down my gullet. And then, on the seventh day . . . I go to a buffet, and binge big-time. I exercise enough afterwards so I'm not so heavy as I'd otherwise be. But I always feel guilty, and nauseated, afterwards."

Then she says, "I'm not sure if what I'm saying directly answers your question, but I wonder a lot of the time how I can be so moderate the overwhelming majority of the time, but then be so immoderate for one meal every week."

"Maybe you're too moderate the remainder of the week, and that makes you rebel at that one meal," says Sara, another student who is a regular at Socrates Café. This elicits a quizzical look from her fellow student.

Sara goes on, "Actually, if you watch everything you eat and tally up calories so zealously, that's not moderate at all. That's extremism. You either eat nothing bad to the nth degree, or you go the other way and pig out. So six days a week, you're extreme in one direction, and then one day a week, you're extreme in the other. You go from extreme self-control to extreme lack of self-control. So moderation can't just be about self-control." The student she's addressing mulls this over for a moment, then nods her head thoughtfully.

Sara then says to all of us, "I think moderation is at least as much about balance as it is self-control, and not just in terms of eating and drinking, but any material goods you buy, any natural resources you use, and in the overall way you live."

This inspires an incredibly hale and hardy senior citizen named Max, who bikes fifteen perilous miles from his home in Phoenix to attend Socrates Café, to say, "There's no such a thing as moderation anymore in the United States. Just look at the way we consume way past any point of contentment or need. Just look at our gluttonous greed for monstrous Enronlike corporate profits—and not just by the corporate bigwigs, but by Mom-and-Pop shareholders—for monster cars, monster stores, monster trophy homes."

Then he says, "We want no limits of any sort, so we don't exercise willpower, a key quality of being moderate." He looks around first to make sure he won't offend anyone taking part in the dialogue before adding, "That's why mega-buffets and mega-bodies are all the rage."

Social critic Eric Schlosser writes in his best-selling book *Fast Food Nation: The Dark Side of the American Meal* that while "(t)he American gene pool has not changed radically in the last few decades," the way Americans live, and the way they eat, has changed dramatically: "The United States now has the highest obesity rate of any industrialized nation in the world." At the time his book was published in 2000, "(m)ore than half of all American adults and about one-quarter of all American children are . . . obese or overweight"— and these numbers soar ever higher. The pernicious results, he says, extend "far beyond emotional and low self-esteem. Obesity is now second only to smoking as a cause of mortality."

"If 'monstrosity' now is the norm in our society, can't one argue that this is moderate?" I muse.

Max shakes his head. "No way. The word *moderate* doesn't enter the equation. These people are *a*moderate. We're just as hedonistic as Epicurus was."

In fact, it wasn't Epicurus, but a group of fifth- and fourth-century B.C. philosophers known as the Cyrenaics who originated the hedonistic philosophy of senseless gorging to which Max is referring. The Cyrenaics subscribed to an amoral "anything goes" code of conduct—whatever gave them pleasure, particularly of the sensual sort, was permissible. Epicurus (343–271 B.C.), on the other hand, lived by a very moderate and even ascetic ethic, because he felt that these qualities led to the greatest individual attainment or satisfaction of pleasure. To Epicurus, recognizing how little one really needed to be satisfied was the path to pleasure.

"So for you," I say to Max, "moderation is . . ."

". . . about setting limits—on what you eat, what you buy, what you use, the land you develop, how much you profit in a business, you name it," he says. "Extremes are destroying our country. Moderation is the key to a sane lifestyle."

"So you're against extremism, which to you is the opposite of moderation," I say.

"Precisely. We have to go back to being a frugal people."

"Are you extremely frugal, or moderately frugal?" I ask.

"Extremely," he says without thinking. Then, with thinking, he says, "Oh, so you're saying *I'm* immoderate." He frowns, and then laughs. "Well, I guess I am. I set extreme limits on the way I live. But the people I'm critiquing are just the opposite. They want no limits of any kind."

Laszlo Versenyi writes in *Socratic Humanism* that Socrates believed that unlimited desire or passion "brings only pain, for what has no limit is impossible to satisfy. Consequently, licentious living is a slave's life, lacking all satisfaction." But must we master all our passions and desires? Must I have to master my passion for good books, good dialogue, good thinking? I would agree with Socrates only if he means that I need to develop and discipline my more constructive passions in such a way that I can enjoy them and benefit from them more than ever.

I now ask, "How do you know when you're practicing moderation?"

"You know, because you're charting a course between extremes," says Paige, another student in attendance.

"Can you give me an example?"

She considers a moment before saying, "Well, I've been thinking about the morals I was brought up with by my parents. I was brought up to believe that I should be a virgin until I got married, that I shouldn't drink, that I shouldn't see so-called dirty movies. Living on campus here is my first time out from under their wing in Ohio. I'm a junior now, and I've changed a lot since I first came to school here. At first, it never occurred to me to break from the morals I was brought up with. But I think I've since broken every moral they've ever tried to instill in me." Her admission is not a happy one. "I think I went too far a number of times, got carried away. But I felt so . . . free for the first time.

"But after a year of partying too much, of doing too much of just about everything, I realized that that wasn't for me. I didn't want to be like my parents, but I didn't want to be the opposite of them either. I'm very uncomfortable with both extremes. So now I've found the middle ground that suits me, that gives me balance. I never get too wild anymore. I still play hard, but I never get too carried away, and now I study hard too.

"I've found what for me is moderation in my life. It isn't my parents' idea of a moderate moral code. On the other hand, it isn't some of my friends' idea either; they think I'm way too 'virtuous' these days. For me, though, it's right—for now, at least. It's something I've had to discover on my own. But for others, my code may not seem moderate, because of their unique values; it may be extremely conservative, or liberal. So every person, I think, has a different idea of what a moderate moral code, or middle ground, would be. But we'd still all share a similar idea that moderation is a middle ground of some sort."

The Greek philosopher Aristotle (384–322 B.C.)—a devotee of Socrates and student of Plato's who went on to found his own academy, the Lyceum, which was devoted to observing and philosophizing about the natural world—developed a "Doctrine of the Golden Mean." In his *Nichomachean Ethics*, Aristotle asserts that one adheres to this doctrine by always choosing the middle path, which lies between the extremes of "excess" and "deficiency." Aristotle says that virtue itself "is a state involving rational choice, consisting in a mean . . . between two vices, one of excess, the other of deficiency." However, Aristotle says, in some cases the mean does not apply, because there are instances of depravity that lie outside the bounds of excess and deficiency, allowing for no possibility of achieving a virtuous middle ground. Instances of this, he says, would include "committing injustice, being a coward, and being intemperate, since then there would be a mean of excess *and* a mean of deficiency, an excess of excess and a deficiency of deficiency"—what some in today's dialogue have been calling *a*moderation.

———

After an extended pause, Shelley, who is receiving her doctorate in education, comments, "It seems like everything we've been talking about, when it comes to moderation, has to do with habits. Moderation is a habit between extremes. If you indulge in some areas, it doesn't always mean you are an extremist. You have to look at your habits in context, and as a whole. If you indulge in some areas, but compensate for your indulgences in others, you can still be considered moderate. It just depends. Like, if you drink way too much, but don't smoke, this doesn't mean you're moderate, because not smoking doesn't compensate for your excessive drinking. But if you overeat, but then exercise strenuously, you are compensating for your eating excesses, and so could still be considered moderate. I think that, to determine whether you're moderate, you have to look at the sum total of all your habits, because moderation is a habit of responsibility."

After ruminating a while, Jeff, a thirty-something who still lives with his parents, and who has told me he still has no idea what he wants to do when he grows up, now says, "This is changing directions a little, but I've been thinking how I drive my parents crazy. I'm constantly turning off light switches behind them. I constantly am on their case if they leave the water running longer than they need it. I recycle everything. I wear my clothes until they wear out, and then some. My parents think I'm an extremist. But I don't think I'm extreme, just responsible. I think if you're moderate, your goal or end is to eat responsibly, exercise responsibly, use nonrenewable natural resources responsibly, practice sex responsibly, indulge responsibly. What that means is you have to be aware of the consequences of your actions, and think in terms of how they affect others." He is quick to add, "I'm not saying I follow these guidelines all the time. I'm just saying that if you strive to be moderate, that's what you shoot for."

This prompts his friend Keith to say, "This makes me think about the word *enough*. Moderation seems to have everything to do with what your philosophy of enough is. Once you have enough food, enough clothing, enough shelter, enough money, enough happiness, enough love, then that will be your barometer of what moderation is."

The woman student who spoke at the very beginning of our dialogue says: "But there are things I can never get enough of. Never enough love, never enough knowledge, never enough time in a day. Is it always bad to feel as though you can never have enough? Can't it sometimes be a great good?"

# EXCESS OF EXCESS, DEFICIENCY OF DEFICIENCY

Is it possible to steer back to some sort of moderate ethic in America? Is it desirable?

For instance, would we want those who steer our market economy to change course and start subscribing to an ethic based on moderate corporate gains—an "ethic of enough," as one participant in the dialogue put it, rather than an ethic in which there is no such thing as enough profit or productivity or growth?

In an interview that was published in the July 2, 2002, issue of *USA Today*, Harvey L. Pitt, then-chairman of the Securities and Exchange Commission, had this to say: "We are coming off a period of enormous and probably excessive exuberance in the markets. . . . I don't want to condemn corporate America. I do condemn the fact that in the excesses of the 90s, people really lost sight of fundamental values."

More likely, it was because people first lost sight of fundamental values that the "excessive exuberances" of the 90s came to pass.

On July 17, 2002, Federal Reserve chairman Alan Greenspan was widely praised for his candor in admitting to the "infectious greed" that has gripped "much of our business community." Yet Greenspan failed to note that his policy of keeping interest rates abnormally low, in order to encourage extreme consumer spending for the sake of unending "growth," rather than enacting moderate policies that encourage sensible consumption and careful savings, can certainly be considered a catalyst of this excessively "infectious greed" he condemns. Moreover, the fact is that in the context of U.S. history, Americans today have become much greedier, and they also have many more "avenues" to "express" their greed—and the type of rapaciousness witnessed in America today resembles the type that occurred in great civilizations of the past as they began an irreversible downward spiral.

In *Spirit of Laws*, published in 1748, the French political philoso-pher Baron de Montesquieu, or Charles-Louis de Secondat, said that the "spirit of commerce" should bring with it "the spirit of frugality, economy, moderation, work, wisdom, tranquillity, order, and rule." Montesquieu said that the role of commerce in society is to "make each poor citizen comfortable enough to be able to work as the others do and bring each rich citizen to a middle level such that he needs to work in order to preserve or to acquire." While ancient "commercial Athens" long embodied this moderate ethic, ultimately it strayed far from a moderate course—commercial leaders wanted no limits on their increasing avarice, which, Montesquieu asserted, gave "sudden rise" to "disorders of inequality"—and it crumbled from within. Many of these same patterns are recurring today in the United States and other wealthy democratic nations.

—

Are there any exceptions to the "infectious greed" that has permeated the corporate world and all those vested in it, any role models worth emulating? What about Bill Gates, chairman of Microsoft? In *The New Imperialists*, author and *Washington Post* journalist Mark Leibovich notes that Gates "has given away his Microsoft stock in multibillion-dollar chunks" as he "gets to try to save the world," via his Bill and Melinda Gates Foundation. The foundation has "total assets approaching $25 billion" and is making "sweeping global efforts to thwart the spread of disease and increase the spread of computers." Leibovich writes: "For as much as one can question the motives of anyone who gives away $23.5 billion, some have ascribed Gates's stepped-up giving to an attempt at image repair," a "balm to the demonization from his rivals and government, as well as the standard resentments that come with having more money than anyone else." Leibovich describes how Gates, his father, his wife, and one associate have formed "a dynamic salon" of four people, who determine how $23.5 billion dollars—"with a lot more where that came from"—will be used to steer the direction philanthropy takes in America.

Is this really a "dynamic salon"? Or would it have to be open to a great diversity of views, from people of many walks of life and experiences, to be in any way "dynamic"? If Gates's salon had more dynamism, perhaps someone taking part would suggest that he cut the price of his products and make more modest profits, so consumers whose pockets are nowhere near as deep as his would have more leeway in determining what to do with their money.

Benjamin Franklin may be a much better role model. Not only was he a prosperous businessman; he was a great scientist and even greater statesman, and the only person who signed all four of the principal documents that led to the founding of the United States. Alfred Owen Aldridge wrote that while Franklin's ethic "reflected the Puritan ethic of individual hard work for all classes of society," it also "realized that widespread human comfort and dignity could not be obtained without joint action and social responsibility."

Thomas Fleming notes in *The Man Who Dared the Lightning* that Franklin believed that "one of the greatest vices . . . was what he called 'the pursuit of wealth with no purpose.' " Franklin had an "ethic of enough." He was "convinced that once a man had accumulated enough money to assure himself and his family of . . . moderate comfort, the good citizen should turn his hand to public service" and dedicate himself to "improving the lot of the common man." Franklin inspired countless others in his era to practice this ethic along with him.

For the poor, wasteful excess is not an option. Nobel Prize winner Toni Morrison writes in her first novel, *The Bluest Eye*, that for the poor, the looming prospect of "being outdoors," of being cast out from your home, "curtailed" all temptation toward excess. "If some-body ate too much, he could end up outdoors. If somebody used up too much coal, he could end up outdoors." What if we all practiced such an ethic? If we don't, will we one day "end up outdoors"?

What if the way we measured the nation's overall prosperity were based in part on how many additional low- and moderate-income people were able to fulfill the American dream of owning their own home, and had good health care? In the pharmaceutical industry, what if growth, in part, were based on how cheaply they were able to distribute their products to the most people, and turn a modest profit? In the food industry, what if growth were measured partly on how their products contributed to the nutritional health of its consumers? What if overall economic growth were measured in part by whether there is an increase in the number of people who earn at least a middle-class, living wage? Is this far-fetched, pie-in-the-sky nonsense?

Corporate muck-a-mucks profess to be soul-searching, after an orgy of irresponsibility. Perhaps they now will be inspired to subscribe to a moderate ethic based on ideals that were widely shared by Franklin and others in this country's early years.

---

Would it be desirable to change our nation's dietary habits, so they were based on moderate and sensible intake, rather than excessive and nonnutritional eating?

Eric Schlosser says in *Fast Food Nation* that we must replace the type of diet proffered us by the fast-food industry with one that is "regional, diverse, authentic, unpredictable, sustainable, profitable— and humble. It should know its limits." In other words, it should be based on moderation—in size, in scope, in profitability, in distribution, in selection based on seasonal availability. "People can be fed without being fattened or deceived." Optimistically, Schlosser says that maybe this new century will herald "a refusal to be kept in the dark, less greed, more compassion, less speed, more common sense . . . a view of food as more than just fuel."

Jeremy Rifkin, president of the Washington-based Foundation on Economic Trends, calls it an "irony" that the food-production system today is such that "millions of wealthy consumers in developed countries increasingly are dying from diseases of affluence . . . brought on by gorging on fatty grain-fed beef and other meats, while the poor in the Third World are dying of diseases of poverty brought on by being denied access to land to grow food grain for their families." For instance, he reports that in the devastating 1984 Ethiopian famine, which cost thousands of lives each day, much of Ethiopia's arable land was used to produce grain "for export to Britain and other European nations to be used as feed for livestock," instead of to feed its own starving people. Is this really "irony," or a disturbing sign that the "haves" simply don't care about the plight of the "have-nots"?

Can we change to a more moderate course in the way we live our everyday lives? Is it desirable, much less necessary?

Thomas Jefferson, principal author of our Declaration of Independence, brooded constantly about the set of virtues that Americans, individually and collectively, must strive to cultivate if America were to be not just a free society, but a morally and intellectually excellent one. As scholar Jean M. Yarbrough notes in *American Virtues: Thomas Jefferson on the Character of a Free People*, Jefferson believed that "(b)oth moral excellence and civic virtue begin with the government of the self. Before we can fulfill our obligations to others, we must first achieve independence and learn to exercise responsibility, moderation, patience, and self-control."

American pragmatist philosopher John Dewey (1859–1952), in writing about Thomas Jefferson, whom he admired as a philosopher and statesman, notes Jefferson's abiding faith and trust in "the people" ultimately to do the right thing. Jefferson's "was a faith in what he sometimes called their common sense and sometimes their reason. They might be fooled and misled for a time, but give them light and in the long run their oscillations this way and that will describe what in effect is a straight course ahead"—what Socrates and Aristotle, Jefferson and Montesquieu, would no doubt consider a moderate, and excellent, course.

## MIDDLENESS IS NEXT TO GODLINESS?

In his panegyric to middleness, philosopher Charles Hartshorne, professor emeritus at the University of Texas at Austin, says in *Wisdom As Moderation: A Philosophy of the Middle Way* that "(w)e truly have monstrous evils to worry about these days," and that these evils "are all related to our underestimation of the value of moderation on all of the many dimensions of life." For instance, the scarcity of many nonrenewable natural resources that were consumed so immoderately compels us "to reconsider many things about our standard of living," and "pay more attention between what we must have for a good life and what we only carelessly imagine we must have."

In the corporate world, he says that "(e)xecutives who command enormous salaries but ask wage earners to accept lower wages [are] unimpressive as models to admire or imitate. Perhaps they need to set better examples of moderation." Hartshorne says he, for one, is content with his middle-class salary, which he considers moderate. But if he considers his salary in the context of salaries people make around the globe, it would be grossly excessive, not in the moderate middle at all.

—

How do we ever precisely estimate moderation in any given circumstance, much less under- or overestimate it? What mean or yardstick do we use to determine whether our conduct is moderate? If we eat sensibly, based on our size and weight, would that be moderate?

Or should we not strive to be moderate at all? In a world in which half of humanity is often on the brink of starvation, should we actually eat considerably less than moderately, until the basic nutritional needs of everyone can be met?

Or, consider that a growing body of hard scientific research shows that if we eat a carefully prescribed, but extremely frugal, diet, we'll live considerably longer (barring the unforeseeable). So, if you aim to live an extremely long time, an extremely frugal eating regimen would be in order. Would that be moderate middleness in action, your longevity balanced by your frugal eating habits?

Is aspiring for the longest life span possible a worthy goal, or is it absurd, given the overcrowding that already exists in many parts of the globe? Even if this weren't so, would it be an immoderate course, no matter how much or little you ate?

Many of those whom I most admire across the ages gave no thought to longevity; they were extremely immoderate in their approach to life and living. They used themselves up quickly, living and loving and creating intensely in their intellectual and humanitarian and aesthetic pursuits; in this respect, they were immoderate to the core.

What does this say about a moderate ethic?

As with any universal approach to life and living, a rigid ethic of moderation is overly formulaic, and in instances it can be counterproductive and downright fanatical to proselytize that the middle way is always the best way. What if the ambitions of the world's great humanitarian movers and shakers had been middlingly moderate? We'd likely never have heard of or read about them, much less been inspired by them.

—

Charles Hartshorne relates in his book that Rabbi Olan, a leader in reform Judaism, recounts that he knows a "modern man" whose "approach to the goods of this world is to use no more than is barely necessary," lest he deny precious resources "to those who have little or none . . . He is a sensitive human being who is very conscious of so many people on earth who possess nothing and use almost nothing," because they have nothing to use. The rabbi says that "(i)t will take a world population endowed with these qualities to reverse the human rush toward self-destruction." While he believes it is "very dim" that there will be "so radical a regeneration of the human creature," he nonetheless holds out hope: "In conditions not unlike our own, the Hebrew prophets offered one hope—if men do justly, love mercy, and walk humbly, they may overcome. Is it too late? This is what Hillel meant when he asked: 'If not now, when?' "

—

Surely, though, there are excellent forms of excess—such as when you test and expand the limits of your aptitudes and abilities, of your courage, of your social conscience—just as there are pernicious forms.

In Plato's dialogue *Charmides*, Socrates concludes that a key quality of moderation is to know one's limits, and that "self-knowledge is at the very core" of discovering these limits. In concluding this, he is not imposing preset limits on what a person can or can't do, should or shouldn't do. Instead, he's saying that every time a person striving for excellent ends acts in the world, he discovers more and more about what his limits are, and aren't—and that this journey of discovery can help him push the envelope further outward as he advances on the road to excellence.

Many assume that because Socrates examined the question "What is moderation?" he believed moderation was a virtue. A more accurate view is that he felt that in order to know when and whether to act immoderately, one first had to know what moderate conduct was. Socrates himself was consummately immoderate in his search for self-knowledge and his refusal to cave in to "national pride" and the concerns of the state over individual freedom.

# JUSTICIA MEXICANA

I am in the Plaza de Las Tres Culturas, or Plaza of Three Cultures, in the Tlatelolco neighborhood, or *colonia*, of Mexico City—named Tenochtitlan by its original Aztec inhabitants—which is the oldest continuously inhabited city in the Western Hemisphere. With a population of well over thirteen million in the city's incorporated limits alone, and at least another ten million in the relentless outward sprawl in the unincorporated limits, Mexico City is the largest city in the world. This is what John Womack, Jr., a professor of history at Harvard, wrote several years ago about this overcrowded and polluted and mesmerizing city:

> Americans tend to think of Mexico as an exotic place, which allows them endless fantasies about it. But Mexico is real. It is a big, complicated, vastly Catholic, still deeply old-fashioned, nevertheless largely modern, and largely poor country . . . (E)xcept for an interlude of populist reform in the 1930s, the Mexican political system has been an intricate collusion of businessmen and politicians. . . . Mexicans love their country intensely. But for most of them it is a hard place to live, work, or do much good.

Pulitzer Prize–winning journalist Andres Oppenheimer says in his book *Mexico, Bordering on Chaos: Guerillas, Stockbrokers, Politicians, and Mexico's Road to Prosperity* that "(n)o single country in the post-Cold War era affects the U.S. national interest in more ways than Mexico. . . . Whether it is illegal immigration, drugs, the environment, the economy, or, increasingly U.S. domestic politics, Mexico is the country that influences life in America on the greatest number of fronts."

Mexico, for me, has become a new home. Since my wife, Cecilia, who is from Mexico City, and I married in 1998, I have spent several months each year in Mexico, holding dialogues and becoming familiar with its wide range of social problems. No one but no one, I've discovered, likes to talk the talk—honest, probing, rigorous, philosophical talk—like Mexicans, or has the comparable stamina to do so for hours on end.

This is my first dialogue at the Plaza of Three Cultures, which has this distinctive name because of the three cultures that coalesce and clash here: It is situated around the ruins of the Great Temple of the Aztecs, which dates from long before the Spanish *conquistadores* arrived on the scene and did their best to obliterate all things Aztec. The temple, which is where Aztecs worshiped Huitzilopochtli, the sun god, abuts the colonial Church of Santiago, one of the first Spanish temples inhabited by the Franciscans after the Spanish conquest led by Hernan Cortez between 1519 and 1521. And it is at the vortex of modern Mexico City's nonstop urban hustle and bustle. So there is an uneasy coexistence of three cultures in this one area, which was once the largest and most well-known Aztec *mercado*.

The week preceding today's dialogue, Cecilia and I had passed out fliers to passersby in the plaza. Plazas are natural gathering places in Mexico for people of all walks of life. There's nothing at all unusual here about a person commandeering a section of a plaza and launching into a discourse on one subject or another—and for people promptly to gather around and take part. Best of all, there are no "gatekeepers" whose permission you have to secure before holding a dialogue in a plaza.

Cecilia and I had chosen this particular plaza for a Socrates Café in part for its significance in modern Mexican history. On October 2, 1968, ten days before Mexico was set to host the 1968 Olympic games, the growing friction between prodemocracy groups and the authoritarian government culminated in a huge protest rally at this plaza.

About ten thousand prodemocracy demonstrators converged here and remained, *en plantón*, their heels dug in, demanding that the government engage them in a dialogue about how to best go about opening up their society. For months, there had been growing tensions between government security forces and the prodemocracy forces. Everywhere that activists held rallies, the military, in what was called its *Guerra Sucia*, or Dirty War, was quick to intervene, trying to curb their momentum before the groundswell could grow any greater.

Everything came to a head on the evening of October 2, when without warning or provocation, government forces opened fire on the unarmed crowd in Tlatelolco Plaza. In the ensuing chaos, hundreds of protesters were injured and killed. The military and police rounded up hundreds more, and took them to military camps for interrogation. Many were held there for years as political prisoners. Many never were heard from or seen again. The nascent prodemocracy uprising, which had been on the verge of burgeoning into a nationwide movement, was effectively quelled.

The government claimed at the time that the protesters provoked the shootings. It appears, though, that Mexico's then-president, the authoritarian Gustavo Diaz Ordaz, or one of his subordinates, apparently fearing the protests would precipitate an international boycott of the games, decided that immediate and decisive action was needed. In spite of the many eyewitness accounts to the contrary, and though there has never been any evidence to support such a claim, the government claimed that "antidemocratic thugs" and "professional terrorists" and "Communist conspirators" were the culprits behind the violence. In truth, the protesters were a motley gathering of idealistic students, faculty members, disillusioned unemployed, and farmers and union workers. They shared a common sense of betrayal by a government that had promised to provide them with a decent standard of living, with decent employment opportunities, but instead put them in worse straits than ever. They were sick of the business-as-usual corruption of Mexico's elite, who reaped everything and sowed nothing. The small concentration of wealthy power brokers who ran the political and business establishments also happened to be the most prominent members of Mexico's ruling party.

Though on paper a democratic country, Mexico had been dominated by one party, *Partido Revolucionario Institucional*, or the Institutional Revolutionary Party (or PRI), since 1921. PRI party machinery, in control of virtually all public funds, manipulated and determined the outcome of every presidential campaign. In the modern era, Mexico had never had a president other than one from PRI. Though an election was held every six years, in reality, presidents were chosen behind the scenes; the current PRI president would select his successor, in something similar to a coronation, from among the party faithful. After what became known as the Tlatelolco Massacre of 1968, President Ordaz's handpicked successor was none other than Luis Echeverria, the PRI interior minister at the time of the massacre at the Plaza of Three Cultures and the person who, it is widely believed, gave government forces the green light to open fire on the protesters.

In shameful disingenuousness, a Time-Life book on Mexico City states that Mexico "has enjoyed more than half a century of economic and social progress under the same constitution, and administrations have succeeded one another peacefully ever since the formation of the party [PRI] in 1929." The truth is that most Mexicans have never "enjoyed" the fruits of this "peaceful" transfer of power, much less any semblance of "economic and social progress."

But times, at last, seem to be changing. As we gather at the Plaza of Three Cultures, it is now over a year since the election of Vicente Fox Quesada, the titular head of the conservative *Partido Acción Nacional*, the National Action Party, or PAN. Fox is Mexico's first non-PRI president in modern history. The charismatic conservative businessman and onetime Coca-Cola executive had based his campaign in considerable part on strident pledges to bring about sweeping reforms. Fox promised at campaign rallies that these reforms would bring a certain measure of justice to the millions of historically oppressed and exploited in the country. But so far, since his election, he has balked at any real reform, lest he antagonize the PRI, which still holds a commanding majority in Mexico's congress, and whose cooperation he needs to pass any new legislation.

Shortly before our gathering, a government commission at last issued a report on what took place at Tlatelolco Plaza in 1968. It pointed the finger of blame and responsibility for the bloodbath at the PRI-controlled government of President Ordaz and Interior Minister Luis Echeverria. Since the report's release, there has been a great clamor for Fox to establish a full-fledged truth commission, and to "bring justice" to those responsible.

It is against this backdrop of violence and oppression that has marked and marred Mexico's history that I now find myself encircled by a sizeable and growing group of ordinary Mexicans and other Latinos from the region.

—

"*Qué es justicia?*" I ask the group. What is justice?

Without hesitation, a man right in front of me replies, "I can tell you what *justicia Mexicana*—Mexican justice—is: If you're well connected and have lots of money, then you can cheat and beat the justice system. If you get caught for any crime, whether it's embezzlement or rape or murder or theft, all you have to do is pay off the authorities, and you get off scot-free."

The government's own Justice Ministry estimates that in the year 2000, of the 1.4 million crimes reported, fewer than 10 percent led to convictions and sentencing. A United Nations report says that 95 percent of all crimes in Mexico go unpunished, and 50 to 70 percent of Mexican judges have been involved in acts of corruption. One of Mexico's most prominent criminologists, Rafael Ruiz Harrell, said in a study for the human rights commission of Mexico City that "impunity is the rule, not the exception."

"On the other hand," the participant goes on, as many onlookers murmur in agreement, "if you're one of the tens of millions who aren't connected, and you run afoul of the law, or dare to complain about the way the law is applied, then forget about it. The people in power will destroy you, they'll make you out to be the bad guy, because you have no rights."

A 1999 Human Rights Watch report concluded that "through willful ignorance and purposeful fabrication of evidence, prosecutors routinely prosecute victims using evidence obtained through human-rights violations, and judges avail themselves of permissive law and legal precedent to condemn victims while ignoring abuses." Even today, over two years since Fox took office, Amnesty International says that despite Fox's pledge to put an end to the country's notorious human-rights violations, few inroads seem to have been made.

I ask the participant for a concrete example of *justicia Mexicana*.

He thinks hard, muttering to himself, "There're so many," before replying at last, "Carlos Cabal, the former head of the failed Mexican banks, Banca Cremi and Banco Unión, was extradited to Mexico from Australia. He was charged with defrauding our government of seven hundred million U.S. dollars. His defrauding schemes were a primary reason your government had to bail out our country's financial system, and caused the huge devaluation of the peso that, almost overnight, impoverished millions of formerly middle-class people like me.

"So now, finally, Cabal is back in our country, behind bars where he belongs, and at last it looks like justice will be done. So what does the 'reform-minded' government of Vicente Fox do? It drops all but two of the fifteen charges against Cabal. Why? A judge ruled that the cases against him hadn't been filed within the appropriate deadline, and that the cases weren't 'in order,' whatever that can mean. Once again, corrupt judicial officials overturned charges against one of the most corrupt people of our era, because of so-called technicalities. This is *justicia Mexicana*. It's classic Kafka!"

In Franz Kafka's great unfinished novel, *The Trial*, the character Joseph K., a bank officer of good repute, was arrested one day without being told what charges he faced. Then he was put in the position of trying to defend himself against unknown charges. Surely the real trial of the novel was how Joseph K. bore up under the bizarre proceedings. Many critics have described this novel as fantastic and even farcical, albeit with tragic aspects. But those who have experienced firsthand life under corrupt authoritarian regimes know that what happened to Joseph K. is a disturbing mirror of their all-too-real life experiences. The term *Kafkaesque* typically connotes that which is alien or incomprehensible. But I think it should signify that which is incomprehensibly unjust, but which is by no means alien, to millions of people around the globe.

"So what you're really describing is, in your view, the epitome of injustice," I say.

"That's right," he says.

"So for you, then, what would justice be?"

"It would be the weak ruling over the strong."

This prompts a man beside him, who has come out from his newspaper kiosk to take part, to say, "I disagree. Throughout history, justice has always been the rule of the stronger over the weaker. That's just how it is."

What he says is strikingly similar to the claim of Thrasymachus, in Plato's seminal work *Republic*, when he tells Socrates that "justice is nothing more than serving the interests of the stronger."

The participant goes on, "Can you really imagine a type of justice in which the weak rule over the strong? It sounds nice, but it would never do. How could the weak ever rule the strong?"

A woman with two children clinging to her skirt says, "I think that justice is where no one person is stronger than any other."

To this, the man who had spoken previously insists, "But the stronger always decide what justice is."

A university student named Mariola now says, "Justice would be where the laws are such that we all are collectively stronger than any single individual, and where we are all protected from any person who'd try to trample on our collective and individual rights."

She pauses before adding, "The system we have now isn't one where the strong rule over the weak. It's one where the weak are completely left out, so those in power can treat them as they will. We need to replace this system with one of ideal justice, where the laws serve all of us, not just a select few."

The participants' focus so far on legal justice *as* justice mirrors that of the classical Greek philosopher Protagoras, who also equated legal justice with justice itself.

"For me," says a woman who just joined us a few moments earlier, and has been straining to pick up the gist of our dialogue, "justice is having a system of laws that apply equally to everybody. So 'Mexican justice' isn't justice at all. Because justice has to be justice for all."

Says a woman standing on the periphery, "I don't think justice is *just* about the laws being applied to everyone. Because first, you have to have laws that themselves are just."

This prompts the man who'd first spoken at our dialogue to reply, "Even if the laws apply to everyone, you have to make sure that the people who apply them are honest, that they're not above the law and don't flout the law."

He directs his gaze my way and says, "I'm a taxi driver. I worked double shifts for years so I could buy a new taxi. Two weeks after I bought it, it was stolen from my driveway. I hadn't yet bought insurance for the car, because I didn't have the money. If I hadn't had an old, backup car for emergencies, I'd have been out of work completely. A few days after it was stolen, I drove by an auto-body shop. There was my car! It was partially stripped, but it still had my license plate! I called the police. They went there, and then reported to me that the owner of the place claimed it was sold to him. I've come to find that that place is a major center for stripping hot cars and selling the parts. The police get *mordiditas*, huge bribes, to look the other way. I can't drive by that place anymore. It makes me sick. I offered to pay the police to help me. They laughed at me like I was crazy, and told me to come back when I could give them twenty thousand pesos."

Then he says, "My point is this: We already *have* laws to bring justice to those who break the law, but they aren't applied. If those who are responsible for seeing that there is justice for all flaunt the system, then the system fails. In this country, the people who represent justice—the police, the judges, the lawyers, our representatives in Congress—are almost all corrupt. You can have all the great laws you want, but if they aren't applied justly—if they don't apply to every person, in the same way—they are less than nothing."

With great emotion, a young man beside him, whom I presume to be his son, now says to me, "You should see our country's constitution. It's a work of beauty. If it were applied as it's supposed to be, Mexico would be the most just nation anywhere."

Modern Mexican philosopher Fernando Salmeron writes that the Mexican Constitution of 1917 promised to "convert the state into the protector of the economically weaker classes." Anyone who has spent any quality time in Mexico knows that it has fallen far short of this promise.

In a soft and halting voice, an elderly man says, "I was an executive at a brewery for twenty-four years and ten months. In two more months, I was to retire with full retirement benefits. What did my employers do? They fired me. Their reason? Incompetence. I'd been a stellar employee all these years, and all of a sudden I'm incompetent? I hired a lawyer and tried to sue—only to find that there are no laws on the books to protect workers from unfair dismissal. I had no legal recourse. I'm reduced now to selling lottery tickets on the street corner to survive."

Then he says, "Until there are laws on the books that afford people like me protection from unscrupulous employers, there can be no justice like that we've been talking about."

After a pause, in which a number of people commiserate with the man, I say, "It sounds as if we need to look at types of 'just laws' in order better to answer the question 'What is justice?' What, to you, is a just law?"

"A just law is one that is balanced," replies Saira, who sells handmade goods at the plaza. "It protects the rights, for instance, of both employers and employees. Like, employers should have the right to fire incompetent employees, but they should never be able to fabricate charges for firing an employee, like what happened to this man here. Any employee who is fired should have a chance to appeal the decision, to argue that the reasons for his firing were not justified. He should have his 'day in court.'"

Her husband, Amado, then says: "I'm an aficionado of American movies. One of my favorites is *The Verdict*. Near the beginning, Paul Newman, who plays a down-and-out lawyer, says that the courts are not here to provide justice, but to give a person the chance at justice. But in Mexico, we have justice like in the movie *True Grit*. When someone asks John Wayne's character, Rooster Cogburn, if he needs a good lawyer, he replies, 'No, I need a good judge.'"

Then he says, "Justice has to be blind, nonpreferential—like that statue Lady Justice, a blindfolded woman holding a set of scales. She can't see the faces of the people she is to judge, so she can judge them impartially."

The first commonplace depiction of justice as an icon of a blindfolded woman holding two balanced scales likely is that of Justitia, the Roman goddess of justice. In all likelihood an evolution of earlier goddesses—in particular, Ma'at, the ancient Egyptian goddess of justice, order, and truth, and Themis, the Greek goddess of divine justice and law—Justitia is one of the few remaining virtues of old that is still regularly personified around the world. Justitia is most often seen in statues and flags in front of courthouses and assembly buildings for national and local governments, and is depicted as a woman of serious mien dressed in a flowing robe. Her blindfold and the scales she holds symbolize her ability to judge both the powerful and powerless without bias, and to carry out the law without prejudice.

The Aztec civilization that once thrived in the Tlatelolco area had a judicial system that, for their era, was a model of the type of impartiality that Justitia represented. As Ramon Eduardo Ruiz writes in *Triumphs and Tragedy: A History of the American People*, "Laws and courts of justice were the anchors of Aztec life," and Aztec justice "was meted out in a relatively impartial way. "Named by the monarch and chosen for their integrity, judges wielded great authority, empowered to order the arrest of even dignitaries."

"I don't want justice to be blind at all," says a woman with a deeply careworn face. "I want justice to be applied with her eyes open to the oppression and wrongs we've suffered." Her voice breaking, she then says, "I have not seen my cousin for over thirty years. He was one of the thousands of students who protested at this plaza in October 1968, and declared 'missing' after being taken by police to be interrogated."

She falls silent and looks away from us. Then she resumes her direct gaze at the group and says, "They were idealists. They just wanted our country to become the democracy it claimed already to be."

The late Octavio Paz, a poet and writer widely considered one of Mexico's greatest intellectuals, said that the Tlatelolco protesters embodied "the civic awakening of an entire generation of young people", with their "wave of hope and generous idealism." The student demonstrators, he wrote, were "a direct expression of the general dissatisfaction of the country as a whole" with the country's endemic political corruption, and were "seeking a public dialogue with those in power."

Then the woman says, "We all know what happened: My cousin and all the others were tortured until they died. Everyone in the government who knew what happened has blood on their hands."

"I don't just want to know the truth about what happened," she tells us. "I want those who committed the crimes to be punished. If you find out the truth, but then are powerless to do anything to right wrongs, where is the justice in that? I don't want just 'the chance at justice'; I want justice."

The woman now says, "At first, President Fox didn't want to establish a truth commission. But now, because so many of us demanded one, he's relented and agreed to form one."

"If he's acceding to the will of the people, is that an important element of the type of justice you're talking about?" I ask.

"I think so, yes. But there's going to be a lot of people—not just in Mexico, but in your country as well—who are going to wish we didn't have this commission."

An article in the July 1, 2002, *New York Times* reported that "the few American documents declassified to date strongly suggest that Washington was well aware of what went on in those years" of the prodemocracy protests, in which the Mexican government "used every power from wiretaps to torture for gathering information on its opponents," and "co-opted and controlled dissent as best it could and, failing that, crushed it," inflicting "what it deemed an acceptable level of violence, including extrajudicial death sentences."

"So for you," I say, "true justice is finding out the truth, and then . . ."

"Giving those who are guilty the punishment they deserve."

"How do you ever determine what anyone deserves?" my wife, Cecilia, asks.

"That's what I was thinking," says Juan Carlos, who manages a nearby restaurant. "Who's to say who deserves or doesn't deserve punishment? Who's to be the final arbiter or higher authority?"

"I think *we* are that higher authority," says the woman who demanded punishment of those involved in the Dirty War. "We the people need to create and set the yardstick for what each individual deserves. For too long, just a few people in power have determined what the rest of us 'deserve,' or get away with. We have to change that."

The woman beside her, a human-rights activist, says, "President Fox named Ignacio Camilo Prieto as the special prosecutor to head the new truth commission. He's a scholar and lawyer with great integrity. One of his cousins was killed in the Dirty War. Right after his appointment, Prieto said he would be 'inspired at all times by the spirit of justice, not the spirit of vengeance.' But why can't vengeance be a legitimate form of justice? Can't we take away—in the spirit of vengeance *and* justice—the billions that the rich in our country have robbed from the rest of us, and redistribute it so that all children get the education and nutrition and medical care they deserve?"

"I think we can," says a philosophy student named Emilio, who attends Universidad Nacional Autónoma de México, National Autonomous University of Mexico, or UNAM, a sprawling university in the south of the city that is frequently a hotbed of social protest. "By taking what the rich and powerful have robbed from us, and then giving it to those most in need, sort of like Robin Hood, it would be both retributive and distributive justice. Of course, the individuals from whom we take these things, and whom we punish, may look at this as vengeance plain and simple. But no one else would."

Scholar Patrick Romanell points out that the ethic of twentieth-century Mexican philosopher Antonio Caso y Andrade was to "forgive and forget former offenses of other Mexicans of whatever political persuasion, economic position, or social caste," and to "unite . . . through an ethic of sacrificing love and unselfish service." Perhaps this ethic of Caso y Andrade, revered for his disdain of power and money, and his willingness to speak out against the country's authoritarian rulers, has more relevance and resonance today than when he was at the vortex of moral thinking in Mexico over six decades ago. But I wonder: Can't one forgive, without forgetting? Can't one punish transgressors, at the same time as they are forgiven? Can't punishment be a form of forgiveness—not the sadistic and purely vengeful types of punishment, but types that aim to rehabilitate, and to inculcate some social conscience?

A man from Venezuela who has come to Mexico looking for work says, "Look at what's happening in my country right now. The rich want to depose our president, Hugo Chavez, because he wants to take away from them and give to the poor what they gained at the poor's expense. The mainstream media tries to paint Chavez as some sort of demon. But all he wants is justice for all."

After considerable reflection, an elderly man says, choosing his words carefully, "I think the system of justice administered by our government, as an institution, has to be above individual notions of vengeance and desert. The government has to develop a system of punishments so that anyone who commits crimes, no matter how rich or poor, and who is brought to justice, will have to pay a price."

Another university student, Ulises, responds, "But first, the system must make sure that the crimes committed are 'true crimes,' rather than the 'crimes' that the authoritarian regime calls crimes in order to maintain power. For instance, until recently, it was a 'crime' to criticize the government, a 'crime' to have public assemblies to protest against them."

"In order for there to be 'true justice,' all crimes must be put under the jurisdiction of civilian justice," says Francisco, an *ambulante*, or street vendor, who with his nine-year-old daughter sells hot dogs and drinks on the plaza sixteen hours a day, seven days a week. "To this day, all the military is immune from civilian justice. They are protected by 'military justice,' so they can literally get away with murder. Look at what happened to Digna Ochoa."

Digna Ochoa, a thirty-eight-year-old former nun renowned for defending social activists, including insurgents such as Zapatista rebels in Chiapas State, was murdered on October 19, 2001, shot to death in her office in Mexico City. Ochoa was a prominent human-rights lawyer in a country whose leaders abhorred those who stood up for human-rights victims. Many of her cases implicated Mexico's police and military, and many now point the finger at the military, and its long-standing history of torture and corruption, as her murderer. Human-rights groups such as the Miguel Agustin Pro-Juarez Center for Human Rights claim that the military is blocking the ongoing investigation into her murder.

"Ochoa was a woman of great courage," Francisco continues. "She spoke out against the military oppressors, even though she was threatened and attacked by them. But she'd never have been able to bring the military to justice. Our new attorney general says the military must now be accountable, but so far nothing has changed."

There is a lull before Raimundo, who works for an outreach program for the city's tens of thousands of street children, says, "I think Fox has to address all the little injustices, not just the 'big ones.' Because these millions of little injustices wreaked on those who are trying to make an honest living add up to a very huge injustice."

He says next, "I think we're taking baby steps in the right direction. At least I no longer fear being jailed for protesting. Maybe Fox had to be pushed, but he seems committed to making Mexican society more open. And he finally seems to realize you can't bury your head in the sand about the past. You have to face it. By doing so, you honor the victims at the same time as you take action against the perpetrators."

"He's absolutely right," says Emilio, the UNAM student. "Fox has done some admirable things lately to bring about justice, like releasing from prison Rodolfo Montiel and Teodoro Cabrera."

Dirt-poor farmers arrested in September 2000, and whom Digna Ochoa had represented, Montiel and Cabrera had spearheaded a successful protest movement, called the Organization of Peasant Farmer Ecologists, against clandestine and illegal logging operations that were decimating the forests of Guerrero State. The army, putatively working hand in glove with corrupt political bosses and private logging companies, subsequently arrested them on what almost everyone agrees were fabricated charges, in which confessions were obtained under torture. A judge sentenced them to ten years in prison. A *New York Times* article on this incident says that "(t)his kind of tale can be heard all over Mexico. Members of the police and the military can bend and break the law without much fear of punishment. Killing, torture, kidnappings and false arrests by law-enforcement authorities are prominent features of the legal landscape . . ." President Fox reviewed the case and then declared there was insufficient evidence to hold them in jail.

"Do you know that Fox's release of these prisoners was actually against the law?" Emilio tells us. "He released them for 'humanitarian reasons.' But he has absolutely no authority to do that, as the laws are currently written. So he actually had to break the law in order to do what was just!"

We've been talking for hours now, and the sun has just set. The person who'd spoken at the very outset of our dialogue about *justicia Mexicana* now says, "I think we can't put all of the burden on Fox to address past injustices, and to make our country more just today. We, the people, have to be 'the strong.' We have to make sure that justice serves all of us in an impartial way."

Gabriela, who works at a nearby museum, says, "We're slowly dismantling our unjust authoritarian system. We no longer accept things with resignation. In the past, most Mexicans considered resignation the supreme virtue. But now, we have *hartazgo*—we are 'fed up' with the corrupt ways of the past—and now we're actively working to change the status quo."

As if surprised by her own insight, she then says, "It turns out that we ordinary Mexicans are 'the strong' after all."

Which prompts her boyfriend, Leonardo, to say, "But I wonder, over the long run . . . will we turn out to be strong, in a better way, than the strong who came before us, or will we become 'just' like them?"

## MACHIAVELLIAN JUSTICE

It seems that almost all of Mexican president Vicente Fox's predecessors were acolytes of the Italian philosopher Niccolò Machiavelli (1469–1527), most widely known for his slender book, *The Prince,* a treatise on how rulers can acquire and then keep their grip on political power. Machiavelli coined the term *virtu* (Latin for "manly" or "manliness"), which is an amalgam of those capacities and skills and strategies a ruler needs to best maintain and prop up the existing political system. As far as Machiavelli was concerned, the means a ruler might employ to achieve these ends can be unscrupulous or immoral, and yet can be considered just, as long as they preserve and defend the state. To Machiavelli, what matters isn't virtuous conduct but efficacious conduct. If one's conduct, no matter how base, props up the state, then to Machiavelli, that person has the quality of *virtu*—what I would call virtueless virtue.

Machiavelli says this in *The Prince*: "There is such a gap between how one lives and how one ought to live that anyone who abandons what is done for what ought to be done learns his ruin rather than his preservation—for a man who professes goodness at all times will come to ruin among so many who are not good."

But many of those who "profess goodness at all times," and exemplify such goodness, are well aware of how their attempts at elevating humanity might be thwarted by the not-so-good and the downright evil. Nishida Kitaro, Mohandas Gandhi, Martin Luther King, Jr., and Digna Ochoa are just a few examples of people throughout human history who have tried to do the greatest good, yet were well aware of the obstacles they faced, and of the possible consequences. While there likely always will be, as Machiavelli says, a "gap between how one lives and how one ought to live," one can strive always, as these humanitarians did, to narrow this gap.

Machiavelli further says that a ruler, "in order to maintain his state, is often obliged to act against his promise, against charity, against humanity, and against religion." This may be so, if a ruler aims solely to maintain his own grip on power. But for the state itself to be long-lived and vibrant, then surely charity *for* humanity is a better guide. Indeed, Machiavelli says that a ruler's sole purpose is to act in ways that preserve his country. For the past seven decades, though, Mexico's rulers have acted in ways that have led to their great personal gain, while the overall soundness and health of their country has steadily deteriorated. So their application of Machiavellianism has been highly skewed. And that is the inherent danger in a code of conduct, such as that formulated by Machiavelli, that attempts to skirt any moral foundation and to do away altogether with the notion of civic virtue. Such a code easily can be misinterpreted, deliberately or unintentionally, to mean that any action whatsoever can be justified if it preserves the state, because the state that is preserved does not have to be a moral one, only one that is arguably viable in some fashion. And for Mexico's rulers and their legions of cronies, it was as viable as it was amoral.

Unlike Machiavelli, Socrates believed that in all our actions, whether we are a ruler or an ordinary citizen, we should strive for the ideal of acting from a strong moral foundation, with the end of becoming more virtuous. To Socrates, if we acted in a way that advances our own interests, but at the expense of others, then we have not acted justly much less virtuously, because we have further fractured society, depleting our store of collective virtue rather than adding to it. In this vein, a just person is one who, in conducting himself in the world, is ever-mindful to act in ways that help liberate and elevate other members of society—not just one's immediate society, but society on a global scale—while one who is unjust acts in ways that oppress and demean, for personal gain.

Socrates did not aspire to the pinnacle of power and all the singular responsibilities that came with it. But his role as gadfly—his willingness to speak out against corrupt tyrants, with the end of creating a more accountable and charitable form of government—was itself a role with great public responsibilities, and considerable personal consequences. While those in power employed any means to perpetuate their grip on the state, Socrates was willing to sacrifice even himself if it seemed the best means of perpetuating humanity over the long term.

While the history of politics in Latin America in the twentieth century has been a history of applied (albeit in a skewed way) Machiavellianism, there are emerging democracies in Latin America, in Mexico and elsewhere, that are attempting to create new political traditions with the types of ends that Socrates had in mind.

The late Octavio Paz defined democracy as "that free arena in which criticism takes place"—and not just "criticism of others," but enlightened "self-criticism." To Paz, in order to "communicate with others, we must first learn to communicate with ourselves." Paz believed that the "democratization" of Mexico, while by no means the "final solution" to the country's social ills, was "the right path to follow" in attaining some measure of social justice, because it best enabled citizens to "examine [their] problems in public, discuss them, propose solutions to them, and organize ourselves politically so as to ensure that these solutions are effectively implemented."

However, a nation's people can become adept at enlightened forms of criticism, and democratic forms of organization, and still be left without the means to bring about significant social change. Mexico, for instance, remains a country in which a stunningly small minority controls almost all the nation's financial and natural resources. Under such conditions, no matter how much freedom of expression and organization the overwhelming number of the nation's poor might enjoy, they still have been stymied in efforts to make much of a dent in remedying their unjust plight. It would seem that genuine social justice cannot be realized without a concomitant measure of economic justice.

## JUSTICE ON TRIAL

In one memorable scene in Franz Kafka's *The Trial*, originally published in 1925, Joseph K. talks with a painter in the court where he is to stand trial. He sees that the painting being worked on looks to be a rendering of the goddess of justice: "There's the blindfold over her eyes, and here are the scales." But then Joseph K. notices she also has wings on her feet, and appears to be in motion. Joseph K. says, "That's a poor combination. Justice must remain at rest. Otherwise, the scales sway and no judgment is possible."

His ideal of justice appears to be one in which judgment is rendered based on standards that never can be altered or budged. But that is precisely what justice is not. Justice's very viability depends on a certain amount of movement, of flexibility, of experimentation. What may remain relatively unchanged are its ends—namely, to see to it that certain human rights are sacrosanct and inviolable, never to be infringed upon by the whims of the corrupt or powerful. The most excellent type of justice is one in which its scales are never at rest—a type that forever strives to realize its function of serving everyone equably, and ensuring that everyone has the opportunity to live equitably.

As Joseph K. continued to look at the painting of the goddess, the light fell on it differently, and it came to look "just like the goddess of the hunt." I think that this marked not a change in the light on the goddess, but a change within Joseph K. He began to "see the light"— to see that the type of "justice" with which he was confronted was anything but, with its bizarre and convoluted proceedings and arbitrary applications. He began to see that he was doomed to a tragic fate, and he gave up all hope of being dealt with justly. Joseph K. no longer protested his unjust circumstances, and eventually a knife was put through his resigned heart.

## RIGHTING WRONGS

Several months have passed since the terrorist attack on the World Trade Center, and I'm holding a Socrates Café in Manhattan, at a café a few subway stops from "ground zero." I'd made arrangements for the gathering a month before September 11, but several who'd said they'd come, particularly those from outer boroughs, had written me to say that now they rarely ventured from their homes at night, and so probably wouldn't attend. To my surprise, every one of them showed up.

There are fifteen of us in all, including several high-school students.

The question we agree to delve into is "What is justice?"

There's a protracted silence. The question lies there. It seems overwhelming. I think we all are thinking about the World Trade Center, and none of us knows quite where to begin.

Finally Jason, an architect who saw the second plane hit the World Trade Center south tower, says, "I think justice is 'righting wrongs.'"

"What do you mean, exactly?" I ask.

"I think justice is what we seek when we feel we've been wronged. And we feel that justice has been 'served' when the wrong has been at least somewhat righted—atoned, or compensated for, or avenged."

"Can you give an example?"

"Well, one obvious example is that we've sent our troops to Afghanistan to avenge what Osama Bin Laden and his Al-Qaeda terrorist network, with the support of the Taliban, did to us. We've almost completely crushed the Taliban, and it looks like Al-Qaeda is just a shell of what it was, thanks to our military action. So that's an example of justice as 'righting wrongs.' We've avenged ourselves somewhat for the wrong they did to us."

Then he says, "I know some people disagree with the way we've tried to right this wrong. A lot of innocent Afghanis have also been killed by our bombs, and furthermore, we were responsible for propping up the Taliban regime back when they were fighting for independence against the former Soviet Union. But I don't think anyone can disagree that the purpose of our military action has been to bring the guilty parties to justice, and right their wrong."

Sheryl, a high-school student from the Bronx, who also works as a volunteer for a homeless shelter, now says, "I agree with Jason's definition of justice. But I don't think anyone will be surprised that I partly disagree with the way our country's chosen to right this wrong. The best way would have been if we'd acted in a way that this wrong never happened in the first place. I guess that would have been 'preemptive justice.'"

Again I ask, "What do you mean?"

"Well, after I began to get over the shock of their horrible attack on us, I began to think, some of those people who flew the planes into the World Trade Center and the Pentagon were easy fodder for fanaticism, because they were uneducated and oppressed. I got to thinking, if they'd had even some of the opportunities in life most of us here have, what happened probably wouldn't have happened."

"But Bin Laden is fabulously wealthy," says Miriam, an investment banker. "He has more than most people here have."

"Often fanatical leaders are from backgrounds of privilege," Sheryl replies evenly. "But I think he would have had a lot more trouble finding people to serve his sadistic ends, while he hides in caves, if the people in that region had even halfway decent clothing, food and shelter, health care, a chance to express themselves and to vote for their own leaders. I'm not saying that would stop all fanaticism or terrorism. I'm just saying it would reduce the pool of people who could be recruited and duped by monsters like Bin Laden. So, at least in addition to bringing Bin Laden 'to justice'—getting revenge against him so he gets the payback he deserves—we should attack the source, attack the daily injustices the ordinary people there live with."

"How is reducing the inequities in the world the same thing as acting justly?" I ask.

Sheryl thinks about this for a bit. Then she says, "If you think, as I do, that poor people not only *need* a certain standard of living in order to thrive, but also *deserve* it, then, by giving them a hand up, you're acting justly."

"I'm not sure I completely follow," I say. "Even if I agree that everyone needs a certain standard of living, among other things, to have a decent life, how can you say for certain that everyone deserves this? Does every person in bad straits, no matter how badly they've conducted themselves, deserve a decent life?"

"Well, I guess I can't say for certain," she says momentarily. "But I still think we should feel sympathy for those who've hit rock bottom, even if sometimes they're partly to blame. We should think, 'There but for the grace of God go I.'"

She goes on, "Like the homeless people at the shelter I volunteer at. Some maybe are down and out by their own doing, but most never had a break from the day they were born. Most were terribly abused and neglected as children, and now suffer from mental illness. Some of them were born to parents who were drug addicts, and they became addicts themselves. So they were wronged from the very beginning, and suffer from scars that are no fault of their own. But at least they know that some people who are better off than they are care about them, and want to see that they get what they need and deserve to improve their situation—they want to right a wrong and 'do justice' to them."

Eventually Bill, a retired city employee, says, "People are donating incredible sums of money—hundreds of millions of dollars—to the survivors of those killed at the World Trade Center. They're trying to right a wrong, by compensating the victims."

Taunya, a classmate of Sheryl's, then says, "I read an article about how they're divvying up the money to the survivors of those who died or were injured. It said that they're calculating who gets how much based on how much their future earnings would have been. That means the family of a man or woman who died, and who'd been making a lot of money, is going to get a lot more from the funds than families of poor people who were victims. I think it should be just the opposite—the poorest of survivors of the victims should get the most. That would be more like justice in action, because they're the most in need."

As the *Washington Post* reported, a "special master" of the September 11 federal victims' compensation fund has been appointed "to put a dollar value on the lives of the deceased, with the size of the awards based largely on lost earning power." Under the plan devised by this special master, "families would receive awards ranging from several hundred dollars up to $4 million, and in some very rare cases, more." The *New Yorker* reports that the formula devised by the special master defies "most notions of equity," since "the more needs a family is likely to have, the less well it fares." And yet, it says, it's the "high-end" families—those who stand to get the most from the fund—who are particularly "infuriated" by the formula, because it limits how much they can get from the fund.

Jason says now, "I think every family of the nine-eleven victims should get the exact same amount of money. This idea of calculating how much each should get based on future needs and future earnings of the victims is nuts. Every single person who died was equally valuable. They each mattered and counted and had loved ones. So in this case, justice would be served—the wrong would be most righted—by giving each family an equal amount. Otherwise, the families who get screwed are going to feel more wronged than ever."

This prompts Cary, an administrative assistant at a philanthropic foundation, to say, "Now I'm wondering: If the survivors of the September eleventh victims are being compensated, shouldn't the victims of the Oklahoma bombing be compensated too, and the victims of the first World Trade Center attack in 1993? Because those were acts of terrorism, too."[1]

1. On February 26, 1993, a massive explosion in the parking garage of the World Trade Center killed 6 and injured over 1,000. Six Islamic extremists were sentenced to 240 years each in prison. On April 19, 1995, a bomb detonated outside the Alfred P. Murrah Federal

"If they're not compensated," she continues, "that doesn't seem fair."

"What is the difference between just and fair?" I ask.

"I think, for something to be just, those who are victims of wrongs like the September eleventh and Oklahoma City tragedies would each have to get what they deserve in terms of compensation. For this to happen, there would have to be a fair protocol in place—in this case, some sort of formula to see to it that all victims of terrorist acts on U.S. soil are treated the same and are all compensated equally. So, fair has to do with the protocol you put in place, and just has to do with the outcome or results."

"But what if the fair protocol doesn't bring about a just outcome?" I ask. "Let's take a simple example. I have an apple pie. There're eight people here with me. I want to devise a fair procedure that ensures a just outcome. How do I do that?"

"That's a no-brainer. You give everyone the same amount," says Miriam.

"But what if one person here, who's always craved apple pie, is very poor, because he takes care of his invalid parents, and so he's never been able to have any in his life?" I ask. "And what if another here is so rich, and such an apple pie junkie, that he eats it ten times a day, at minimum—in fact, has already eaten two pies? And further, what if one person here hates pie? And another is allergic to apples. And another has just committed armed robbery, stealing a poor couple's monthly pension check and their fresh-baked pie. And another plans to trade his slice of pie for drugs. And still another gave all his millions to the poor, and another has made his millions off the poor who worked in his sweatshops. Should they each still get an equal slice?"

---

Building in Oklahoma City killed 168 people, including 19 children. Timothy McVeigh, a twenty-six-year-old Army veteran, eventually was convicted of murder and federal conspiracy charges for the bombing, and put to death. His accomplice and former Army friend, Terry Nichols, was convicted of manslaughter.

"That's a stickler," replies Jason after a while. "If you didn't know any of these things about these people, then yes, you should give each an equal slice. Or if you'd promised each an equal slice before you found out all these other extenuating circumstances, then you should keep your promise. But if you *did* know some of these things, then you'd have to come up with a different formula of distribution, since it seems that part of our working definition of justice is that it consists of allocating to each person what she deserves." He thinks a bit more before adding, "The bottom line is, all you can do is do your best to put a fair mechanism in place to distribute the pie. There's no such thing as a perfectly just outcome—you can only try to be more just, rather than less."

"I think the difference between just and fair is that fair has nothing to do with morals," says Miriam. "In the first example you gave, before we knew anything about the people who were getting a slice of pie, it would've been fair to give each an equal slice. But after we know more about them, and see how unjust the distribution is, because of the way some live or have behaved, then morals enter into the equation. So fair only has to do with a situation where there're no ethical conundrums.

"So now I'm thinking, unfair as it may be," she continues, "that I don't think any of the donations for the nine-eleven victims should go toward anyone or anything else, no matter how worthy. Because we're not talking about morals; we're only talking about giving them money that's pledged to them by the people who made the donations. When the Red Cross tried to divert some of the donations they received for September eleven to use for other disaster victims, the people who'd made the donations cried foul. The Red Cross finally gave in and earmarked all the money for the September eleven victims, but only after its reputation was badly tarnished."

"You're right, this money was specifically promised for reparations to the September eleventh victims' families," says Bill. "But it *is* a moral issue, and so an issue of justice, because there're people deciding exactly how much each family gets, based on what they say each deserves. As soon as desert enters the picture, so does justice."

Amanda, a teacher at a magnet school for underprivileged children, says, "If I were a victim of the Oklahoma City attack, I'd think this was very unjust. The government should step in to make sure they receive similar compensation if the public doesn't voluntarily step in to do so. Because they deserve compensation just as much as anyone else."

Then she says, "This idea of compensation, or reparations, for horrific acts like this—for crimes against humanity—is widely accepted now as justice at work. For instance, many Jewish victims of the Holocaust have been suing German companies for decades, along with the German government itself, for reparations over what happened in Nazi Germany. And well they should.

"Now, descendants of black slaves are asking for reparations from the U.S. government and U.S. corporations that existed back then and condoned slavery—and again, well they should. I know a lot of people say this is far-fetched, but I don't think so. Those who condoned these atrocities, or looked the other way while they knew they were going on, should be accountable."

"But in this instance," I say, "it would be the government and certain corporations that are being asked, or coerced, to pay the victims. In the case of the nine-eleven tragedy, people from all over the world, even from extremely poor countries, are voluntarily donating money for the victims' families. There's no hue and cry that governments such as Saudi Arabia that may have supported, or at least condoned, what happened on September eleventh should be made to ante up. Isn't there a big difference in how justice is being served in these cases?"[2]

"Maybe those who are voluntarily donating *do* feel obligated to,"

---

2. The Associated Press reported that among the contributions to the 9-11 victims was a "$5 check from . . . Malawi, where the average annual income is $180."

says Nick, a high-school student from an outer borough with whom I have been in regular correspondence since he read my first book and then started a Socrates Café with some fellow students. "Maybe they feel it's not fair that they go on living their lives in a vacuum, while the survivors of the victims suffer. Maybe they feel that the least they should have to do is give generously."

Yusuf, a hotel manager whose family immigrated from Ethiopia when he was six year old, says now, "My cousin's youngest son died of malnutrition when he was three. Tens of thousands died in Ethiopia during that awful time of starvation, while the rest of the world looked the other way. I think that was unjust. It *should* be the law that people who live in great wealth in the rest of the world have to share their bounty—especially if their wealth is earned off the blood and sweat of the world's poor. I think it should be a crime against humanity that half the human race is living without sufficient food, much less education and health care and shelter, while the other half has many times more than it needs."

In his slender book, *Utilitarianism*, the British philosopher and economist John Stuart Mill (1806–73), who was a reform activist on behalf of the underprivileged and underrepresented, writes that those who are "just" in any given society resent "a hurt" to others, when that hurt is one in which "society has a common interest." But Mill didn't address how, or whether, members of one society should feel about hurts inflicted on members of another: Should, for instance, citizens of developed nations feel a "common interest" in alleviating the "hurt" of the poor in the Third World? If so, to what lengths should they go in order to alleviate or eradicate this global hurt?

Mai, a computer programmer who arrived midway through the dialogue, tells us, "The most difficult thing to come to grips with, I think, is something that is almost unacceptable: that life is terribly unfair *and* unjust. Many good and decent people never get what they deserve, even though they play by the rules, and many suffer terrible misfortune, through no fault of their own, while many bad people get away with bloody murder, and even thrive on the misfortunes of others."

Yusuf seems on the verge of responding, but before he does, Mai says softly, "I'm from Cambodia. My mother and I, and two of my brothers, escaped from the Khmer Rouge. My father and older brother were killed in the reeducation camps. After several years being bounced around from one refugee camp to another, we were relocated here. American citizens who were complete strangers to us sponsored my family. They helped us get settled and start our lives here. Thanks to them, we were able to build a new life, and I was able to go to college. They were very compassionate about our plight, and in many ways I think of them as a second family."

She then says, "I think all help of this nature should be voluntary. I know that because of the compassion I was shown, I feel an obligation—a voluntary one—to do what I can to help others in need, particularly people who've been victims of great injustice."

"I'm not comfortable with this idea that the best way to atone or compensate victims of terrible wrongdoing is by giving them money," says Liliana, after a lull. A musician, Liliana had to abandon her apartment near the World Trade Center after the attack, because of its potentially unsound condition, and is staying with friends. "Too many people give money as 'compensation' for staying at arm's length from the victims. What we need is for people to reach out to victims— corny as this may sound, to hug them and let them know they 'feel their pain.' That would be the best way, not to right a wrong, but to *heal* a wrong. I don't think a wrong can ever be righted, only healed to some degree."

After some reflection, Sheryl asks, "Shouldn't we *have* to help make the lives of victims of tragic circumstances less unfair?"

"We should feel *inspired* to help others a lot more than we do," says

Taunya. "We should want to give till it hurts—and as Liliana said, not just give money, but give of ourselves—because we should be hurting for all those in bad straits. That would be a just response. But I don't think making it a law is the answer."

"We can't help everybody," says Miriam. "You have to pick and choose whom you help, turn a blind eye to some worthy causes, no matter how unfair it is. Because we have limited resources, limited energies."

To which Yusuf's spirited reply is, "But too many people turn a blind eye to *all* the hurt in the rest of the world. I think the answer is to open people's eyes to how connected we all are, in the sense that everyone hurts sometimes, everyone has suffered hardship of some sort. When something extremely horrible like nine-eleven happens, it really bursts your bubble, and brings home this connection. It makes you realize that we're all in this together."

"I think all the donations that have poured in show what generosity people all over the world are capable of," says Mai. "I disagree that most who donate do so to compensate for being aloof. I think it shows that they *do* hurt for others, and that they're willing to give till it hurts, once their nobler sentiments are aroused."

Nick nods in agreement and says, "I think we just have to keep the momentum going now, harness all this goodwill and steer it into other areas, so we can, as Taunya said, make the lives of all the less fortunate a little less unjust. I'm going next summer to Afghanistan with a group of volunteers around the world who are going to help rebuild and repair their communities. I don't have any money to give, but I'm a good carpenter, so I can give them my labor."

Then he says, "I think all giving of this sort is justice in action—a form of restoring some peace and harmony in the lives of people who've been wronged in the worst way. We can never completely right a wrong, never undo an injustice. But we can contribute to the healing process. I think this is a big part of how we reduce the chances that these worst kinds of injustices will ever happen again."

## JUSTICE AND FAIRNESS

In *A Theory of Justice*, which many consider a landmark work, Harvard philosophy professor John Rawls asserts that if each of us were behind a "veil of ignorance"—if each of us had "no information" about anyone else, knew nothing about their beliefs, their actions in the world, their race, their socioeconomic status, their sex, their singular needs—then we would all strive to distribute goods in such a way that each of us would conclude we were treated as fairly as possible. Rawls posits that if we act from this "original position"—namely, in a vacuum—then in a situation such as the pie-distribution dilemma discussed at this Socrates Café, the only just and rational solution would be for each person to receive an equal slice.

One insurmountable problem with Rawls's self-described "justice as fairness" approach is that such decisions are not made in a vacuum—and should not be. Contrary to what Rawls asserts, even in the most simplistic of distributive conundrums, you can only attain the end that he has in mind—of "securing" the most cooperative society possible—*if* you know as much as possible about each individual. Consequently, it is necessary to examine distributive dilemmas in a range of contexts. Among other things, you must assess carefully each individual's needs (something you can do only if you know a great deal about the individual's social history); you must look to see if there are other competing claims among those involved; you must determine whether each individual has been treated equitably in the past (including whether each who stands to receive a slice of the distributive pie has been treated as equitably as the others); and you must know some of the ends that those involved have in mind, or come to an agreement on what the ends should be. Only then can you begin to examine fruitfully whether giving everyone an equal slice is really the fair, to say nothing of the rational, thing to do. And only then can you determine whether there is a moral dimension to the circumstance that would bring the notion of justice into the picture.

Even if we all agreed that justice is a virtue (much less that justice is always equivalent to fairness), surely justice isn't the *only* virtue.[3] Socrates, for one, believed that all virtues must be employed in equal measure in order to act in the most excellent manner possible. Even in the pie example, if there is a moral dimension involved, Socrates would say that we must take into account and incorporate such additional virtues as courage, piety, moderation, and goodness, and that the only way to know *how* to incorporate them is first to know a good deal about those involved in the situation, and about the social and historical context. If you subscribe to this Socratic ethos, there would likely be a much wider range of choices in even the most simplistic situations than Rawls would have us think. Indeed, there would rarely if ever be a distributive situation in the real world that would lend itself to Rawls's view that there is typically just one overridingly rational and fair choice that stands out above all others.

The premise of Rawls's theory of justice is that "each person possesses an inviolability founded on justice that even the welfare of society as a whole cannot override," and that "the rights secured by justice are not subject to political bargaining or to the calculus of social interests." But Rawls does not seem aware that even this foundational view on the

---

3. And surely distributive justice—the type Rawls deals with—isn't the only type of justice. Among other types, there is retributive justice, transformative justice, social justice (which may be composed of retributive, distributive, and transformative justice).

"inviolability" of his narrow notion of justice is based on such "bargaining." All notions of justice, far from being transcendent concepts that come from otherworldly sources, are human constructs based on political, social, cultural, and ethical considerations. Consequently, justice of any type can only be secured within the "calculus" of society, whether on a local scale or a more global scale. And since individual justice and social justice are inextricably intertwined, the "welfare" of one clearly hinges on the "welfare" of the other.

## MAKING GOOD AGAIN

In an article in the *Atlantic Monthly* that appeared over ten years ago, journalist Michael Z. Wise recounts how the efforts of Nahum Goldmann, founder of the New York–based Conference on Jewish Material Claims Against Germany, compelled the Federal Republic of Germany to pay "more than $50 billion in the form of reparations to the state of Israel and indemnification to Holocaust survivors." Since the publication of this article, at least an additional $10 billion has been paid out. And it appears that billions more still will be paid in reparations in the years to come, as Goldmann's group continues to seek monetary reparations "for tens of thousands of survivors who have still not been indemnified."

Wise writes that "what the German government calls *Wiedergutmachung*, literally meaning 'making good again,' can never truly be completed."

Should such reparations ever end? Can they ever "make good" on past injustices? Is that really their goal?

In the book *Nahum Goldmann: His Missions to the Gentiles*, author Raphael Patai quotes Goldmann as saying in 1966 that the German policy of "compensation and reparations is . . . quite singular. . . .

There is practically no precedent for a government paying out indemnities to the victims of a former regime," much less "to those who are not even citizens of that country."

Should the descendants of those who committed such atrocities be made to pay for the sins of their ancestors? In a poll taken ten years ago, Michael Wise says that "66 percent of Germans believed that reparations should stop," that enough is enough. But, he writes, "the bottom line" in German reparations "is not just deutsche marks but the principle of accountability," and that in a world in which "genocidal impulses and 'ethnic cleansing'" show that man's atrocities against his fellow man continue unabated, "the precedents that have been set" by *Wiedergutmachung* "may be needed again."

Patai asks, "Has the murder of even one person been atoned for by these payments?" His answer: "Of course not. But it made life easier for the individuals who suffered under the Nazi regime but survived, and for Jewry as a whole—the only people singled out by the Third Reich for total extermination."

Is that what justice amounts to—"making life easier" for those who have suffered unimaginable wrongs?

In *The Victim's Fortune: Inside the Epic Battle over the Debts of the Holocaust*, John Authers and Richard Wolffe write that "one fact seems incontrovertible" in the matter of German reparations—namely, that many of "(t)he victims themselves . . . do not share the same sense of success that exists among the lawyers, companies and governments who waged these fights." For instance, "Jaime Rothman, receiving his German slave labor compensation in New York, voiced sentiments shared by thousands. 'The point is always the same,' he said. 'Too little, too late.' But even if it had been earlier or larger, it would have been no more moral."

If, as such victims believe, direct financial reparations do not "make good" in any moral sense, can these payments be perceived in any way as bringing about any measure of justice? Do they at least serve as some means for preventing future crimes against humanity? And if so, doesn't this in fact make reparations a moral issue?

One scholar is quoted in Raphael Patai's book as saying that the German government's policy of reparations "represents a symbol of hope to the entire world and a warning to all lawless and amoral totalitarian governments." Still another says that the accord "can and must serve as a beacon for future modes of international protection of individual human rights on the international level." And in *The Guilt of Nations*, Elizabeth Barkan writes that restorative justice is "a new international system," the "centerpiece" of which is "the willingness of governments to admit to unjust . . . past policies and to negotiate terms for restitution or reparation with their victims based more on moral considerations than on power politics."

However, it seems that acts of genocide have continued unabated, in such places as far-flung as Serbia and Algeria and Rwanda, and that the governments that masterminded or sponsored these acts were completely heedless of any possible retributive consequences, such as having to pay reparations. Moreover, when the various people made the comments I cited above, they didn't—couldn't—take into account the unprecedented 9-11 tragedy, when a small group of fanatics, without affiliation to any particular country or government, killed thousands.

What measure can be taken to "serve as a beacon for future modes of international protection of individual human rights on the international level" against terrorist acts such as this? Should all the countries that in any way, knowing or not, abetted these terrorists have to pay reparations? Or does this incident show that the prospect of reparations ultimately serves as no effective deterrent to the "lawless and immoral" of the world, for the very fact that they are lawless and immoral? Does it also show that when a crime against humanity is committed by a group operating outside all national and governmental parameters, it is impossible, or at least exceedingly difficult, to point the blame at any particular government? Or is it that victims can blame, and demand reparations from, the nations' governments that created fertile ground for such fanaticism, by never giving their citizens the right, much less the opportunity, to live with any semblance of decency or dignity, to become autonomous individuals?

—

The 9-11 tragedy seems to have created a new form of reparations: People around the globe are voluntarily donating what collectively is an enormous sum of money to the survivors of victims. While there always have been outpourings of generosity in times of tragedy— from earthquakes and other natural disasters, as well as from acts of violence and other perceived injustices—the amount given in this instance is unprecedented. Does this outpouring of generosity to the September 11 victims mean that in the future, how much, and even whether, any amount of reparations is paid to victims of violent tragedy should be left up to the will of the people? Does the 9-11 tragedy show that when enough people are sufficiently informed and moved, they voluntarily will compensate victims, virtually obviating the need for government intervention or reparation? Or does such an outpouring make it all the more incumbent for governments to compensate victims of similar types of tragedy when there isn't similar voluntary generosity from the public? Most of all, is such compensation tantamount to justice?

A number of descendents of those kidnapped centuries ago from Africa and brought into bondage to the United States, where, if they survived, they were treated in every respect as less than human, are now seeking reparations. Some assert that the reparations policy in Germany should serve as a standard of the type of reparative justice that slave descendents claim should be carried out by the U.S. government, and by U.S.-based corporations, that at least tacitly condoned slavery.

Should it make any difference that it was their ancestors, rather than they themselves, who were victimized? And if survivors of victims of the September 11 tragedy believe it their just dessert to receive hundreds of millions of dollars in donations pledged to them, after losing loved ones in one heinous act of terror, should those whose ancestors lived their entire lives in terror feel justified in asking for many times more this amount?

In *The Debt—What America Owes to Blacks*, Randall Robinson, founder and president of the Transafrica Forum, dedicated to improving conditions for the perennially oppressed in the African world, writes that there must be reparations to descendants of slaves before there can be any semblance of justice being served. In making his case, he writes that "only slavery, with its sadistic patience, asphyxiated memory, and smothered calluses, has hulled empty a whole race of people with intergenerational efficiency." He calls slavery "a human-rights crime without parallel in the modern world," because "it produces its victims *ad infinitum*, long after the active stage of the crime has ended," evidenced by the fact that "(e)very artifact of the victims' past cultures, every custom, every ritual, every god, every language, every trace element of a people's whole hereditary identity" was "wrenched from them and ground into a sharp choking dust."

Robinson believes that today's descendents of slaves *are* direct victims. Consequently, he believes that it is their just due to receive generous compensation, and that this would be tantamount to "making good" on—doing justice to—what happened to them. Robinson asserts that the example of Germany compensating Jewish victims of the Holocaust serves as precedent. "It paid Jews individually. It paid the state of Israel. . . . Jews have demanded what was their due and received a fair measure of it." Yet, he says, while "(f)or two and a half centuries, Europe and America inflicted unimaginable horrors upon Africa and its people . . . Europe not only paid nothing to Africa in compensation, but followed the slave trade with the remapping of Africa" as a means of "further European economic exploitation." And America, he asserts, has never compensated its victims, though to this day there exists a "yawning economic gap between blacks and whites in this country" that "was opened by the 246-year practice of slavery," and that "has been resolutely nurtured" ever since then, "in law and public behavior."

Would reparations serve as a type of "just" atonement that would bring this bleak period of U.S. history to closure, or, as is the case with Germany, should reparations be ongoing, with closure neither to be sought nor attained? If the public were sufficiently informed about their plight, would it voluntarily start a fund, similar to the September 11 fund, to compensate them?

Can victims of such injustices ever be compensated sufficiently? Is it ever possible completely to make good on the wrongs of the past? And where, if anywhere, should one draw the line in such compensation, and determine definitively that the situation has been "made good," and so "justice has been served"?

Booker T. Washington, for one, believed that ultimately one needs to escape from and efface the "victim mentality," and use the hardships one has suffered in the past to one's best advantage. Washington (1856–1915) was born into slavery in Virginia and overcame incredible odds to receive a formal education. He became president of Tuskegee Institute, which he turned into one of the leading institutes for black education, and he was one of the most influential black leaders of his time (he was advisor to numerous presidents and to major leaders of American industry). In his book *Up From Slavery*, written a full century before Randall Robinson's book that argues for reparative justice, Washington writes that he pities "from the bottom of my heart any nation or body of people that is so unfortunate as to get entangled in the net of slavery." He goes on to say that he has "long since ceased to cherish any spirit of bitterness" against those who perpetrated "the enslavement of my race."

His controversial perspective on slavery is that "when we rid ourselves of prejudice . . . and look facts in the face, we must acknowledge that, not withstanding the cruelty and moral wrong of slavery," those who were most victimized by it now "are in a stronger and more hopeful condition, materially, intellectually, morally, and religiously, than is true of an equal number of black people in any other portion of the globe." I don't think the "facts" would ever support such a claim. Surely the hundreds of thousands who did not survive, and instead died at the hands of slave owners and slave traders after being forced from their homeland, would disagree with Washington. Moreover, Washington conveniently chose not to examine whether black slaves and their descendents were "in a stronger and more hopeful condition" than their white counterparts in the United States.

Washington stresses that he did not make these remarks "to justify slavery . . . I condemn it as an institution. . . . ," but rather he made them "to call attention to a fact, and to show how Providence so often uses men and institutions to accomplish a purpose." Washington, who extolled such virtues as selflessness and industry and optimism, says that whenever he has been asked "how, in the midst of what sometimes seem hopelessly discouraging conditions, I have such faith in the future of my race in this country, I remind them of the wildernesses through which and out of which a good Providence has already led us."

But many descendents of slaves continue to live in "hopelessly discouraging conditions." Maybe one more "wilderness" still has to be traversed; maybe it still remains for us as a nation to face squarely the issue of slavery and the toll it continues to exact on many of its descendents. This is not to say that reparations definitely is the most appropriate or "just" response, only that it may be part of any response, and that it is time fully to broach the issue.

—

Is reparative and restorative justice too backward-looking? Are there more forward-looking forms of justice that will better advance the long-term ends of humanity?

Ruth Morris advocates a type of justice called transformative justice, which, she writes, is realized by the healing "power of forgiveness." She stresses that "(t)his is not to deny that many traumas carry lasting pain. You don't forget the loss of a child, or the betrayal of values. . . . (b)ut . . . forgiveness has in it the most powerful satisfaction of all. It holds the riddle of how we can live together in community in this crowded world, where everyone's life-space intrudes on someone else's."

Would that be an unthinkable notion even to consider, that we should forgive those who committed mass murder on U.S. soil? Even if we can forgive, or even as we forgive, is it sometimes still necessary to act aggressively to prevent future crimes of humanity from occurring, even if it means committing violence ourselves? It partly depends on our ends, which should not include paying vague lip service to "preserving freedom." Rather, our ends must include taking concrete measures, as part of a lasting commitment, to create a type of world in which ever-more people can live in dignity in open societies. If we became fanatics for such ends, it would be much less likely that there would be much fertile ground for fanaticism of the extremely pernicious sort Bin Laden foments.

Morris writes that "we cannot guarantee that floods, falls, human violence, or other disasters will avoid our doors, however much structural security we build. But we can provide the best insurance system when we build a caring community for all."

But what are the conditions for such a "caring community for all," which Morris seems to think is a type of "justice for all"?

Booker T. Washington himself points to a possible answer, in tacitly equating the function of justice with that of making sure everyone in society has the opportunity to live in a "stronger and more hopeful condition, materially, intellectually, morally and religiously." Perhaps realizing this "more hopeful condition" is, in effect, justice in action.

A commitment to eliminate endemic inequalities would never altogether eliminate crimes against humanity. But over the long term, such a commitment should enhance our prospects of becoming a more excellent species, tilting the global balance toward "more hopeful," rather than more hopeless.

## NO SUCH THING AS JUSTICE

I am in the central historic plaza of San Cristobal de las Casas, in Chiapas State in southernmost Mexico, not far from the country's border with Guatemala. I'm encircled by about thirty indigenous people who live in outlying communities, or *ejidos*. Most are dressed in bright hand-sewn traditional clothing, and many women and girls have babies strapped to their backs in multicolored *rebozos*.

San Cristobal is an insular city located at over seven thousand feet above sea level. It is named after Fray Bartolome de las Casas, a Catholic bishop who strove in the sixteenth century to end his fellow invading Spaniards' *encomienda* system, which legally allowed and encouraged them to enslave the indigenous people (those they didn't wantonly kill).

While today San Cristobal is a huge tourist draw, especially for Europeans, beneath its beautiful veneer is great tension. The picturesque colonial city once again has been drawn into the vortex of the struggle for indigenous people's rights, since New Year's Day 1994, the day the North American Free Trade Agreement, or NAFTA, took effect. That morning, a rather ragtag group of *guerrilleros* descended from the surrounding mountains, converged on the city, and after a brief skirmish that left several dead, took over control of the city from the Mexican military.

Their faces hidden behind red handkerchiefs, or *paliacates*, the group of invading rebels called themselves EZLN, Ejercito Zapatista Liberacion National, or the National Liberation Zapatista Army. They'd named themselves after Emiliano Zapata, a Nahua Indian who'd spearheaded the Mexican Revolution of 1910 that toppled the dictatorship of Porfirio Diaz. After assuming power, Zapata called for extensive land reform, so that the disenfranchised indigenous people could again live in dignity. "All of the land, all of the forests and natural resources that have been stripped from their rightful owners," Zapata declared, "will be immediately restored to the villages or citizens to whom they legally belong. . . . so that they can have their own *ejidos*, townships, fields for crops." But in 1919, before Zapata could implement reform, his conservative enemies had him assassinated.

While, from time to time since then, there have been tepid efforts at land reform, and some *ejidos* have been allocated to the indigenous, for the most part, the same issues plague this region that created great strife for hundreds of years. There remains the same oppression and exploitation of the indigenous people, the same virulent racism against them, and the same unresolved issues of land reform.

Frustrated over their continued marginalization and exploitation, many decided NAFTA was the last straw. The land-reform process had long since stalled, and those who had been given land often had not been allocated what or how much they were promised, after an agonizing yearslong wait. And often as not, the land that was meted out to them by the federal government overlapped with that already ceded to other communities, sowing the seeds (perhaps intentionally on the part of the government) of conflict between indigenous groups. To add insult to injury, their primary means of subsisting—selling their basic staples such as corn and coffee and nuts—was undercut by NAFTA, which enabled U.S.-based transnationals to import their own corn and coffee into Mexico and sell it cheaper than the indigenous people could sell their own products.

From the standpoint of the indigenous people, all of them of Mayan descent, NAFTA was the latest and greatest in an unending series of betrayals by the Mexican government. Because the government refused to remedy the situation, many felt their only recourse was drastic action.

The New Year's Day uprising in 1994 was led by an enigmatic *ladino* (non-Indian) who billed himself as Subcomandante Marcos, though there is little question that his true identity is Rafael Sebastian Guillen, a university graduate in philosophy and onetime university teacher whose father was a successful furniture salesman. According to John Ross, author of the American Book Award–winning *Rebellion from the Roots: Indian Uprising in Chiapas*, Marcos/Guillen, who was influenced by the French Marxist philosopher Louis Althusser, said the uprising took place as a protest against NAFTA and "how cheap U.S. grains that NAFTA would pour into Mexico would obliterate the possibilities of commercializing Mayan corn," forcing the indigenous people here to live in more extreme poverty than ever. Marcos said, "To us, the free-trade treaty is the death certificate for the ethnic people of Mexico," and marked the death knell of all attempts to bring justice to the region. Harvard historian John Womack, Jr., a leading authority on the conflict and its historical underpinnings, asserts that the poverty itself "justifies the revolt" in the Chiapas highlands.

The EZLN occupied San Cristobal for a mere thirty hours before they disappeared back into the surrounding Lacandon jungle. But in that short time span, they'd succeeded in thrusting the plight of the region's indigenous people into the international limelight.

As I got set to hold my latest dialogue here, it had been over six years since the EZLN launched its initial salvo, and all had been relatively quiet on the southern front, except for a skirmish here and there. Mexico's new president, Vicente Fox, had recently taken office, replacing president Ernesto Zedillo, who, after exhaustive negotiations, had backed out of a formal accord reached with the indigenous people that would have guaranteed them the right to live autonomously, and that would have expedited land reform. Zedillo instead chose surreptiously to install more military fortifications in the area—yet another in a long series of deceptions by the Mexican government, made all the worse because Zedillo had vowed frequently and strenuously to reach an accord.

Now it was Vicente Fox's turn. He'd promised famously in his presidential campaign to resolve the indigenous conflict in "fifteen minutes." His first act in office was to submit to Congress the accord that Zedillo had reached with the EZLN and indigenous leaders, and then had backed out of. But the Mexican Congress had diluted the bill to the point where, even if it were approved, it served to diminish further the few rights of the indigenous people, rather than enhance them. As a result, the Zapatistas cursed the government and retreated once again from public view, presumably to hatch their next offensive.

These are tense times. The plaza is platooned with soldiers and police with automatic weapons. They'd brought in a new *guerrillero* prisoner earlier in the day, while my wife Cecilia was holding a "classroom without walls"—giving reading and writing lessons for the indigenous children, who, instead of going to school, spend all day and night selling handmade purses and belts and *pulseras*, or bracelets, to tourists who stroll the plaza.

This is not the first time that soldiers have glared at me when I've held a dialogue; but it is the first time that so *many* have. When I'd first tried to strike up a dialogue with the indigenous people, most looked at me as if I were loopy. None would respond to my overtures. When I asked Cecilia, who'd been a teacher in an indigenous community before we met and married, why holding a dialogue with them seemed like Mission Impossible, she told me, "Probably because no one has ever before asked them what they think. And if no one's ever asked them, they probably haven't asked themselves. Hang in there. They'll soon see that you want to learn from them, and they'll respond."

She was right. Slowly but surely, they came to know me and trust me, and even to look forward to our dialogues, which take place late in the evening, when there is a lag in tourism, and they can relax from a fourteen-hour workday, in which they try to sell enough of their products to eat a decent meal and buy a few necessities.

Tonight, as we gather around and sip hot tea I've brought to share, I ask, "What is justice?"

Chuno, who has been in the plaza all day selling a variety of nuts that he and others grow on their collectively owned *ejido* two hours away, says to me in Spanish, "In our native language, Tzeltal, we don't have a word that is the equivalent of justice."

This answer takes me off guard. "Surely you must have *some* word that is similar or equivalent."

"There isn't," he assures me. "We've never felt like we needed it."

"How can that be?" I say. I'm sure I look bewildered. "You've been fighting for years now for 'justice.' How can you say you don't have or need the word?"

"Oh, we know the Spanish words for justice and injustice, *justicia* and *injusticia*, all too well," he tells me. "We've been victimized for centuries by outsiders. But what I'm saying is that in our language, we have no word for justice, or for injustice, because we don't need them—*in our language*. Because in our communities, when we're just among ourselves, nothing like injustice ever takes place. So why would we need a word for it or for its opposite, justice?"

No such thing as injustice? No need for the word justice? In exasperated perplexity, I manage to say, "Why?"

Chuno replies patiently, "In our *ejidos*, we make all major decisions together. Everyone has his say. We sit in a circle and talk, for nights on end if necessary, until everyone comes to an agreement on what we should do."

A man whom I know to be a Zapatista sympathizer, if not a member of the EZLN, now says to me, "If there weren't unanimous agreement, then someone in our community might feel he was dealt with unjustly. But if we all agree—not in a forced way, but in a way where we each present our views, and then discuss them and hash them out until we reach agreement—how can there be injustice?"

I say nothing. He goes on, "So we don't need such words. But I can see why Mexicans have these words, *justicia* and *injusticia*. The Mexican government is injustice incarnate. If they want to build a highway, or bulldoze nature to build a building, even if it is against the will of the people, they just do it. But in our indigenous community, if we decide to cut down a single tree, all the people first have to agree that it needs to be done."

John Womack, Jr. writes in *Rebellion in Chiapas* that "none of the Indian languages" have "words for 'command' or 'favor' or 'rights,'" much less justice. To have such words, to apply them to their conflict with Mexican authorities, "(i)t took new Spanish words."

Maruch, a Tzotzil indigenous woman, says now, "If we had a word similar to justice, it would be something like 'resolution' and 'restoration.' Because when there's a conflict in our community, we try to bring about a peaceful resolution, and restore harmony. This way, everyone emerges from the conflict as more of a *batsil winick*, a true human being."

"We see the conflict between us and the Mexican government as one between two communities," she goes on. "But they don't see it that way, because they are powerful and have been able to exploit us at will for centuries. Under such circumstances, it's impossible to restore harmony."

Her husband, Petul, says now, "Many of us here have been waiting for years for the government to allocate us our own *ejido*. We live in shacks on the outskirts of this city. We have no community to call our own, and so we have no ways to remedy conflicts, because we live outside our traditional rules of *ejido* law. So even if we had a word for justice, those of us here without an *ejido* couldn't put it to use, because we have no community."

What he says jibes with Aristotle, who in his *Nicomachaean Ethics* said that "justice exists only between people whose mutual relations are governed by law." F. A. Hayek, a Nobel Prize winner in economics, says something similar in *The Road to Serfdom*: "Nothing distinguishes more clearly conditions in a free country from those in a country under arbitrary government than the observance in the former of the great principles known as the rule of law." Hayek says that rule of law means "that government in all its actions is bound by rules fixed and announced beforehand—rules which make it possible to foresee with fair certainty how the authority will use its coercive powers in given circumstances, and to plan one's individual affairs on the basis of this knowledge." But Hayek fails to distinguish between just and unjust forms of rule of law. Just because one knows beforehand what a law is doesn't make it a *just* law. Laws that are on the books in an authoritarian state often are no better than arbitrary rule. People still can't plan their affairs "on the basis of knowledge" of the rule of law, when individual liberties are highly restricted, if not completely curtailed.

—

After a considerable lull, Anton, a soft-spoken man who is sitting beside me with his wife, Peti, and four children, says to me, "I also live with my family in shacks outside of San Cristobal. But not because we didn't have a community to call our own. We were fortunate to have lived in an *ejido* all our lives—until the Zapatista conflict. My family, and many others, were kicked out of our *ejido*, because we didn't agree with the strategy of Subcommandante Marcos and the EZLN in the conflict with the Mexican government."

He then tells me, "Each indigenous community held meetings to decide whether or not they were going to fight along with Marcos. We all sympathize with Marcos, with what he says he hopes to do on our behalf. But that doesn't mean we all agree that armed conflict is the answer. Over many evenings, our community discussed what to do. But we never reached agreement. I and many others refused to fight alongside Marcos. But the majority of members in our communities sided with him. So they kicked us out. They said there was no room for opposing views."

Peti now says, "They said, 'If you aren't with us, you're against us.' They forced us to leave our community, and to live here in shacks. They imposed the same type of arbitrary authority that they accuse the Mexican government of imposing. So when some here try to tell you that all indigenous communities resolve conflicts peacefully and through universal agreement, and that we have no need for words like *justice* and *injustice*, it's not true."

A number of others nod in agreement, and I can see that they are angry. I see also that those who earlier described indigenous communities as oases of harmony are agitated over this debunking of their assertions.

Finally, a Zapatista sympathizer says, "It was for their own good. If they'd stayed in the community, and the Mexican army came, they would have been arrested along with us. The military would have thought they were on the side of the EZLN."

Another woman says softly, "We didn't want them to leave. The EZLN told us we *had* to make them leave."

Scholar John Womack writes: "Where communities voted for war, the EZLN tolerated no dissent or pacifism: The minorities had to leave. Not only then did different organizations in communities separate, but old friends too, . . . once-trusted comrades, members of the same family, fathers and daughters, mothers and sons. The expelled were now displaced persons, migrating again, thousands of them." And just as the person here says, they were allowed only to "take with them what they could ride, lead, or carry." In what I would call a travesty of justice, these communities were now divided, their traditions usurped, by the very group that claimed to be fighting to allow them to preserve their traditions and live autonomously by their traditional ways.

"But you'd told me that you only made decisions after there was universal agreement," I now say.

"All of us agreed that Marcos's fight was, as you say in Spanish, *justo*, just," says the Zapatista sympathizer. "We all agreed that he was on our side. What we didn't agree on was whether we should join Marcos or not in his fight."

This is a less than complete answer, but it is all I can get from him.

Salvador, whose family also was kicked out of their *ejido*, says, "We did sympathize with Marcos. We think his heart probably is in the right place. But we already had Bishop Ruiz on our side, helping us organize and fight for our rights, but in a peaceful way. We're devout Catholics, and we felt that a nonviolent path had to be taken. We felt that armed conflict would be a setback."

Before the EZLN made its memorable entry into the long-simmering conflict in Chiapas, Bishop Samuel Ruiz, who had been bishop in Chiapas for nearly fifty years (he'd just retired as this dialogue takes place), had been the central figure advocating for the indigenous people. John Womack, Jr., writes that Ruiz "emphasized the egregious inequality and injustice in his diocese . . ." When Ruiz first arrived in Chiapas half a century ago and traveled the state for the first time, he quickly came to the realization that "the trouble was the Church itself, its alienation from the Indians." Ruiz determined to stand up to those who treated the indigenous people as if they had no rights. He said, "I came to San Cristobal to convert the poor, but they ended up converting me."

Womack writes that since becoming bishop in 1950, Ruiz has been instrumental in helping the region's indigenous people take "a new, critical attitude toward old beliefs . . . and collectively . . . act on a new sense of right and justice." Because of Ruiz's efforts, they refused any longer to be resigned to their exploitation, but instead became instilled with a *toma de consciencia*, an awareness of their plight and their potential to change it.

Minco, with whom I've spent many hours over the weeks engaging in thoughtful one-on-one dialogues, when he isn't shining shoes at five pesos a pop, now says, "It's not even right that we all agreed about Marcos's motivations. Marcos took complete control of EZLN, and of the indigenous-rights movement. He's the exact opposite of Bishop Ruiz, who empowered *us*."

———

There's a long silence. Finally Mario stands up. The Chol indigenous man walks each day two hours to San Cristobal to and from his *ejido*, and attends the local university at night and sells nuts and fruits during the day, to support himself and his young family. He makes eye contact with each and every one of us, and then says, "Even though we may not have a word for 'justice' in our language, I do think there is an answer to this question, 'What is justice?' My answer is that justice is equality—not just under the law, but in how we human beings see one another. To have this justice, we would have to do away with racism. We would all have to see each other as equals.

"You can have as many laws as you like," he continues, "but unless people feel in their hearts that we are all equal, that we all deserve to live a good and hopeful life, there can be no justice of the type I speak of. So first, we have to change people's hearts and minds, before there can ever be just laws. Racism is the biggest obstacle to achieving this justice for the indigenous in Mexico."

His wife, Carmela, nods and says to me, "The fact that no Mexicans will take part in these dialogues with us speaks volumes. They want to have nothing to do with us, because they think themselves superior. Here in San Cristobal, we can't eat in the restaurants. The police, with their *macanas*, or batons, harass us if we sit down in this plaza for very long, even though it's a public place. Some local Mexicans push us to the ground when they pass us. Until a few years ago, we weren't allowed to walk on the sidewalks here; we had to walk on the road and risk being hit by a car."

"We have the highest illiteracy and infant mortality rates," she continues, "work the longest hours for the worst wages, and it is tolerated and supported, because of the color of our skin. The racism just seems to get worse . . ."

Her friend Pashku, a university student and a human-rights activist, says, "Mexico is terribly racist. Even though most Mexicans are *mestizo*, of mixed Indian and Spanish blood, they 'act white,' meaning, they distance themselves completely from their indigenous roots—and so have nothing whatever to do with us—and associate completely with the small part of their blood that is European. There will never be justice of any kind until we do away with this racism monster."

After a pause, she then says, "This land we're fighting for in Chiapas, it was ours before the Spanish *conquistadores* came; yet we're treated like third-class citizens. It was ours before the Mexican government and their functionaries took control of it, after the Spanish were finally defeated. They have the legal documents to say it's theirs. Legally, it may be, but morally, justly, it is ours. I understand that we'll never get it all back. But we need *some* land, so we can all have communities to call our own. They must give us our proper share, so we can live like human beings."

Ten-year-old Veruch tugs at my shirtsleeve, indicating she wants to speak. She has been teaching me her language of Tzotzil over the past month, and refuses to accept any money for it—she says friends don't pay friends for help—even though she earns less than a dollar a day selling *pulseras* and has no family of her own. She says now, "Isn't justice sharing what you have so everyone has enough?"

## RACISM AND JUSTICE

The Mexican philosopher José Vasconcelos (1881–1959) of the state of Oaxaca, which has an even larger indigenous population than Chiapas, dwelled deeply on the country's racist heritage. Vasconcelos—both an academic and public philosopher who twice was forced into exile for his antiauthoritarian stances against the dictators of his era—sought, as scholar Didier T. Jaen notes, "another dimension for man and society." Vasconcelos believed his homeland was capable of taking a "new road," one in which Mexico "would march at the vanguard of all other nations, which would follow her guide, tired as they were of an economic materialism that lacked human dimensions."

In his seminal essay, *La Raza Cosmica*, or *The Cosmic Race*, Vasconcelos argued that to be of "mixed race" should not be viewed as a stigma at all, but an asset. He asserted that the most advanced civilizations have come to the fore at times when they were composed of "a mixture of races and cultural currents." Such varied peaks of civilization as the Golden Age of Hellenic Greece and the Second Empire of Egypt, when the pyramids were built, were great "*mestizo* periods"; and he viewed "powerful North America," with its great and flourishing "melting pot" of races, as filled with "the most vigorous drive" of all other nations.

Vasconcelos, who elaborated his perspective on race in the 1920s, on the heels of the Mexican revolution, held that when "the various races of the earth . . . intermix," they typically give rise "to a new human type," in which civilizations are at their most flourishing and vibrant. Prior to 1920, as scholar Julio Moreno notes in *Yankee Don't Go Home!*, "Mexicans preferred to identify with their local region, the patria chica, rather than with the nation as a whole." But "the revolution triggered efforts to define national ideals and find a common ground with which Mexicans from different regions could identify." Mexicans began to embrace "the country's indigenous and mestizo background," seeing this heritage as a rich and unifying "symbol of national identity." Consequently, Vasconcelos's notion of "the country's 'cosmic race' " served as a "key to national progress." Didier Jaen observes that this pervasive celebration of Mexico's mixed ancestry was a richly humane counterpoint to the notions of racial purity, advanced in that era by Aryan theorists, that eventually were "carried to aberrant imposition by Nazism."

In his provocative essay, Vasconcelos wasn't arguing that people of various races and cultures should mix out of any necessary compulsion. Rather, as Didier Jaen writes, Vasconcelos believed that mixing of races would occur naturally when "sexual unions . . . cease to be founded on necessity or on norms of convenience to society." He surmised that if men and women were only "guided by the free choice of love, beauty, and joy," they would quite often choose partners of races or ethnicities other than their own. He said that "such unions will be more like works of art rather than the social contracts our present marriages are . . ." As a result, "ethnic barriers will lose their force, and the mixture of the races . . . will increase to the point that a new, fully mixed race will emerge, in which the better qualities of all the previous races will survive by the natural selection of love." A race created by the "natural selection of love" would culminate in what Vasconcelos coined "the Cosmic Race."

As deeply racist as Mexico is, it need not look elsewhere for examples of how to overcome its racial divides. It has acted in the past in a way that shows it can serve as a beacon to other societies grappling with divisive ethnic and racial dilemmas. The fact is that Mexico once was so inspired by an indigenous man, Benito Juarez, to transcend their baser inclinations, and envision nobler possibilities for themselves, that they elected him their president. In *Mexico: Biography of Power*, Juarez is depicted as an Indian who refused to "lower his gaze" before others, who had an unparalleled "will to emancipate himself," and who refused to accept that racism had to keep him from achieving his aspirations. A Zapotec Indian from Oaxaca State, Juarez was born in 1806 into dire poverty, his parents illiterate peasant farmers. But he was determined to educate himself, and through dogged persistence he managed to gain entry into seminary, and then to go on to get his law degree. Juarez then immersed himself in public life, and in 1847 became governor of Oaxaca State. There, he set about changing a political system that, he said, had for centuries sanctioned the "poverty . . . brutalization . . . degradation and . . . enslavement" of the nation's indigenous people. Juarez railed against "the torpid poverty that submerges our brothers" and the "heavy exactions that still burden them."

But his blunt statements against the endemic corruption and

racism promoted by General Santa Anna, the nation's then-dictator/president, forced him in 1853 into exile in New Orleans. When Santa Anna was overthrown, Juarez returned to Mexico and was appointed minister of justice by the new president. In this post, he enacted the famous "Juarez Law," which did away with the sweeping powers of the Catholic Church, whose powers he believed had been wielded largely to oppress the indigenous people. Building on this success, Juarez then implemented social and legal reforms that further restricted the powers of the Church and undermined the wealthy landed interests. He did away with special military courts, so soldiers could no longer brutalize the indigenous people with impunity, and he worked tirelessly to implement economic, political, and land reform on behalf of the indigenous people.

Juarez touched a chord with a nation weary of oppression, corruption, and racism, and in 1861 Mexicans made him their president—their nation's first and only indigenous president. Though reelected, Juarez died before he was able to overcome the trenchant opposition by the conservative majority in Congress, preventing implementation of his sweeping reforms. Mexico then regressed, to the detriment of its indigenous peoples, to the type of authoritarian and corrupt rule that has defined it ever since.

Most who write about Juarez's ascendancy to the pinnacle of power say it was an aberration. But the fact that this excellent aberration occurred, I think, shows that it can occur again. To do so, it likely will require a person with the same set of virtues as Juarez: someone of vision and will and moral courage, who puts the long-term interests of his country, and humanity itself, above all; and someone who speaks to people's nobler sensibilities. But it also will require a person who, like Juarez, is not overly seduced by and mired in the "blame game," and instead uses his history of oppression as a source of inspiration to overcome all obstacles.

—

At the beginning of John Womack's book on the tragic situation in Chiapas, there is this quote from a twenty-four-year-old Zapatista *guerillero*: "I want there to be democracy . . . I am looking for a life worth living . . ." I wonder: If you examine your life in the spirit of Socrates' famous saying that "the unexamined life is not worth living," and discover that you live in virtual shackles, would it have been better never to have examined your life in the first place?

Bishop Samuel Ruiz strove not only to inspire the indigenous people to examine their oppressive circumstances, but also to help them help themselves make their lives more worth living, by organizing politically and demanding the rights that were their due. In doing so, he went up against every vested interest imaginable—from the Mexican government, to powerful Mexican landowners and businessmen, to transnational corporations, to his local superiors in the church, to the Vatican.

Like Fray Bartolome de las Casas, who was among the first to practice "liberation theology," Ruiz believed it was hypocritical to claim to care for the souls of the poor, and yet to do nothing (and care less) about liberating them from their abject situation. As Leonardo and Clodovis Bof write, "(T)he historical roots of liberation theology are to be found in the prophetic traditions of evangelists and missionaries from the earliest colonial days in Latin America," and "churchmen" such as Fray Bartolome "questioned the type of presence adopted by the Church and the way indigenous peoples . . . were treated." Now Ruiz is among a group of "charismatic bishops and priests" who since the 1960s, when "a great wind of renewal blew through the churches," have made it their "social mission" to better the plight of the poor.

The variation of liberation theology practiced by theologian Gustavo Gutierrez in Peru is, to me, the most admirable of all. Gutierrez doesn't just advocate a policy of liberating the poor from poverty. Instead, he abandoned a relatively cushy existence to live with the poor, and is committed to doing so, until they are lifted out of poverty. He writes in *A Theology of Liberation* that "if the ultimate cause of human exploitation and alienation is selfishness, the deepest reason for voluntary poverty is love of neighbor. Christian poverty has meaning only as a commitment of solidarity with the poor, with those who suffer misery and injustice." Like EZLN leader Marcos/Guillen, Gutierrez is a devotee of Paul Ricoeur, and he agrees with Ricoeur that "you cannot really be with the poor," and cannot help bring any measure of justice to their cause, "unless you are struggling against poverty" yourself.

—

Andrew Reding, who directs the Americas Project of the New York–based World Policy Institute, wrote that "the revolt among the Mayan population of Chiapas is a wake-up call to the unacknowledged reality of racism in Mexico." He contends that if Mexico is to transcend its racist heritage, it will need "the same sort of consciousness-raising that has spurred change in the United States and Canada."

Reding acknowledges the critical role of the "liberation theology wing of the Catholic Church" in this regard. He particularly lauds the efforts of Bishop Ruiz, who was vilified by his superiors for interpreting "too literally the gospel that all human beings are created equal," and consequently were irked that the indigenous began "to demand treatment as human beings fully equal to the descendants of the conquistadors who continue to dominate southern Mexico." Still, he says, there may be a "silver lining in the cloud of rebellion over Chiapas"—namely, "that it has begun to force Mexico's unacknowledged racism into the open."

If bringing racism into the open in and of itself is a silver lining that somehow will catalyze the creation of a more just society, he may be right. But nearly eight years after he wrote this essay, the acknowledgment of racism in Mexico has not led to enlightenment, and in cases has fomented even deeper hatred of the indigenous people among many Mexicans; it seems to have led to deeper divisions, and the indigenous inhabitants now live in more oppressive circumstances than ever.

John Womack, Jr., indicates that the United States might play a vital role in efforts to overcome racism in Mexico. But he says that our lack of understanding about our neighbor to the south is a great hindrance: "Our problem is not merely the media, or our notorious inability to learn another language. It is our entire evasive and mendacious culture," which "deafen(s) us to crying injustices . . . "

Rigoberta Menchu, on the other hand, thinks that the most vital role to be played in overcoming racism in Latin America is by Latin American citizens themselves. A Quiche Indian and Mayan descendent who lived most of her life in a dirt-poor community in Guatemala, Menchu was an unlikely winner of the 1992 Nobel Peace Prize. For thirteen years, until early 1994, she had lived in exile in Mexico, escaping there from Guatemala after her parents, both longtime leaders in the indigenous-rights movement, had been brutalized and murdered by government security forces. In her 1983 book *I, Rigoberta*, written at age twenty-three, she relates her tragic story. In her book, she says her cause "wasn't born out of something good," but rather was "born out of wretchedness and bitterness," and was "radicalized" by the poverty, exploitation, and discrimination in which her people live.

In an essay written in 2001, she says, "There will be no peace if there is no justice. . . . no justice if there is no equity. . . . no equity if there is no progress . . . no progress if there is no democracy. . . . no democracy if there is no respect for the identity and dignity of the peoples and cultures in today's world." Menchu, who used the $1.2 million she was awarded with the Nobel Prize to found a nonprofit group to carry on the struggle for social justice in the region, sees reason for hope. In her native Guatemala, she says that the *ladinos*, or the region's nonindigenous, are "beginning to realize that they themselves are only another ethnic group," rather than a superior race. She envisions, over the long term, the emergence of a new type of society, in which there will be "new relationships" among peoples at all levels. Such a society, she believes, will radically change the political and economic and military structures of Latin American countries, and serve as a model for healing racial and ethnic rifts throughout the world. "Every day," she says, "we fertilize the seed to build a new relationship between indigenous and nonindigenous peoples"—and, as a result, inch a little closer to realizing her version and vision of justice.

# GOOD TO BE HUMAN

It is bitterly cold outside, but inside, where I'm seated by a fireplace with six others in a student center at a university in the north-central United States, it is quite cozy. After reading my book *Socrates Café*, the students here asked me if I might hold a dialogue with them. They told me that they were a "fellowship of six students," three Jewish (two from Israel, one from the United States), and three Arab (one of whose family is in the Palestinian territory, one from Saudi Arabia, and one from Egypt). They said they get together once a week just . . . to get together. They said they do this, in part, in response to the increasingly violent situation in the Middle East, where the quest for a Palestinian homeland seems more remote than ever, as the violence between both sides ascends to ever-greater heights. They said that they hoped, in their modest way, to help increase understanding by regularly having "friendship gatherings."

Today, as we meet, the Israeli army has just surrounded the compound of Yasser Arafat, chairman of the Palestinian Liberation Organization, after a particularly horrific string of homicide bombings by Palestinians. To date, since the Palestinian *intifada*, or uprising, began in September 2000, more than 1,700 Palestinians and 700 Israelis have been killed.

The question the students examine with me this evening is "What is good?"

"In Hebrew, the word *tov* means 'good,'" says Dorothy, a third-year student from Israel. "A person who is called *lev tov* is a person of 'good heart.' Such a person always thinks first of others, and how she can act in the world in a way that will have a positive impact, or ripple effect, on everyone else in her world, so they'll be inspired to be *lev tov*. A person of good heart sees the good in everyone, and helps them bring out the good in themselves."

"This is very similar to what we call in Arabic a *tayyeb*, a person who is virtuous and good, and so is blessed by Allah," says Iyad, an earnest young Palestinian Arab who is double-majoring in literature and international relations. "He's a person who suffers when others suffer. A *tayyab* gives of himself constantly. His goal is to ease the pain of others."

"That sounds almost exactly like a *lev tov*," says Lance, who is a freshman from Michigan. "Such people recognize that human good is what Primo Levi once said: to never forget that all humans *are* human. Levi said that in the concentration camps, the victims were stripped of their humanity—that the Nazis didn't just see them as *less* human than they were; they saw them as *Untermenschen*, less *than* human."

Primo Levi, an Italian-Jewish writer trained as a chemist and part of the antifascist resistance, was sent to the Auschwitz concentration camp. He was one of only a handful of people still living when the camp was liberated by the Soviet Red Army.

Lance goes on, "Levi said in his book *Moments of Reprieve* that too many humans 'are too dazzled by power and money' and forget their 'essential fragility.' "

"There are people on both sides of the conflict between Israel and Palestine who see themselves as more human than the other side," says Jehan, a psychology major from Egypt, "and some who don't even look at the other side in terms of fellow human beings."

She then says, "In places like Serbia, what happened there, the ethnic cleansing, as well in Iraq, Saddam Hussein's atrocities against the Kurds, and the Basque terrorism in Spain; they're all examples of this. They see their enemy as subhuman, so they can justify doing *in*human things to them without a twinge of remorse. And what is happening now in the Middle East, between Jews and Palestinians, is that there's a type of hate among many on both sides where each is convinced that the person they're killing or murdering is not really a person."

"So to treat one another as equally human is good, or what you call human good," I say.

She nods.

"But does it end violence? Or does it just mean that you respect your enemy? And if so, what is the ultimate good in that?"

"Well, I think having that respect is the first step to ending violence over the long term," says Suad, a premedical student from Saudi Arabia. "In my country, our leaders still don't recognize officially Israel's right to exist. So that tells you how they 'respect' them as fellow humans."

There is a pause before Dorothy says, "Good is that bridge that exists between two humans. When you genuinely communicate with another human, you no longer are the person you were before you communicated."

She goes on: "What is happening between the leaders of Israel and the Palestinian territory right now is that they've closed themselves off to communicating with one another. So they've closed off all possibilities of human good."

Dorothy turns to Iyad and smiles. She then says to me, "Iyad and I take the same international relations course. At the beginning of each class, we discuss current events. One day, near the beginning of the semester, we discussed the situation between Palestinians and Jews. We got into such an argument. We were both sure we were right. We yelled, got mad, I mean really mad. The other students just watched us shout at each other. I eventually stormed out of the room, even though class had just gotten under way."

Iyad, looking all the while at Dorothy, picks up the thread: "I promised myself that I'd never speak to you again. Then, after class, a student came up to me and said he was on my side, on the side of the Palestinians. At first, this made me feel good. Then he went into this rant about how the Palestinians are justified in any act of violence they perpetrate against Jews. He called Jews names that I wouldn't repeat. He was just a student from white-bread America. I don't know what hate literature he was filled with, but I know I didn't want him to be on *my* side."

Iyad looks at me and says, "He made me think, 'How do I really see that person I was yelling at in class? Do I see her as a stereotype? Do I have a lot of the same irrational hate as this student who was 'on my side'?"

He continues, "When I saw Dorothy the next day, I came up to her. She sort of flinched when she saw me. I apologized to her and then said, 'I don't even know you, but I was arguing with you worse than I do with my brothers and sisters.' She laughed, and said the same went for her. Then I invited her to have a cup of coffee."

Dorothy tells me, "I accepted, and after we started talking, I realized how much we had in common. We both want to be diplomats. We both have huge stamp collections. We love to learn different languages—I'm learning Arabic and he's learning Hebrew. And of course, we both want peace in the Middle East."

"Well, after that," she continues, "we kept getting together, and soon we each invited a couple of our friends to join us." She nods to the others who are with us. "At first, we didn't talk much about the situation again in the occupied territories. We weren't avoiding it exactly, I don't think. But we just were talking, about things that people who are becoming friends talk about."

Iyad says, "After another suicide bombing, our international relations professor again brought up the subject of the Middle East conflict at the beginning of class. Dorothy and I were both hesitant to speak. We didn't want to get mad at each other. Then we did start to speak, but carefully, still saying what we felt we had to say, but also being sensitive to the other's feelings. And we listened carefully to each other's responses. We realized we had similar concerns and hopes—to live free of fear, to have security for our families, to have some control over our lives, our futures."

"Instead of trying to win an argument," says Dorothy, "we voiced our concerns, but also we really opened ourselves up to the concerns of the other."

"And now, that's what we often do here when we get together on our own," says Suad. "Our shared concern is How can we reach a solution that addresses all our shared concerns? How can we ever inspire people on both sides to look at our concerns as equally valid? Because once you recognize how legitimate each other's concerns are, then I think you *have* to go the next step and address them."

"My cousin is in service in the IDF, the Israeli Defense Forces, in Israel," says Lance, after a pause. " In her first letters to me, she said being in the military made her feel like part of something greater than herself. She liked that everyone from every walk of life has to serve in IDF, and that most do so willingly because their democracy is so precious to them. But lately, she has said that you can get too caught up in it, lose your sense of humanity. She said some of the Israeli soldiers, without provocation, have mistreated Arabs, and worse. Yet many Israelis look at them as heroes. In her most recent letters, she's begun to question what's going on there."

In late December 2002, B'Tselem, Israel's leading human-rights monitor in the occupied territories, called on the Israel Defense Forces to investigate "abuse of Palestinians by IDF soldiers," which it says "occurs daily." It also called on the IDF to punish soldiers guilty of abuse, in order "to send an unequivocal message that violence, abuse, or degradation of Palestinian civilians is absolutely prohibited." B'Tselem says that as long as the Israeli Army refuses to punish soldiers who abuse civilians, such acts "will continue to occur."

"You have to look at your enemy as a *human* enemy, as someone who probably has a girlfriend or wife and family, who hopes to have a house, a decent job," says Ephraim, from Israel. "You may think his way of attaining these goals is misdirected, maybe in the worst way, but if you lose sight that he's a human being, all is lost."

Iyad says, "The leaders of Hamas and Islamic Jihad now have younger and younger people, and now even women, doing their deeds for them. They've filled them up with such a hate frenzy, convinced them that regular Israeli families are legitimate targets."

He pauses before going on. "I knew one of the bombers who committed suicide, who killed and wounded Israelis. He left a note behind, a long rambling note about how they must rid this world of Israelis if there is to be peace. His parents, you just can't believe how distraught they were—and angry that their child was manipulated by the leaders of the Islamic Jihad. He was a good soul with a brilliant mind, and now he's gone, used up by extremists. Where is the 'good' in that?"

He continues, "Everyone is afraid to speak out against Hamas and Islamic Jihad and Al-Aqsa Martyrs Brigade. They can kill you for criticizing them. They've killed many Palestinians for being 'informers,' but really were just people who dared criticize them. They kill without due process anyone they think is against them. What they do and believe is the exact opposite of human good—it is evil, what the Quran calls al-*Khabees*."

We're silent for a while. Eventually Dorothy says, "Yitzhak Rabin, our former president, didn't like Yasser Arafat, but he saw him as equally human. Rabin was a genuine *lev tov*. His only concern was for the long-term good of humanity. But an extremist Jew hated Rabin for being that way, and assassinated him . . . "

"Rabin was the same as Anwar Sadat, our president, who was a *tayyeb*," Jehan says now. "He was also assassinated. If Rabin and Sadat were alive today, I think we'd have the framework for a lasting peace."

Ephraim says to me, "Like, in your country here, some leaders had the courage to sacrifice their lives, to advance with the civil rights movement. They knew losing their lives was a distinct possibility, but they still moved ahead, because they thought foremost of the greater human good. Now, we have these jaded leaders all over the world—from Clinton and Bush, to Sharon and Netanyahu. They take no risks for the good of humanity.

"As Dorothy said, when Rabin treated Arafat as an equal, and vice versa, that was human good. They were trying to understand each other, their thinking, their concerns, their aspirations for their people. When you open yourself up like that, you can't emerge unchanged, in the best sense."

"None of us here agrees exactly on what 'the' solution is that will give us all hope and optimism for the future," says Iyad. "We argue sometimes, and a few times, some of us have gotten very angry at one another. But we never let that keep us from getting together. So far, thankfully, no one in any of our families has been killed. I don't know if we'd still gather like this if they had . . . "

We again are silent for a while.

Then Dorothy says, "One thing I've learned, because of my studies here at the university, is that in all great social movements, in which it seemed like impossible mountains had to be moved, impasses were broken and progress was made only after people from opposing sides got together and talked to one another—and refused to quit talking to one another, no matter what."

Ephraim now says, "When I was younger, I used to think that we had to build walls around those who wanted to do violence—walls so high that they couldn't escape to do any harm. And I think I wanted to put a wall around myself. Now I think that we have to tear down all walls—like this wall of security Israel is building now. We need to tear down all walls and build bridges—bridges of human good."

"I think, to know beyond a doubt that human good is bridging the space between people," Suad says next, "all you have to do is to look at what happens when people quit trying to bridge these gaps—human evil automatically fills the void."

"I keep thinking of my baby brother back home," says Dorothy. "He doesn't yet know hate. I wish that this could be resolved before he's old enough to learn that he should hate or fear. And I wonder, once I return home, if I'll still be so 'objective,' or if I'll change incredibly."

"I used to think everyone else had to change," says Iyad. "I tried to change my mother's opinions. I tried to change the opinions of the people here. I didn't really want to listen. But then I realized that the person who had to change was me. All I can do is be an example of a person who's trying to bridge the gaps."

"I just finished reading Edith Wharton's *The House of Mirth* for my American literature class," Jehan tells us. "There's this one section where Wharton talks about a person's 'quickened intelligence of the heart' that is 'disciplined by long years of contact with . . . suffering,' one's own suffering and that of others. Wharton writes that when you really reach out to others, there is a 'current of rare contact, one of those exchanges of meaning which fill the hidden reservoirs of affection.'

"I think that's what happens every time we reach out to another human being. We fill a hidden reservoir—what I'd call build an invisible bridge—of love. When we do that, we are doing the greatest human good possible."

## NOT-SO-ORDINARY VIRTUES AND HUMAN GOOD

Scholar Robert Gordon writes that Primo Levi enumerated over his writing life a "category of virtues" that were unique in their "rather stubborn ordinariness"—virtues that steer away from "the 'heroism' of classical notions" of virtue, and instead affirm "ordinary life—the life of marriage, the family, and the home, of work and production." He says Levi makes this the "proper center of moral life . . . , of notions of dignity and integrity, rather than . . . the banal backdrop against which the self struggles to a higher ideal."

Gordon maintains that to Levi, ordinary virtues are "beyond heroism, politics, and even history," because even the Holocaust, with its unprecedented "system which cut its victims out of public history, precluded the dynamics of politics, war, or heroism," did not lead to their extinction. But I don't think that this makes these virtues in any way "beyond heroism or politics or history," but rather even *more* heroic, and even *more* integral to history and politics. Those who consistently practice so-called ordinary virtues tend to be extraordinarily rare, and their efforts serve as a beacon for anyone trying to become more fully human.

For Levi, there is no single set of ordinary virtues. In his book *La Tregua*, he writes that "we all build our own" set of virtues "in the wake of our experiences or those of others we have taken on board"; and what distinguishes them as ordinary is where they are practiced, such as the home and workplace. To Levi, no list would ever be definitive, but rather, for each person, it would be somewhat "homemade, eccentric." But to isolate these virtues in the more mundane spheres of our lives diminishes them. There were all too many in the Nazi era who were adept practitioners of these ordinary virtues at home, yet took part without a twinge of remorse in heinous atrocities elsewhere—the latter negates, and makes a mockery of, the former. Surely these ordinary virtues, in order to be genuinely ordinary, must permeate all spheres of one's life in order to realize the human good of which the students spoke. Levi himself is a paradigm of such a person.

According to Gordon, Levi, in his search for ordinary virtues, did find that even though there is no definitive list, some virtues tend to recur, and could be called universal: "acknowledgement, attention, attentiveness, care (attending to), patience, listening, dialogue, sensitivity, a sense of proportion and perspective, an ability to see and draw lines of connection," as well as the "virtue of listening," and "all forms of apt or right looking." Most of all, to Levi, the "characteristic . . . nature" of any set of ordinary virtues is that they are permeated by the "dynamics of human acknowledgement," as opposed to "the degraded and denied looking of the camp world" of the Holocaust. To fail to see any longer a human face—"to be faceless"—is "to deny and be denied one's very essence, to be denied even the slimmest chance of survival or of life embodied in the ethical 'eye contact' between human beings . . . "

—

Levi might have been sympathetic to the work of the German-born Jewish philosopher and theologian Martin Buber (1878–1965). One of the few philosophers to elaborate a philosophy of dialogue, Buber, in his renowned work *I and Thou*, distinguished two ways of relating to humans—the I-Thou, in which we are open to others, to their perspectives and experiences, and in which we engage in dialogue with them as equals, and the I-It, a form he deplored, in which we look at others more as objects rather than as fellow subjects, and whom we treat as inferior to ourselves and our own ends.

Both before and after he moved from Germany to Palestine in 1938 at age sixty, Buber tried to apply his philosophy of I-Thou dialogue to the ongoing debate on the type of state that would eventually be established there. For Buber, dialogue with Arabs as complete equals was a moral imperative, and the only route to achieving human good. He wrote of the need for Jews to adapt a policy of "all-embracing and fraternal solidarity with the Arabs"—of seeing them as equally and fully human—and he believed that the only way to reach a worthy, lasting, and peaceful agreement was by taking such a path. Five years before Jewish statehood was established in 1949, Buber wrote of the need for "tremendous daring," for "courageous and independent thinking" among Jews in order to achieve this goal. Buber said Jewish statehood must not come at the expense of others who also have historical and spiritual ties to the region; he believed passionately that the "return to the land" should not be accompanied by the desire "to suppress another people or to dominate them." But contrary to Buber's hopes for "joint sovereignty," some 750,000 Palestinians suddenly found themselves strangers in their homeland.

In a seminar for Jewish-Arab understanding delivered three years before he died, Buber said that it was incumbent for each individual to be an example, despite the social opprobrium he might face as a consequence, of someone who is willing to engage in I-Thou dialogues with one's putative enemy. He said "an open-eyed faith . . . in the possibility of influencing someone else by one's own positive and constructive behavior justifies itself . . . " To Buber, this philosophy of changing the world by personal example, when applied by Jews "to the field of our relations with the Arab minority . . . , means that we are obliged to grant that minority truly equal rights to the degree permitted to us by the conditions of our security. No more, but also no less." Buber contended that the camp that "willingly or unwillingly, consciously or unconsciously," considers conflict inevitable "collaborates . . . in bringing about war," while the camp that "refuses to believe that we cannot prevent the outbreak of war . . . does his part to advance the cause of peace."

Rabbi David Hartman, a modern Israeli philosopher who is a member of the department of Jewish thought and philosophy at Hebrew University of Jerusalem, furthers this line of thinking when he says that Israel either can "recognize" the "fundamental human desire" of the Palestinians to have their own homeland, "and seek to accommodate it, while at the same time building safeguards so as not to weaken our own national security, or we can create a society that rules by force and intimidation over a million and a half vehemently resentful people." In his book *Conflicting Visions*, Hartman asserts that even if rule by force and intimidation could be deemed "militarily and politically feasible, it would inevitably undermine the moral and religious significance of our national renaissance. During two thousand years of wandering and waiting, we never imagined a Jewish nation that would find itself obliged to suppress and humiliate an entire people. Palestinians as homeless victims will make us constantly feel like strangers in our own home."

—

Sari Nusseibeh, an Oxford-educated professor of philosophy and president of Al Quds University in Jerusalem, who was born and raised in Jerusalem, agrees largely with the perspectives of Buber and Hartman—namely, that good can only be accomplished in a conflict when each side sees the other as fully human. A prominent Palestinian intellectual and Islamic philosopher, Nusseibeh is an ardent advocate for a peaceful resolution between Israelis and Palestinians in the occupied territories. In 2001, after spending years away from political turmoil in order to focus on his scholarly pursuits, he accepted Yasser Arafat's appointment to serve as the PLO's high-level political commissioner for Jerusalem. He said he did so in order to play a role in bringing "reason to prevail on both sides."

To Nusseibeh, humans "must strive to be closer to each other and cooperate . . . " So it follows that "(t)he average Israelis are just the same as the average Palestinians . . . and just as human. . . . " In *No Trumpets No Drums: A Two-State Settlement of the Israeli-Palestinian Conflict*, published in 1991, Nusseibeh writes that, in his view, "the principle of mutual recognition, the recognition by each side of the other side's right to self-determination," is the only guarantee to a lasting peace. To date, his outspokenness against both the Palestinian homicide bombers and the Israeli occupation has incurred the wrath of both sides. Hard-line Palestinians regularly call for his ouster, and the Israeli military deems him such a threat that he has been put under surveillance.

In an interview in the *Jerusalem Post*, Nusseibeh maintained that "no peace [is] possible except a warm and open peace." This is similar to the view of the Nobel Peace Prize–winning author Eli Wiesel, a Holocaust survivor, who said in a magazine interview that "the mission of the Jew was not to make the world Jewish but to humanize it, to make it a warmer, more hospitable, more human welcoming world."

—

Another kindred thinker is Mubarak Awad, a Palestinian psychologist and philosopher born in East Jerusalem, who has long advocated a nonviolent solution to the Middle East conflict. Awad is the founder and director of the Washington, D.C.–based Nonviolence International, as well as the Palestinian Center for the Study of Nonviolence in Jerusalem, both devoted to educating people on how to bring about justice via nonviolent resistance.

In an April 2002 essay, Awad writes that "recognition and acceptance" by both sides are "central ingredients" to a lasting peace, just as they were in South Africa, and just as they are "being currently practiced by the Catholic Church, Germany, and Poland who are seeking forgiveness from the Jews." First and foremost, he says that Israelis "should extend an apology to the Palestinians for Israeli abuse of Palestinian basic human rights," and that Palestinians "should apologize to the Israelis for Palestinian acts of violence against Jews. Both must forgive, and accept apology graciously."

Awad believes that the "Palestinian, Arab, and Muslim worlds need to view acceptance of Israel and the Israelis as an acceptance of the humanity of other people who were born in the land and have a right to stay. This acceptance does not reflect a belief in the superiority of the Jews but affirms that Arabs and Jews are equal in all aspects of life." For harboring such "radical" views, Awad was expelled from Israel as an agitator.

—

In the *Nirvana Sutra*, Buddha says that "the sufferings of all other living beings are his own sufferings." If this notion of "shared suffering"—when one person hurts, we all hurt—became fixed in the consciousness of most human beings, this in and of itself, I think, would make tremendous inroads in eliminating acts of inhumanity.

It was the notion that the late president of Egypt, Anwar Sadat, subscribed to when he made unprecedented overtures to Israel that were aimed at paving the way for a lasting peace. In his historic speech before the Israeli Knesset on November 20, 1977, Sadat said that "(a)ny life that is lost in war is a human life, be it that of an Arab or an Israeli . . . Innocent children who are deprived of the care and compassion of their parents are ours . . . be they living on Arab or Israeli land." It was "(f)or the sake of them all," he said, "for the sake of affording our communities the opportunity to work for the progress and happiness of man, feeling secure and with the right to a dignified life, for the generations to come, for a smile on the face of every child born in our land . . . ," that he made his decision to go to Israel "with an open mind and an open heart, and with a conscious determination so that we might establish permanent peace . . . "

This view was seconded by the late Yitzhak Rabin in his Nobel Prize acceptance speech: "There is one universal message which can embrace the entire world, one precept which can be common to different regimes, . . . to cultures that are alien to each other . . . It is a message . . . found in the Book of Books: *V'nishmartem me'od l'naf-shoteichem*—'Therefore take good heed of yourselves'—or, in contemporary terms . . . the message of the Sanctity of Life."

Rabin says next that the "one radical means" for achieving this ultimate good of "sanctifying human lives" is to work toward "a real peace" that is founded on the view that all humans are equally human, and equally deserving of the opportunity to live with dignity.

## GOOD VERSUS EVIL

In an article in *Time* magazine that came out a year after the September 11 tragedy, President George W. Bush is quoted as saying, "Look, my job isn't to try to nuance. I think moral clarity is important, if you believe in freedom . . . And one of the truths is, they're [the Palestinians are] sending suicide killers in because they hate Israel. I know people don't like it when I say there's evil, this is evil versus good. But that's not going to stop me from saying what I think is right."

The president, however, confuses "moral clarity" with "moral certainty," just as he is confused about what each means. First, he equates moral clarity *with* moral certainty. When a person is "certain" that he knows what his and others' morals are, or should be, he certainly does bequeath himself a type of moral clarity—but it may be far from an honest or accurate type. President Bush habitually breaks down moral action, vision, and thinking into clear-cut categories of black and white, good versus evil. In doing so, he fails to recognize that virtually everyone's morals are murky to some degree, as evidenced by the contradictions between our stated values and many of our actions.

When, in 1976, the president was arrested for driving while intoxicated, thus a deadly threat to innocent people on the road, did he consider himself evil, and should we? Or would this only be the case if he had killed someone while driving in such a condition? Or, in either case, would he simply have been a basically good, but troubled, person—and could the same be said for many essentially decent people who are troubled or confused, and are brought to commit an uncharacteristically bad or even evil act? If the president's abuses of alcohol led his own children, or other young people, to think that it's okay to drink to excess, as long as they think they do no harm to others, and only to themselves, would he consider this an evil? Or would this be evil only if it was his intent for impressionable young people to think this?

An integral part of possessing a genuine moral clarity may be to recognize that rarely, if ever, does any moral situation boil down to an instance of absolute good versus absolute evil. In all likelihood, the Palestinian homicide bombers also consider themselves to have "moral clarity" and "moral certainty," and this is what gives them license to feel they can commit such abominable acts. This same type of muddled sense of moral clarity and certainty no doubt gives some Israeli leaders and soldiers the skewed notion that it is perfectly okay to kill innocent Palestinians in retaliatory measures.

Genuine moral clarity involves ceaseless and rigorous questioning and evaluation of one's works and deeds and ends in life, and the means one chooses to realize one's works and deeds and ends. It is a process, not a destination. Anyone who claims to possess moral clarity, and feels no need to question his acts and convictions, is morally confused. Certainty is not clarity, but blindness.

## GOOD FOR GOODNESS' SAKE

To learn more about good, I decided I needed to find some of the charter members of the original Philosophers' Club. Starting in 1997, I'd philosophized thrice weekly with a group of children in the Mission

District of San Francisco, where many recent immigrants to the area reside, and which is known at least as much for its cultural vibrancy as it is for its perennial problems with gangs and drugs. While the Philosophers' Club members had never been known as academic standouts, I found that their ability to engage in scintillating philosophical discourse, and their use of the "fourth R," reasoning, typically surpassed that of their peers, even those with all the advantages.

In 1999, my wife and I had reluctantly moved from the San Francisco area, and so I had to leave the Philosophers' Club, during the peak of the dot-com boom. When prices for everything skyrocketed in the area, it prompted a mass exodus of people, many of them devoted to creative social and aesthetic pursuits and who, like us, lived on shoestring budgets.

Luckily, three years later, I was able to track down several members of our club, all of them now middle-school students. I was delighted that all the Philosophers' Club members I was able to contact were still in school, given that at-risk kids in the area drop out at a significantly higher rate.

It is a joyful reunion as we gather on a breezy Saturday at a park in the Mission District, and over a pleasant picnic, examine the question "What is good?"

Ever-precocious Wilson, now a sixth-grader, is quick to reply, "Good is when you behave your best even when no one else is looking."

This is a typically Wilsonian response, in that it is completely different from any response on this question that I'd ever heard.

"Can you explain?" I ask.

"Let's say I'm all by myself, and I find a wallet stuffed with money, and I don't have a penny of my own. Well, if I'm good—meaning, if I do the right thing—I would bring the wallet, without taking out any of the money, to a newspaper office and let them put an announcement in the lost-and-found section."

I ask Wilson now, "What do you mean when you say good is the same as doing the right thing?"

"My mom always says to me those words in that Santa Claus song, 'Be good for goodness' sake.' That's the same as doing the right thing. You are good without expecting a reward, or praise."

"My mother always tells me, 'Even when you're at school, I can see you. So you be sure to behave,' " says Pilar, who lives alone with her mom, since her dad abandoned them and returned to Mexico. "I know she can't really see me, but I pretend she can. It helps me make sure I always do the right thing."

"One time," says Arturo, "these gang members were bullying this little kid when no one was around. At first, I laughed along with them, because I wanted them to think I was cool. But then I thought, What would I do if my dad could see me? I knew he'd want me to stand up for the kid. I knew he'd think I was being good, like he'd taught me, if I did that. So I did—and they hit me, too!"

"When there were riots where I lived in Cincinnati, it was like, everyone was invisible," says Keisha, who's just moved back to the Bay Area. On April 7, 2001, the police in Cincinnati had shot and killed an unarmed nineteen-year-old black youth, an act that many in the black community viewed as just the latest in a string of unjustified acts of violence by the police against blacks. In the ensuing week, mass rioting and looting—the worst in over thirty years—had broken out in the city center. "There were so many people breaking storefronts and stealing stuff, that they were as good as invisible. That's why my mom moved us back here. She didn't want any part of that. She thinks people are cowards if they just make themselves invisible within a crowd."

Rafi—a "special education" child when I first philosophized with him, but who is now in regular classes, where he has demonstrated he is quite up to par with his peers—says, "Like, these people who run corporations that cheat people out of billions of dollars, so they don't have any money to retire on. My mom says none of them can ever be blamed, because it's impossible to tell which of them did what. It's *like* they're invisible."

"If you can be invisible, then you're not human," says Estefania. "If you can do things that no one can see you do, then you can do things like rob and kill and cheat—bad things, inhuman things. So it's better not to be invisible. Because there would be no morals, no rules, no laws. Who would want that?"

This reminds me of a section in Plato's *Republic*, when the character Glaucon tells Socrates and company a tale about a shepherd named Gyges, who happens upon a ring. Gyges puts the ring on and discovers, hey presto, that it makes him invisible. The upright shepherd suddenly loses his uprightness and succumbs to the ring's powers. He seduces the queen of Lydia, and then conspires with her to kill the king, after which he becomes the new ruler. Plato's intriguing question is: Would anyone in the same situation behave differently? Is it "human nature" to take advantage of invisibility powers to do as one pleases, or is there such a person who would shun the powers to go on being human, and honest?

"That's why I like Frodo Baggins in *The Lord of the Rings*," says Jennifer, referring to the book by J. R. R. Tolkien. "Frodo doesn't want the Ring of Power. But one of the great big men in his fellowship, Boromir of Minas Tirith, said he would use the ring to defeat the Dark Lord Sauron, and then 'do good' for his people. But Frodo knew Boromir was kidding himself, and that if he had the ring, maybe Boromir would start out by doing good, but soon, he would become just like Sauron and 'do evil,' do everything he could to exterminate or enslave others for his own gain. Because when you have more power than any human should have, you become bad."

Then she says, "Frodo just wants to get rid of the ring, to destroy it in Mount Doom in Mordor, so he can go back to being a simple, visible Hobbit. He's greater than the ring. He knows that the greatest good he can do is get rid of it."

"What do you mean by 'greatest good'?" I ask.

"The most good for the most people over the greatest period of time," she says. "As long as the ring exists, there will be the chance for great evil, to harm people in the worst ways. But as soon as the ring is gone, then people can live in peace for a long time."

After a pause, Wilson says, "That's why I don't think as much of Harry Potter as I do Frodo. Harry Potter uses that invisibility cloak of his to break the rules. Even though he's trying to do good, to help people, he shouldn't use the invisibility cloak to do it. He should just go in, visible, and take his chances. The cloak gives him too much power. And the more magic he learns, the more powerful in a superhuman way he'll become. Soon he'll have too much power for his own good."

"I don't know. . . ." This from Rafi. He seems lost in thought, worlds away from us. Then he comes back to earth and says, "I think you never know how good you are until you have more power than maybe you should, like, if you're stronger than everyone else, or you have the power to put anybody you want to in jail—or if you have a ring of power or an invisibility cloak. If you have all this power, and you still are gentle and kind and fair, then isn't that the real test of how good you are?"

## HIGH HOPES

"I think hope is good—the greatest good" is the first response I get from a participant at this Socrates Café, after they've chosen the question "What is good?" to explore.

"How so?" I ask.

He doesn't respond at first. Our room is windowless, yet he looks piercingly at the wall, almost as if he could see through it to the outside on this stiflingly hot midsummer day. Finally, he looks at me and says, "Good, for a person, is having something to look forward to. Hope is that looking forward."

"So good is the same as hope?" I query.

"No, good is made up partly of hope. You can't do good, or be good, or create good, if you don't have hope." Then he says, "Some days, I'm right on the edge, between hope and hopeless."

Everyone else around me taking part in the dialogue looks at him. They seem surprised by his candid response. There are thirteen of us in all. We're in a maximum-security prison. Most surrounding me have been convicted of some of the most violent crimes imaginable.

There is a prolonged silence. The only sound is the clattering old fan set in the corner of our room, which seems only to push the hot air into our faces. Eventually another inmate says to the one who'd just spoken, "I hear you, Lou. I was taking college classes, and I was six credits away from getting my bachelor's degree. I'd been taking classes for eight years. Then they yanked the program. I asked one of my professors why. She said the politicians decided that inmates at a maximum-security prison shouldn't be taking college classes—that it was 'bad' to offer us classes, because it meant we were being treated 'too good.'"

The inmates here had been taking a wide variety of courses in a unique bachelor's program in the humanities and social sciences—classes in subjects like "human autonomy" and "freedom" and "the rise and fall of civilizations"—until the program was summarily curtailed two years ago.

Another then says, "This place is called a 'correctional and rehabilitation institute.' But now they don't give us a chance to correct or rehabilitate. Now the mentality is 'lock 'em up and throw away the key.' They want us to live with the absence of hope. I think that's the opposite of good." Everyone nods.

"Is it evil?" I ask.

"It is," says Mike, "if it's intentional."

I say to the group, "But didn't some of the crimes you committed take away hope from victims and their families? Wasn't that the 'opposite of good' in a much worse way than someone taking away your college classes?"

Only one seems angry or upset by my question. There are no immediate responses. At last, Eric replies, "I think what you say is true. So now they're doing the same to us—though like you said, there's no comparison between taking away our college classes, and what we took away from people that put us in here. But they're both 'bad'; it's just that one is a much worse degree of bad than the other. The mentality of the politicians is: an eye for an eye. But we're supposedly here to be rehabilitated, not just punished. Society's institutions, like this one, are supposed to be 'more good' than any individual member. But society wants us to rot here. What does that say about the level society has stooped to?"

What he says brings to mind a comment that the psychiatric social worker who paved the way for my visits here made to me when we first met. He said that the elected officials who determine funding for correctional institutions no longer care about rehabilitation, because most of their constituents do not. Ever-cognizant of those who put them in office, politicians, he says, reflecting their constituents' views, see rehabilitation-oriented programs as a "luxury" for inmates that they don't deserve. Anne Larson Schneider wrote in *American Behavioral Scientist* that "by inflicting harsh punishment upon criminals who are socially constructed as deviants, violent and undeserving, elected officials can gain the accolades of the general public without incurring any noticeable political costs from those actually receiving the punishment."

Tommy, another inmate, now says, "I was taking classes in psychology and social studies. A teacher came in once a week, and we sat in circles like this one, and discussed what we'd read. I was learning about myself and other people in a way I don't learn in everyday rap sessions, or group encounter sessions, or reading on my own."

Nodding toward the person who'd spoken before, he says, "It looks like our professors will never be able to come back. So they've taken away from me some of the hope I had of becoming a better person. I don't just mean better like 'better educated' or 'better smarter'; I mean 'better wiser.' I took classes because it gave me hope of becoming 'better wiser,' of learning about what makes me and others tick, and how to take the bad things inside of me and turn them into good things."

According to a National Institute of Justice study, the recidivism rate for inmates who earn a four-year degree while serving time in prison is only 12.5 percent, compared to a staggering 66 percent of the entire population of 105,000 inmates studied. Robert Ellis Gordon, who for eight years was a creative-writing teacher in Washington State prisons, until the program was canceled, says that this "dramatic set of statistics" is "one that ought to be as meaningful to governors, state legislators, law-enforcement officials, and other policy makers as it is to educators and social workers," and anyone else "who professes a belief in crime prevention." He goes on to say, "Lacking education, which is to say marketable skills, confidence, and an expanded sense of possibilities"—which seems to be the essence of hope—"it is inevitable that many of these released prisoners . . . will return to what they know best: the life of crime. Thus, the polity's desire for vengeance is being fulfilled at the price of public safety"—and, it would seem, at the price of good.

"I don't expect anyone to feel bad for us," says Steve. "I'll never get out of here. But I think we all need hope in order to get out of bed in the morning. I need to hope I'll understand better why I did some of the things I did that got me here, and how I can improve upon myself.

I need hope that I can become better—and this 'becoming better' is to me what good is all about."

"He's going to think we're feeling sorry for ourselves," another inmate, Mark, now says, looking directly at me. "I guess we are, in a way. But all we're saying is that even in a place like this, you have to have a reason to hope. The greatest good is to be able to look ahead, like Lou said at the outset. You know, to see yourself as 'better wiser' than you are today, or than you were when you did what you did to get in here."

Randall, who is sitting next to Mark, now says, "Hope itself is something you learn about. I mean, you learn that there's good hope and there's bad hope. I only used to know bad hope."

"What do you mean?" I ask.

"Well, the only thing I used to hope for was money to get good clothes, a good car, a good high, so I would be the man. I thought it didn't really matter how I got these things, as long as I got them and got away with it. That was bad hope. I was only out for me. Now, I have different sorts of hopes, good hopes, because I don't want just what I think is best for me, but what's best for everyone. What I mean is, I think now that something can't be best for me, if it's not also good for everyone else. To learn that, I needed to take classes, so I wasn't so ignorant anymore about these things. I mean, how can I become 'wiser better,' if I never have a chance to learn to 'know better'?"

As Socrates scholar Laszlo Versenyi notes, Socrates believed that "if a man chooses and does evil rather than good," he does so "because he is overcome by ignorance," and so "makes the wrong choice." But genuine good, according to Socrates, is to think of the "long-term results" of one's actions, and how, if they are good, they are "useful" and "beneficial" to the "well-being"—what the ancient Greeks would call *eudaimonia*—of the individual; and how, if they are bad, they are "ruinous." What Versenyi doesn't make as clear as he should is that

Socrates believed that good acts are those that contribute most and best both to the *eudaimonia* of the individual *and* of society as a whole. While this is always a delicate balancing act, and while such well-being and fulfillment are never achieved absolutely, in Socrates' estimation striving for *eudaimonia* is the end of all properly informed and educated citizens.

Randall then says to me, "People I studied, like Nelson Mandela, spent decades in jail, but for trying to do good things. White society in South Africa tried to take away his hope—it *hoped* to take away his hope. That was an evil kind of hope, because white South Africa was showing it didn't care about reaching out to all the people of its country. It only cared about maintaining the status quo for the privileged few, so they could continue with the 'good life' just for themselves. But Mandela's dream, to bring social justice to everyone, was a good hope, because it was a kind where there couldn't be a good society unless everyone had a shot at the good things in life. And if you look at South Africa now, where there's no more apartheid, you see that he inspired everyone, white and black, to get over their ignorance and 'know better'—to know that over the long haul, you can't have a good society if it only benefits a few."

There's a stretch of silence. We all seem in deep thought about all that has been said so far. At last, Darryl says, "I hope someday that I have the right to hope that the families of those I wronged can forgive me, maybe not all the way, but at least some of the way. But before I can hope that, I first have to feel like I've changed enough. So first, I hope that someday I feel like I can be in a position to forgive myself, maybe not all the way, but some."

He looks at me and says, "I've been here fourteen years. I know I'm not in any way the person I was all those years ago. But I'm still not sure I deserve to hope for these things. I'm still trying to understand that person I was, why he was so angry and even evil."

Another now says, "It's hard to be the 'better' person you know you've become when a lot of the guards who work here still treat you like you're the same 'bad' person who walked in here all those years ago. I wish I could say it didn't get to me. Every day, when I wake up, I hope and pray that I can be a bigger person than they are. That's a good hope."

Now, one after another, without any prompting, the inmates take turns revealing their 'good hopes':

"I hope that if I get out, people I used to live around will no longer see me as, or expect me to be, that person I used to be. I hope I live by my expectations, rather than anyone else's."

"I get out in three years. I was hoping to be educated by then. But I'm just part of the way there. I hope to find a way to get back in school and finish up my degree. When I'm out, I want to be a drug counselor for youth."

"I hope someday to wake up and have the sun blinding me through my bedroom window."

"I hope that my kid still recognizes me. And I hope he isn't a thing like me when he grows up. It scares me how much like me he is. He looks like me, carries himself around like I did when I was his age. I hope I can drill some sense into him never to be like his dad."

"I hope to be more a part of the solution than the problem. Right now, my way of doing this is, no matter what the people who run the prison system do to me, I will not let them take hope away from me. They can take away my college classes, they can take away my privileges, they can take away my dignity by talking to me like I'm a nobody, but they can't take my hope. That's my way of doing good. Because once, I didn't have hope. I didn't care, so I didn't care what happened to me, or to others. That's why I'm in here. I'll never let that happen again."

I think everyone has said all they have to say, but then Randall says,

"I'm starting to think that maybe it's how you act when you have no hope that's the measure of good.

"How so?" I ask.

"It's when you're the most down-and-out, the most without hope, that determines your character, what you're really made of on the inside, whether you're made of good or bad stuff. I'm in here because when that happened to me, when the last drop of hope within me disappeared, I acted in an 'I've got nothing to lose' kind of way—in a bad way. But you can also act in a 'you've got nothing to lose way' in a good way. You can keep on keeping on, keep trying to overcome your circumstances, especially when you've lost hope."

To which Mark responds, "I live with hope *because* I feel I have nothing to lose to live this way. I've seen and tasted the bad type of 'nothing to lose,' and I hope I've gotten that type out of my system for good."

## HOPE AND DELIVERANCE

Pak Kyong-ni, widely considered one of the greatest contemporary writers in the Republic of Korea, writes that if life were idyllic—"no tears, no separation, no hunger, no waiting, no suffering, no oppression, no war, no death"—then there would no longer be any need for either hope or despair. Such a state of affairs, she contends, would not necessarily be good, because "(w)e would lose those hopes so dear to us all."

What would life be like without despair born of the worst forms of suffering and oppression? Without such despair, would anyone have reason to hope? What would we humans be like if we had no need to hope? It seems to me that there are good and bad—redemptive and nonredemptive—types of despair. A good type may be one in which you set lofty goals for yourself, because you are blessed to be in circumstances to do so; but still, at times, you may despair that you will realize your highest hopes. Still, you persevere, more so than ever, because it is what makes life worth living, and because you have the choice and opportunity to persevere. A nonredemptive type may be experienced by a mother of a child born in poverty. She may despair that her child will never have enough to eat, will never live in safety away from gangs and drugs, will never have a decent education or job opportunities. Her stark life circumstances may lead her to despair that is utter hopelessness.

The noted writer Bharati Mukherjee, born in Calcutta, says in her book *The Holder of the World* that "(t)here is surely one moment in every life when hope surprises us like grace." If so, this would suggest that all of us are touched by "good" at least once in our lives. Unfortunately, I suspect that tens of millions of people living today, and billions throughout human history, have never been graced with even one moment of the type of forward-looking hope of which she speaks.

—

In the United States alone, for many disadvantaged children and youth who run afoul of the law, the message passed on to them today from the system is that they are not worth the effort of being helped to turn around, so they can have a decent future. Many are in essence told that they are hopeless cases. In *Bad Kids: Race and the Transformation of the Juvenile Court*, Barry Feld, professor of law at the University of Minnesota Law School, writes that "within the past three decades, judicial decisions, legislative amendments, and administrative changes have transformed the juvenile court from a nominally rehabilitative social welfare agency into a scaled-down second-class criminal court for young people." At-risk children and youth are treated and tried as adults, and they are written off by society. Yet juvenile court was created in 1899 by progressive reformers to "do good" in a way that jibed with Socrates' notion that good actions were those that struck a balance between benefiting individuals and society as a whole over the long term. Feld writes that juvenile court was founded to provide "individualized treatment" and a "rehabilitative alternative to punishment," not to enact "punitive policies." Today, however, Feld says juvenile court is a "bankrupt institution with neither a rationale nor a justification," where "punitive juvenile justice policies impose harsh sanctions disproportionately on minority youths," and young offenders are given "neither therapy nor justice." Consequently, the will of those directing the juvenile court system today would seem to be to give no forward-looking hope for at-risk juveniles—such a will, by Socrates' count, would be tantamount to evil and "ruinous."

—

What about the inmates in our correctional system who are adults? Is it okay for the rest of us to give up hope that they can ever be rehabilitated? If we give up hope, is it the same thing as telling them they should give up hope in themselves?

Peter G. Herman writes in *The American Prison System* that "to appreciate the importance of incarceration in contemporary American society, one need only look at the statistics. The United States has more prisoners than any other country in the world: With approximately two million people behind bars, it holds 25 percent of the world's prisoners, though it comprises only 5 percent of the world's population." The United States imprisons "six to ten times more . . . than any other industrialized democracy," with "73 of every 1,000 people" behind bars; and "almost one-third of African-American men between the ages of twenty and twenty-nine are under the control of correctional institutions." What's more, Herman points to U.S. Bureau of Justice statistics for the year 2000 that show that "the total number of men and women behind bars, on parole, and on probation has reached 6.3 million, more than 3 percent of the U.S. adult population."

If, as the statistics indicate, citizens in the United States largely determine whether their society is "good" by how safe it is, then has our penal system made our society safer? Anne Larson Scheider, a professor in the School of Justice Studies at Arizona State University, contends that just because there are more people than ever behind bars doesn't mean that fewer crimes are being committed, much less that society is any safer. No matter how many people are put behind bars, she does not think society, as a consequence, will be much safer, because while crime may go down over the short term because of harsher punitive measures, the societal factors that play an integral role in the commission of so many criminal acts have not been addressed in a way that likely will lead to lasting long-term reductions.[1] "Perhaps prisons will never be effective enough in producing public safety," Scheider writes, "because public safety is more contingent on societal factors, such as families, communities, schools, nonprofits, economic opportunities, and the absence of race and class discrimination"—factors that are the bedrock of hope for the nation's underprivileged.

Author John Edgar Wideman, who describes himself as "a descendant of a special class of immigrants—Africans—for whom arrival in America was a life sentence in the prison of slavery," writes in *Behind the Razor Wire* that "(f)rom every category of male relative I can name. . . . at least one member of my family has been incarcerated." He notes that "*which candidate is tougher on crime* was the dominant issue dramatized in TV ads during the last election campaign," and says that what bothered him was "the absolute certainty that . . . the ones they were promising to lock up and punish, by design, would never be their people. Always somebody else. Not their kind."

1. After an eight-year decline, in 2000, the murder rate in a number of major cities—from New York to New Orleans to Los Angeles—once again began to rise steadily. In 2001, the FBI reported that the national crime index rose by 2 percent. And by the end of 2002, violent crime showed no sign of abating, with murders rising 11.5 percent and forcible rape rising 3 percent in suburban counties, which had been considered relative havens from these types of crime.

—

What if we enacted correctional policies based on these questions: If my son or daughter, father or sister, committed a crime, a terrible crime, what would I want the system to do to them, for them, with them? Would I want the system to do them "any good," to help them in any way become rehabilitated?

What if, as Wideman suggests, "we expand our notion of prison to include the total institution of poverty"? If we could help more people escape from poverty, would we also help ensure that they much less frequently took drugs to escape from hopelessness, and that they much less frequently committed crimes undertaken in part out of a nonredemptive nothing-to-lose attitude? If statistics are to be believed, very few rich and middle-class people are incarcerated in comparison with the poor, a gap that can be attributed not only to the fact that the well-off have greater access to much better lawyers when the well-off are in trouble with the law, but also to the fact that they are born into a world of comparatively unbridled opportunity and privilege, and that there is considerable class and racial bias when it comes to law enforcement and sentencing. So helping people escape from poverty would seem to be an enormous part of any long-term public-safety solution. Will enough people in a position to effect such radical social change—which clearly would be for the good of society over the long term—ever care enough to make this happen?

—

Is a "good society" one which, among other things, creates the most favorable conditions for assuring that the fewest people possible will set foot in prison, or return to prison once they've served their time?

Many who claim to cherish the sanctity of all human life are also the most strident supporters of get-tough-on-crime policies, and favor, at minimum, the "lock 'em up and throw away the key" brand of punishment. Many pay only lip service to endorsing the implementation of the types of national social-services programs that hold promise of improving the quality of life for the marginalized, and so reducing the chances that people will have to be put behind bars, or worse, in the first place. Those who claim to cherish the sanctity of all human life yet do not espouse the right to a *quality* life, and do not work tirelessly toward seeing to it that everyone has a decent chance at such a life, would not seem genuinely to practice what they preach.

In *A Sin Against the Future: Imprisonment in the World*, a landmark look at incarceration around the globe, Vivien Stern, who was director of the National Association for the Care and Resettlement of Offenders, asserts that the prison system "urgently needs to be reviewed," because today prisons provide "a setting in which profound abuses of human rights can be carried out under the reassuring justification that this is needed to protect the public." She contends that "imprisonment no longer fits modern societies and their needs," and that it is riddled with the type of inefficiency that "in many cases gives rise to more problems than it solves"—that it does more bad than good. In posing "a threat to our future," Stern says this state of affairs makes the future for us all more bleak.

It seems that many in society who hope primarily for a safe world put most of their stock in building more prisons and passing more stringent punitive laws. If they put at least as much energy and resources into eradicating the conditions that lead to the commission of crimes born of hopelessness, wouldn't they stand a much greater chance of having their hope for a safe world fulfilled.

A number of countries are at the forefront of prison reform, but the United States is not one of them. In South Africa, for instance, where Dutch and English colonizers once imported their prison system, Stern notes that the postapartheid government is now looking at how to reinstitute the precolonial "reparative model" of the nation's indigenous people. In this model, "the values and processes of traditional African law" are incorporated, in which the ends are "a respect for human beings, reparation of damage, and personalizing the relationship between the offender and the victim and the involvement of the community in finding justice are all principles worth resurrecting." These ends would seem to be consummately "good" ones for individuals, and for society as a whole.

## GOOD SOCIETY

What is a good society?

In his book *The Good Society: The Human Agency*, the Harvard economist John Kenneth Galbraith equates a good society with one in which "voice and influence" are not "confined to one part of the population," as is the case in the United States, where "money, voice, and political activism are now extensively controlled by the affluent, very affluent, and business interests," in an "unequal contest" in which "the socially and economically deprived" are marginalized. To remedy this, Galbraith calls for "a coalition of the concerned and the compassionate and those now outside the political system."

Galbraith further elaborates his conception of a good society when he says it is one in which "all . . . citizens have personal liberty, basic well-being, social and ethnic equality, the opportunity for a rewarding life." Over the long haul, he contends, a good society cannot be confined within national bounds, but must go global. "Humans are human beings wherever they live. Concern for their suffering from hunger, other deprivation, and disease does not end because those so afflicted are on the other side of the international frontier." He says this is so even though "no elementary truth is so consistently ignored or, on occasion, so fervently assailed."

It seems to me that all too many who live in privilege consider it an "elementary truth" that they deserve to live as they do, and that those who live in squalor are not their problem, and likely are "meant" to live as they do.

Additionally, in my travels, I have come to know many poor people who enjoy none of the types of well-being Galbraith says must exist for there to be a good society. Yet many, I find, possess a remarkable "affluence" of social and mental, spiritual and communal well-being. They seem to be consummately good people who live in societies that could not care less about them.

## WHEN BAD IS GOOD

"*Yo creo que lo malo es lo bueno, o por lo menos, lo malo puede ser lo bueno,*" Esmeralda, who is in her thirties but is much more wizened than her years, says to me. "I think that bad is good. Or at least, bad *can* be good."

There are about ten of us taking part in this dialogue. We've just started examining the question "What is good?" The participants reside in a homeless shelter near Madrid, Spain. Out of a population of nearly 40 million, Spain's homeless population hovers at around 273,000, one of the highest percentages in the European Union. This at a time of relative prosperity for Spain, as evidenced, for instance, by the fact that more Spaniards own second homes than people in any other European Union nation. And also at a time when upwards of 15 percent of Spain's available housing is unoccupied, the highest rate in Europe. Yet Spain's commitment to provide public housing—usually called "counsel housing"—has waned dramatically. In 2001, it halved its budget for housing for the poor.

"How can bad be good?" I ask Esmeralda.

"You learn more about yourself in bad times than in good times," she replies. "That's good, if it helps you become a stronger person."

The single mother goes on to relate how she and her two children found themselves homeless. "I lost my job as a motel housekeeper, after being accused of stealing jewelry from a guest room, though I'd been an employee there for over ten years, and had a spotless record. Then my landlord refused to give me extra time to pay rent. My children and I ended up begging on the streets and sleeping in alleyways. I'd hoped they'd never have to experience life on the streets. It is how I lived my childhood—my parents were pushed from one place to another by Spanish authorities—and I did not want it for my children."

Esmeralda is of Gypsy heritage—the Spanish Gypsies are called *Roma*—and is part of the country's largest ethnic group, with a population of over five hundred thousand. Gypsies first entered Spain in the fifteenth century. For the first three hundred years after they arrived here, they were subjected to draconian laws, ranging from restrictions on how many they could travel with, to how they dressed and spoke (their traditional dress and language were forbidden). During the long-running dictatorship of Generalisimo Francisco Franco Bahamonde, who ruled Spain from 1939 until his death in 1975 (soon afterwards Spain became a democracy), the Gypsies were targeted more ruthlessly than ever, and they became an even more reviled and entrenched part of Spain's permanent underclass. The Gypsies remain victims of racism and discrimination, and a disproportionate number are homeless or live in substandard housing. They have few employment and education opportunities, and little access to health care and social services.

"I kept telling myself, 'It has to get better,' " Esmeralda continues.

"No matter how bad it got, we made it through each day, even when we were treated abusively by police and others. Eventually, we were placed in this shelter. Now my children are able to go to school, and I'm taking job-training classes. I hope I'm never on the streets again like that, but I learned how strong I am. I think, over the long run, it's good that I discovered this reserve of strength in me.

"So bad is good, if good is discovering what makes you stronger, and bad is what allows you to discover that."

"In bad times, you see the real good or the real bad in others," says Beatriz, who looks to be about eighteen. "When times are good, you think you know who your friends are. But when times are bad, you *know* who your friends are. Many people abandoned me when I became a drug addict. But one stayed with me, and wouldn't give up on me. She found me the shelter, and the good people there who are helping me overcome my addiction and move on with my life. So you really discover 'the good' in people in down-and-out times."

"And 'the good' in people is . . . ?" I press.

"It's their willingness to open themselves up and reach out to those in need. People seem to react in one of two ways when you cry out for help. They either close themselves up all the way, or they open themselves up to you all the way."

Then she says, "It took goodness in others for me to see the goodness in myself. I used to think I was extremely bad, that I deserved to be beaten by my husband. But the people at the shelter helped show me how wrong I was, and that I was a good person who had been taken advantage of and who'd been fooled into thinking I was bad."

She then says, "I think it takes an extremely good person to reveal to you the extreme good that is within you. Seeing this good in me put me on the road to becoming clean of drugs."

A woman named Farah, looking at Esmeralda, says, *"Como ella, nunca me daría por vencida,"* she says. "Like her, I'm not a quitter."

"She then says, "I immigrated from Morocco. There're no jobs there, no hope."

Morocco, which is only fourteen kilometers from Spain, used to be a Spanish possession, and Spain still has territory there. It is the primary country from which people flock to Spain, despite Spain's tough anti-immigration stance and the fact that many have lost their lives making the short but dangerous voyage across the Straits of Gibraltar.

"I paid my life savings to be smuggled over here on a boat, after hearing that Spain needed 'guest workers,' " she says. "But even with two jobs, I wasn't able to get ahead. Then the subsidized housing we lived in burned down, and there was no place for us to go."

Then she says, "I used to blame all of my misery on everyone else, and in many ways I had good reason to. This country destroyed my homeland. My husband died here in an on-the-job accident when he'd come two years before me.

"But some things, you can't blame others for. Or at least, if you do spend all your time blaming, you don't have the energy to overcome your circumstances. Sometimes, bad things just happen."

"What is a bad thing?" I ask.

"It's something that keeps you down, that keeps you from moving forward in life," she replies. "Sometimes, others keep you down, sometimes you keep yourself down. But sometimes, things just happen— like when our home burned down.

"In all these circumstances, you have to fight the things that can keep you down. But you need help. I got help at the shelter, when there finally was room for them to take us in. I'm also taking job-training classes, for a high-tech job. I think I'll come out on top. But the first step, the step toward good, is to quit focusing on blame and start focusing on how to make tomorrow a better day for you and your loved ones."

Then she says, "The shelter is 'good,' because it's made up of good people. They don't see themselves as above us. They just see us as people in need. Here, we're able to send our kids to school, we get public-health care, counseling, job training. We realize we're fortunate in many ways. We all have friends who are on the streets."

"I think we all have good and bad within us," says Maria Isabel, a teenage runaway, after a spell. "Two people can experience almost the same circumstances, and one can turn out bad and one can turn out good. My mother and father were abused as children. It made my mom become extremely gentle, but it made my dad abusive. Some people say you can't decide how you turn out—that it's all 'in the cards.' But I think you do decide whether you turn out bad or good. No matter how bad the things are that happen to you, you decide whether they inspire you to become bad too, or the opposite."

Then she says, "I'm not saying that you can always overcome the bad things that happen to you on your own. If I could, I wouldn't be here. But you can decide how they affect you on the inside. You can decide if the 'good' or the 'bad' inside is going to win."

Another says to her, "I think these aren't just 'bad things' that you're describing. When a parent abuses you, that's an evil thing."

"What is the difference between bad and evil?" I ask.

"Bad is the act of abuse itself. But evil is what's inside the person who does the abuse, who is 'inspired' to abuse you."

"Can't an act be evil, too?" I ask.

She mulls this over. "Yes, I think so. Like, I think if a parent *wants* to do harm, and *does* do harm, then that parent is evil. If a parent, without thinking, hits a child out of anger or worry, that's bad. But if a parent hits a child, on purpose, I mean really hits, then that is evil."

"Is evil the opposite of good, or is bad the opposite of good?" I ask.

"*Depende*," says Seve, a man who has been listening intently. "It depends." One of only three men taking part in the dialogue, Seve is diagnosed as severely mentally ill and has spent his entire adult life in and out of shelters. Then he says, "I think we all have bad impulses, like laziness, that we can overcome, if we choose. These bad impulses are the opposite of our good impulses, like love. But I don't think all of us have evil impulses. Evil is a decision you make. I'm thinking of the terrorists of the ETA. They kill innocent people, including women and children."

Since it began its campaign in 1968 to gain independence from Spain, the Basque Separatist movement, or ETA, based in northern Spain, has acknowledged killing at least eight hundred people throughout the country.

"The ETA terrorists were not born with these evil impulses," he says. "They've made conscious decisions to 'do evil.' Yet they consider themselves do-gooders who have to do evil things to achieve their good. They're lying to themselves. You can't intentionally do evil and achieve good."

Sixteen-year-old Manuel, a Gypsy who has been on his own since age eight, when his parents were killed in a robbery, now says, "The good that's the opposite of evil is this part of you that you're not born with, but that you decide to create. It's the part where you decide, no matter how bad others are to you, you're going to be the opposite, or the world will never become better."

He then says, "While I think we all have a choice whether or not to be evil, I don't think we choose the bad part that's inside of us. Bad is just there. And I don't think it's possible, or desirable, to get rid of it completely."

This draws a quizzical look from several. I ask him to explain further.

"I don't think you can 'be good' or 'become better,' if you don't 'know bad,' " he says. "Just as I don't think you can 'do good' if you're not aware of the evil in the world. The question is, what do you do when the bad or evil enters your life? What kind of person do you let it make you become?"

Esmeralda's eleven-year-old daughter, Mercedes, her voice barely above a whisper, now says, "In school, we just read *Belleza Negra*—*Black Beauty*. And *Black Beauty* says that the world is as bad as it is 'because people think *only* about their own business, and won't trouble themselves to stand up for the oppressed . . . '"

She looks at me and asks, "Is *Black Beauty* saying that if we see wrong or cruelty, and we can stop it, but do nothing, we're bad or evil too?"

## WHEN BAD IS BAD

In the international bestseller *When Bad Things Happen to Good People*, Rabbi Harold S. Kushner says that "(i)n the final analysis the question of why bad things happen to good people translates itself into some very different questions," in which we seek not only to understand why bad things happen, but also whether and how we might respond to them. One of the principal questions that arises from personal suffering or tragedy, Kushner writes, is: "Are you capable of forgiving and accepting in love a world which has disappointed you in not being perfect, a world in which there is so much unfairness and cruelty, disease and crime, earthquake and accident? Can you forgive its imperfections and love it because it is capable of containing great beauty and goodness, and because it is the only world we have?"

It is a commonplace that there always will be "senseless" tragedies, such as the untimely death of a loved one, or "earthquake and accident." But there are other types of tragedies that are unspeakably senseless, because they are so preventable. There are billions in the world who are illiterate, who do not have enough to eat, who die of preventable diseases, who have no permanent shelter. The resources to do away with these tragedies exist.

To Kushner, one "satisfying" response to the slings and arrows that come our way is to "forgive the world for not being perfect, to forgive God for not making a better world, to reach out to the people around us, and to go on living despite it all."

But at minimum, I would hope that our own travails would inspire us to do more than just to "reach out to the people around us." I hope we might be further inspired to seek out people whom we typically may have never paid attention to, because they are on society's margins and their experiences are so alien to our own, and make them part of our world, make their suffering ours. To do this, we need to expand the world around us so that such people naturally are a part of it, and are naturally within our reach.

The French author and social critic Voltaire (1694–1778) said, "Every man is guilty of all the good he didn't do." How many of us in a position to do so devote even a fraction of our lives to doing what we can to make the world a place with less preventable suffering and cruelty? Should those of us who are privileged to live in relative plenty forgive ourselves if we do not do everything we can to alleviate the preventable suffering that is all around us?

Of course, there are degrees of suffering, and different types of cruelty. I'm not sure that the isolated instances of suffering and cruelty that many of us in the developed world have had to deal with can remotely compare to the daily and lifelong tragedies that the world's abjectly poor and oppressed have to face. At the very least, in addition to cultivating such "virtues" as forgiveness and acceptance for the tragedies that befall us, what is even more direly needed is the cultivation of a type of social and intellectual conscience that inspires, and even commands, us to do everything we can to make the world "a better place" for others.

For this to happen, the chronically poor and abject would have to be less invisible to people of relative privilege. Journalist Barbara

Ehrenreich says in *Nickel and Dimed* that in the United States today, where the divisions between rich and poor are greater than ever, "(s)ome oddly optical property of our highly polarized society makes the poor almost invisible to their economic superiors . . . " She accounts for the "blindness of the affluent" by the fact that they "rarely see the poor, or if they do catch sight of them in some public space, rarely know what they're seeing"—so even more rarely still do they know what the poor are saying and feeling and experiencing.

For many people of privilege, life may go on smoothly for a long time before any sort of tragedy or hardship strikes, even though we know full well (unless we live in a vacuum) that people all around are suffering. For those who fall in this category, maybe an even more compelling question than those Kushner poses is: Should those who suffer chronically and abjectly forgive us for having blinders on, and feeling no connection with them, until and unless something unfortunate befalls us?

—

The late Walter Kaufmann, a social philosopher at Princeton University, who as a youth barely escaped the Nazi Holocaust, writes that the "deepest difference between religions," as well as that between "theism and atheism," is "not nearly so profound as that between those who feel and those who do not feel their brothers' torments." He notes that even though Buddha "did not believe in any deity," he nonetheless was "like the prophets and the Greek tragedians," in the sense that they all opened their hearts "to the voice of their brothers' blood." On the other hand, Kaufmann says, "There is no inkling" of such feeling "in the callous religiousness" of many who "find some proof in . . . the existence of a God or gods, and . . . pray to ensure . . . speedy passage into heaven."

To Kaufmann, "the only theism worthy of our respect" is one that professes belief in God "not because of the way the world is made, but in spite of that." He believes that "one of the most admirable attitudes possible for man" would be "to try to fashion something from suffering, to relish our triumphs, and to endure defeats without resentment . . . "

While Rabbi Kushner says we must "forgive God for not making a better world," the brand of theism Kaufmann casts in a favorable light seems to be one in which such forgiveness is beside the point. Following Kaufmann, it seems that we must accept the way the world is, and accept that there will always be suffering and senseless tragedy—but never accept, over the long haul, that the types of human suffering that are preventable always have to be as pervasive as they are now. Most of all, we have to acknowledge the all-important role each of us who live in relative privilege can play in making the world a "good" one, a world with less suffering, where as few senseless tragedies as possible come to pass.

In *Dark Hollow*, Irish author John Connolly sets forth this compelling perspective:

> What matters is that you understand that others suffer, . . . some . . . worse than you could ever do. The nature of compassion isn't coming to terms with your own suffering and applying it to others: it's knowing that other folks around you suffer and, no matter what happens to you, no matter how lucky or unlucky you are, they keep suffering. And if you can do something about that, you do it, and you do it without whining or waving your own . . . cross for the world to see. You do it because it's the right thing to do.

# COURAGE OF 9-11

It's almost exactly three months since the September 11, 2001, tragedy, and I'm in Montclair, New Jersey, a socioeconomically and ethnically diverse bedroom community of Manhattan, facilitating a dialogue in the city where I first inaugurated Socrates Café in 1996. Whenever I come here, which now is only once or twice a year, it feels like a homecoming. Still about ten of the original or "charter" members attend the weekly gatherings, and there are about ten others who almost never miss a Tuesday. Also each week, about five to ten new faces venture inside to get an idea of exactly what this is all about; many end up coming back at least on occasion.

Tonight, the question the group chooses is "What is courage?"

At the outset, no one seems ready or willing to answer. Finally, Ann says, "I think courage is walking into a building that you know could collapse at any minute, to try to save others."

"Why is that courage?" I ask.

She ponders a bit more and then replies, "If your goal is to save someone's life, and you put your own life at risk, then that's courage."

"If you're trained to save someone's life in such a situation, and you know the risks involved, does that still qualify as courage?" I ask.

Before she can speak again, Frank, a retired fireman, says, "I've been asking myself, and been asked, that question a lot lately. I think that if you're trained for such a situation, then you're doing your job, your duty. Some people have said to me that because I've risked my life for people I don't even know that, even though I got paid—but not very much—it qualifies as an act of courage."

"And it's because you were risking your life for people you don't know?"

He thinks about this. "Yes," he replies at last. "If my loved ones were trapped in a building that was on fire and on the verge of collapse, it wouldn't be an act of courage for me to risk my life to try to save them. It would be what I'd expect of myself, and surely what others would expect of me."

"But couldn't you say that you also expect of yourself, as a trained professional, that you would try to rescue strangers in a fire, and that's what people expect of you as well?"

"Yes," he says after some hesitation. "Which I think is exactly my point. That neither, for me, is an act of courage, because it's expected of me. Only people who risk their lives, and aren't expected to, would have acted in a courageous way."

He pauses a good while before then saying, "But when I think of my colleagues who died on September eleventh, some of whom went all the way up to the seventy-eighth floor of those buildings to rescue people trapped in there . . . those circumstances were so unusual and so dangerous, so above and beyond the call of duty, that I consider them courageous."

Then he says, "One of my friends said to me that they mustn't have thought the building would collapse like that, or so soon, or they wouldn't have entered it without hesitation. But I disagree. I think that if they thought they had the slimmest chance to rescue just one person, they'd do it. It's second nature to them to do it."

"If it's second nature to them, no matter how extreme the circumstances, is it courage?"

Frank replies, "Well . . . no. What *is* second nature to us firemen, I think, is our love of life, and to do all we can to protect and save lives."

The journalist David Halberstam, who in his book *Firehouse* profiles Engine 40, Ladder 35, a firehouse brigade in Manhattan which lost twelve of the thirteen firemen it sent to respond to the September 11 tragedy, writes that "love is a critical ingredient in a fireman's code, which demands that you are willing to risk your life for your firehouse brothers"—and for complete strangers. Halberstam notes that "the word *coward* . . . is not used in the world of firemen," and that New York's citizens long have held "a quiet sense of admiration for firemen, for their courage, for the . . . way they go about their jobs, and for the fact that they constantly have to deal with terrifying fires in the high-rises that surround us."

"I think a person who does something that is considered an act of courage would never qualify it that way himself, because of his humility," says Benjamin, a house painter. "I think humility and courage go together."

"Can you explain a little more?" I ask.

"Anyone who tries to rescue someone, in a situation where he could die, obviously values the other person's life at least as much as he values his own. He doesn't put himself above them in any way. I think that takes great humility. It makes me think that if all the terrorists, and all the others who eagerly have waged war throughout history, put strangers' lives on the same level as their own, there wouldn't be so many acts of this nature."

"Amen," says Sal, an imposing, burly man with a gravelly voice, and one of the most gentle souls I've ever met. A decorated veteran, he says, "For me, an act of courage can't just be one that some government official decides is above and beyond the call of duty. It has to be something out of the ordinary, something that probably most other people in the same situation wouldn't do."

"Such as?" I press.

"Well, maybe it at least has to be something that's not expected of you. Like, on one occasion, a newspaperman who was following our platoon around saved my life when he killed an enemy soldier lunging at me. He wasn't trained to do that, that wasn't his role there, yet he did it anyway. That man's act was one of courage—because it wasn't expected of him, and because his goal was to save the life of another human being."

WHAT IS COURAGE? 209

"I think that's right," says Erica, another of the Socrates Café's charter members. "Like, someone like Evel Knievel, who does something extreme like jump over the Grand Canyon on a jet-propelled motorcycle. That may be brave, certainly something that few others would do. But it's not courage, even though he risked life and limb, because his goal was only to perform an extreme act, and make gobs of money. It had nothing to do with saving other people's lives, or making the world a better place. The *reason* you do something has everything to do with whether it's an act of courage or not."

Eventually, thirteen-year-old Amy says, "I've been thinking about what Frank said. I think if you do the job you were trained to do, in a situation where your life is at risk, you're maybe not *as* courageous in certain ways as someone who does the same thing who isn't trained. But maybe, in some ways, you're *more* courageous, because you know what may happen, while someone who isn't trained may be ignorant of what might happen."

I now say, "It seems as though everyone who has spoken so far, instead of defining courage in a static, dictionary-definition sort of way, sees it in a dynamic way, as a type of act where the end has to be to save someone's life."

Those who've spoken so far, and many others, nod in agreement.

"But is that the only way to answer the question 'What is courage?' Does it always have to be an act that saves someone's life?"

Tamara, a career counselor, says softly, "My nephew Henri is showing me that how you die can have as much, or more, to do with courage as how you live. He has inoperable cancer. But he doesn't feel pity for himself. He says there're many people much younger than he who've died from diseases, from wars and accidents, and that he feels fortunate just to have been alive. He lives every moment as fully as he can. It's not like he's just putting a brave face on things; this is the way he is. And I think being this way is a way of courage: Henri has so much dignity in the face of death, and he's a role model and inspiration to others, by showing us that it's more important than ever to keep our heads held high, and live fully, till the moment we die."

After a protracted silence, Rebecca, a graduate student in English at nearby Montclair State University, says, "I think it takes courage to speak honestly your point of view. When I first started coming to Socrates Café a year ago, I never said a word. I was scared! I was afraid someone would put me down, or that what I had to say wasn't worth saying. But these days, I'm a regular blabbermouth." Everyone laughs.

Then she says, "I think it takes courage to face your fears. If you're afraid of loving someone because you might get hurt, but you leave yourself open and vulnerable anyway to falling in love—especially after you've been burned—then I think that that's an act of courage. If you're someone who has no problem speaking in public, then to do so isn't an act of courage. But if you speak out, and in doing so are overcoming a fear, it might be an example of courage. Because to me, a quality of courage is that of overcoming."

Now she covers her mouth and blushes.

I give her a "what's wrong?" look, and she explains, "Well, now I've gone and called myself courageous. And of course, if I call myself that, it can't be courageous, because I haven't shown humility."

The swashbuckling Alan Breck in Robert Louis Stevenson's *Kidnapped* would certainly disagree. Breck "had a great taste for courage in other men, yet he admired it most in Alan Breck."

Frank says to Rebecca, "No, you are courageous. I've seen how you've blossomed since you first came here. You have every right to consider overcoming your fear of speaking in public an act of courage."

Then Ronnie pulls out a photo from his wallet and shows it to me. "That was me 'before,' " he says. In the photo, he's about two hundred pounds heavier than his now-svelte self. "It didn't take courage for me to lose weight. But it took courage for me to get to the point where I made the commitment to lose weight—to look at myself in the mirror and ask myself why none of the weight-loss programs I'd tried ever worked. I had to ask myself, 'Why I am slowly killing myself with all these extra pounds? Why don't I care? How can I inspire myself to care?' Asking, and answering, those questions took courage."

"I think you can never know if you're courageous, or how much courage you have, until after the fact," reflects Susy, an elementary-school teacher. "No matter how well trained you are, or aren't, to rescue people, what have you, it's not until you are put to the test that you can really know."

In Stephen Crane's *The Red Badge of Courage*, the protagonist, Henry Fleming, a raw Union recruit in the Civil War, felt a "crisis" before he was pitched into his first battle, because he had no idea how he would hold up. "Whatever he had learned of himself" previously, Crane writes, "was here of no avail. He was an unknown quantity. He saw that he would . . . be obliged to experiment . . . and remain close upon his guard lest those qualities of which he knew nothing should everlastingly disgrace him."

Eventually, Karl, a former corporate executive, says, "Since nine-eleven, I've been thinking a lot about the way I've been going about living my life. A tragedy like this—several people in this immediate area were among those who died—really hits home. And it makes me realize, it shouldn't take that much courage to do what you really want to with your life. Those clichés are true: You never know when your time is up, so if you have a dream, you'd better get busy making it come true."

Then he says, "What I've always wanted to do is be a special-education teacher. My brother was learning-disabled at a time when there weren't any services available, and I'd always wished I'd been able to help him more. But I can help other young people today. I'm matriculating in the education program here at Montclair State with a specialty in teaching the learning disabled. When I get a job in the field, it will mean a salary cut of about nine-tenths. Many of my friends, and my parents, weren't thrilled by my choice. But it's what I want to do—what I need to do. I was surprised when my wife said she supported me one hundred percent. I guess it helps that our house is paid for, and we have sizeable savings for our kids' education. But I'm still scared, a little."

"I think what you're doing is a form of courage," says Meryl, a dancer. "You're taking a big risk, and going against the status quo, to make a difference. Too often we measure success by how much money you make, instead of how many people you help."

Then Dana, a high-school student, says, "I think one of the greatest forms of courage can be dissent, at least in a democracy. Because dissent means you're challenging the way things are. Whenever you do that, you're putting yourself at risk, to change things for the better. I think putting yourself at risk, perhaps sacrificing your career or reputation or even your life, for the benefit of humanity, is what courage is all about."

"I think it's more courageous to dissent in a country like China than it is here in a democracy," says Paola, a graduate student from Colombia. "There, when you dissent, you could be risking your life, not just the ill will or criticism of others."

This prompts Clementina, an administrative assistant at an insurance company who immigrated to the United States from Cuba, to say, "But even here in the U.S., it's scary these days to dissent. Last week, I went into the post office for stamps, and they immediately gave me flag stamps. I said to the postal worker, 'Don't you have anything else? I'm so sick of these flag stamps. All I see, everywhere I go, are flags.' And she looked at me in a way that made me feel very uncomfortable, in a way I hadn't felt since I lived in Cuba. I actually felt she was going to write my name down and report me. Many people right now think that to criticize is to be unpatriotic in a cowardly way, when it's actually one of the most courageously patriotic things you can do in a democracy. Now, whenever I go to the post office for stamps, I demand that they give me *anything* besides flag stamps. You might think this is silly, but it's my form of dissent in a time when many are afraid to speak out against this empty form of patriotism."

The progressive intellectual author Arundhati Roy says that "(t)he only thing worth globalizing is dissent," and that dissent should be the "common virtue of global citizens." But there's nothing noble or worthwhile, much less courageous, about dissenting just for the sake of it. As always, it depends on your motivations, and your ends. Many people in politics, for instance, dissent just to impede social progress, rather than to expedite it.

Caitlin, a Socrates Café regular I met tonight for the first time, says, "I think of the attorney general of New York, Eliot Spitzer, who went after the dishonest corporations, as a person of courage. He was willing to sacrifice his career, his reputation, his friends, to do the right thing."

She goes on, "Many said it was 'unpatriotic' of him to do it at a time when the nation was reeling. But it was even *more* patriotic of him to do his duty at a time when the nation was reeling, to do what was right when the great majority felt he should do what was wrong. The cowards were the dishonest corporate executives who took advantage of the nation's people, and hid behind the events of nine-eleven to fend off any investigations into their corrupt dealing."

Jim Holloway, an uncommonly perceptive person and a dear friend, says after a while, "I think that this country is being tested right now. It's sort of teetering on the brink between courage and fear. The initial impulse since nine-eleven has been to build walls around us. I've been worried that our country would become so fearful—closing all our borders, stopping all immigration—that we'd lose sight of who we are."

"I think the jury's still out on whether, as a whole, we'll take the path of fear or of courage," he continues. "We've been talking about courage tonight mainly in terms of individual acts. But I think we need to look at courage on a societal scale, and examine whether we, as a society, are responding to what happened on September eleventh in a courageous way, or in a fearful way. Are we giving in to our understandable fears and closing the rest of the world out? Or are we people of courage, and being more open than ever, in spite of our fears, because that's what our country is all about?

"Having a democracy is an act of faith. There's always a danger of terrorism, especially in an open society. And I think a big part of courage is faith—in this instance, faith that we can remain an open society, and face uncertainty with courage, rather than letting our fears get the best of us."

Then he says, "I used to think that it was up to the president to lead the way. But don't you think it's up to people like us?"

## A PROFILE OF COURAGE

Ernest Hemingway famously described courage as "grace under pressure." But I think courage can sometimes, maybe most of the time, be awkward and clumsy. It may present itself in fits and starts. For instance, in addressing a perceived social wrong, it may mean that you don't quite know where you're going or what you're doing, only that you have to do *something* to stem the tide, say, of intolerance or discrimination. The first courageous—and awkward and clumsy—step may be to speak out, in the face of some social opprobrium. The next step may be to formulate, via a stumbling progression, your unique way of combating or resolving this social dilemma, in spite of your fears, in spite of the risks, because of your conscience.

John F. Kennedy said in *Profiles in Courage*, written when he was a U.S. senator, that when one acts courageously, one just "does what he must—in spite of personal consequences, in spite of obstacles and dangers and pressures—and that is the basis of human morality." By Kennedy's conception, "to be courageous . . . requires no exceptional qualifications, no magic formula, no special combination of time, place and circumstance." Kennedy believed that "sooner or later," the opportunity to be courageous "is presented to us all," and that "(i)n whatever arena of life, one may meet the challenge of courage, whatever may be the sacrifices he faces, if he follows his conscience—the loss of his friends, his fortune, his contentment, even the esteem of his fellow men—each . . . must decide for himself the course he will follow." While tales of courage, such as those included in his book, may serve to "teach" and "offer hope" and "provide inspiration," still "they cannot supply courage itself. For this each man must look into his own soul."

—

Are all people who demonstrate such courage heroes? What is a hero?

The Scottish-born historian and critic Thomas Carlyle described a hero poetically as someone who possesses "what of divinity is in man or nature." But I think endowing a person with attributes from a superhuman or divine source, rather than acknowledging that he musters these attributes from within his own frail nature, diminishes a person's potentially heroic stature. Sidney Hook, a noted pragmatist philosopher in the tradition of John Dewey, says that heroes typically "are not great historical figures," but rather people who can be quite unheralded and yet admired "for the risks taken beyond the call of duty, their great sacrifice, their fortitude in adversity, their refusal to compromise with corruption, or their independence of judgment." To Hook, anyone who possesses and acts upon one of these attributes is a hero. I wonder, though, if one must in some fashion possess *all* these attributes, and most importantly, act with humanitarian ends in mind, to be of heroic stature.

These days, anyone who rescues someone from drowning is hailed as a hero, and the rescuer is automatically lauded for his or her courage. But is that all it takes? What if you are trained to rescue drowning people? Or what if the person you're rescuing is someone you know to have done great harm to others, and everyone around you tells you not to rescue him, but you do so anyway, because you believe in the sanctity of all human life? Does that make you more courageous, or less, because of your "independence of vision and judgment," your "fortitude in adversity," your "refusal to compromise"?

Charles DeBenedetti, professor of history at the University of Toledo, writes in *Peace Heroes in Twentieth-Century America* that American heroes are "avatars of change, who tried to move other Americans into seeing that their national interest was merely a part of a greater human interest in global peace, security, and justice." Such people, says DeBenedetti, all have "courage and principle," and share "commitments in conscience to humankind's higher good." Can a hero be someone who rescues another with no thought of "humankind's higher good"? What if you don't have time to consider such lofty notions, and act without thinking? Would it be even more heroic, or less, if your only consideration was to save a human life, with no thought to long-term consequences? What if you act without regard to your own well-being to rescue another—from drowning, from poverty, from torture—before you can know whether the person you are rescuing is good or bad?

I think that the act itself is an articulation of your "conscience to humankind's higher good," because by acting in such a way, you're demonstrating your reverence for the sanctity of all human life. I think courage is a quality of all such acts.

—

DeBenedetti's encomium to American heroes includes such luminaries as: Albert Einstein, who "used his public identity as the paragon of the rational scientific enterprises that had opened the Atomic Age as a means of arguing for the control and abolition of nuclear weaponry"; and Jane Addams, who "built her personal and public identity as a progressive American reformer upon her determination to serve and nurture the weak and powerless."

I've yet to come across a book on American heroes that included César Chávez, the farmworker and labor organizer who in the mid-60s began his daunting years-long battle, for little or no pay, to found the United Farm Workers of America, and in the process stand up to a range of powerful vested interests—from state and local governments, to the Teamsters, to California growers, to multinational corporations. In the end, Chávez succeeded in forming a union for farmworkers, who until then had been terribly exploited, and succeeded in winning a contract between the union and growers, though of course the fight to end completely labor exploitation and improve working conditions for farmworkers continues to this day.

As noted in *Cesar Chávez: A Triumph of the Spirit*, the significance of Chávez's accomplishments is "largely moral." In a time and clime when there was a pervasive "lack of moral values. . . . Chávez stands out as . . . proof that America still has men and women of rare courage and conviction who base their lives on a righteous cause." I think, rather, it was Chávez's rare conviction—his commitment to humankind's higher good—that gave him this even rarer type of courage.

Chávez's life, the book asserts, was directed by such "fundamental moral principles" as "self-sacrifice for others, courageous struggle despite overwhelming odds, respect for races and religions, nonviolence . . . and a faith in the moral superiority of the poor, as well as a central belief in justice." I'm not at all sure that Chávez believed that the poor have "moral superiority" simply because they are poor. I think, rather, he believed that anyone with a humane moral code would hold that the poor and disadvantaged have the same right to live with dignity as everyone else.

In his autobiography, Chávez says that "(f)ighting for social justice . . . is one of the profoundest ways in which man can say yes to man's dignity, and that really means sacrifice. There is no way on earth in which you can say yes to man's dignity and know that you're going to be spared some sacrifice."

Do all acts of courage imply a certain type of sacrifice, with the end of elevating "man's dignity"? If so, do they all imply that you must have strong moral convictions? Can it be, sometimes, that you don't realize what your convictions are until after you act? Or are actions and convictions discovered and revealed simultaneously?

## THE COURAGE TO ENDURE

I am with a group of sixteen seniors, all Native Americans, equally made up of men and women. We are at a powwow—a gathering of a number of tribes, held to create fellowship—in the western United States. I was appreciative that they'd agreed to take part in this dialogue, to say nothing of the fact that so many attended, given their experiences with outsiders, who, several told me, typically don't care to learn from them, but instead talk down to them as they preach and proselytize.

Now, as we gather in a circle, I ask them, "What is courage?"

"I think endurance is courage," says Herman, a Navajo, through an interpreter. Of Navajos over age seventy, at least 80 percent speak only their native language.

"How so?" I ask.

"The U.S. soldiers and settlers tried to kill us all off when they took our land, but we endured. Then they tried to kill us during the Long Walk, but again, enough of us were able to endure—what we call *nineel neeh*—for our people to survive."

In 1863, the governor of the territory of New Mexico decided he wanted to obliterate the Navajos, so thousands were ousted from their homeland and forced by the U.S. Army—after it destroyed their homes and killed their herds of livestock—to walk nearly four hundred miles to Fort Sumner, New Mexico.[1] The tortuous trek was called the Long Walk. At Fort Sumner, the Navajo lived for four years as virtual prisoners. Thousands died in the inhumane conditions.

"Then," Herman continues, "when we were given a reservation, after we signed a treaty with them in 1868, they tried to kill our culture. They punished us if we practiced our traditional ways, or even dared speak Navajo. In spite of all the hardship and poverty and oppression we've been put through, we've endured. We've stood up straight and faced whatever has come our way, and refused to bend. To me, this is courage, or *t'aa bizaaka.*"

Yale University history professor John Demos writes in *No Small Courage* that "Indians did not simply surrender; rather they responded to their losses with courage, flexibility, and a sometimes extraordinary resourcefulness. . . . to make a new stand against continuing white encroachment." He says that survivors "preserved carefully

---

1. Some, such as Navajo Chief Carbona and Ganado Mucho, thought it best to fight it out against Kit Carson and his soldiers, rather than go on the Long Walk, which they felt was a walk to their doom. But after suffering from terrible starvation, those still living finally had to surrender in the winter of 1864.

for the future" their "ancient tribal traditions—the customs, beliefs and values at the core of their historical experience."

As if as an afterthought, Herman now adds, "I think, long after others are not here anymore, Native Americans will still be here, enduring, and the Native American culture will be strong."

Another Navajo elder says, "What would have happened if we hadn't kept speaking our language, in spite of the punishment we faced? The U.S. military wouldn't have had a language to use as a code to communicate with each other—one the Japanese couldn't understand.

"Navajo were called into service in World War Two to become code talkers. The military—the same that had tried to destroy us in the previous century—now asked Navajos to risk their lives for 'the good of the nation.' And they did it, and were praised as courageous for it."

The Navajo language, called Dineh (which is also what the Navajo call themselves), was used by over four hundred Navajo code talkers, all U.S. Marines, to provide rapid and stealthy radio communication from 1942 to 1945 in the Pacific theater during all Marine operations—from Guadalcanal and Tarawa to Peleliu and Iwo Jima. In two separate events in 2001, hundreds, some posthumously, at last were recognized for their contribution to the war effort and received in Washington, D.C., either the Congressional Silver Medal or the Congressional Gold Medal, two of the most distinguished awards that can be bestowed by Congress.

Then he says, "At the ceremony, the military said that if it hadn't been for code talkers, they wouldn't have taken Iwo Jima, and so maybe wouldn't have won the war.

"The military kept what the code talkers did a secret for decades. They said it was classified information. But the code talkers wouldn't have talked about it anyway. It's not our way. If you do an act of courage, and you brag about it, then it's not really an act of courage. Courage is about self-sacrifice for others, not self-glory."

"I wasn't a code talker, but I volunteered for World War Two," says Raymond, a Sioux. "I don't take part in any Memorial Day parades, or things like that. I volunteered to serve because I'm a warrior, a *hashke*, and warriors have the virtues of duty, honor, commitment, sacrifice, patriotism."

Then he says, "I think to have the kind of courage we're talking about, you need first to have these virtues, which you can't have without being physically and mentally and spiritually strong, or you won't endure."

Jacqueline Keeler, a member of the Dineh Nation and the Yankton Dakota Sioux, wrote, in a segment for Pacific News Service, that her great-great-grandfather, Big Horse, who fought the U.S. Army during the time of the Long Walk, said his father taught him this about being a warrior: " . . . a warrior is someone who can get through the snow-storm when no one else can." This seems a fitting metaphor for the type of endurance of which Raymond is speaking.

Another, nodding in agreement, now says, "You fight a war because you have to, because sometimes it's necessary if your group is to endure, even though you hate violence. You don't do it to receive medals. I think most Native Americans who have served this country during wartimes feel this way."

Native Americans have quietly served their country with distinction from the War of 1812 to today's wars—in fact, disproportionately so. Native Americans have the highest record of service, per capita, of any other group in the United States. And most of them who have done so have been volunteers.

"I think our warrior code of courage is very similar to the Marine code," says Dennis, who is from the Chippewa tribe. "Their '*semper fi*' means 'always faithful'—not just faithful to your fellow Marines, but faithful to yourself, to who you are, to your beliefs, to your ancestors. It's a kind of faithfulness where you're willing, if necessary, to sacrifice yourself for those ideals. Native Americans have made these sacrifices with no hope of honor or rewards."

Indeed, while many U.S. servicemen came home to promising futures, most Native Americans came home to wrenching poverty and no job opportunities. And the rest of the nation promptly put them out of mind.

"I think an act can only be called one of courage if you do it with no expectation of being thanked," he then says. "We went to serve our country because we hold dear certain ways and values. When warriors are called on to defend their country, they go, no matter how badly they've been treated by their country in the past."

"We don't do things for personal glory," says Hal, who is Shawnee. "The type of courage we believe in, sometimes it means we have to do physical acts of courage, put ourselves in physical danger, but it's because of our values that we do this. Our values are to endure, to persevere, to overcome, if the goals are worth fighting for."

After a pause, one of the men says, "If you have strong beliefs, it's easy to act, even if you're afraid. You act because of your strong beliefs, in spite of fear."

"I admire Tecumseh a great deal," he continues, speaking of the chief of the Shawnee Nation (1768–1813). "Tecumseh said that 'the three most dreadful calamities were folly, inactivity and cowardice.' He said this when he was urging other Indian nations to join forces with him to defeat the whites in the early nineteenth century. He asked, 'Have we not courage enough remaining to defend our country and maintain our ancient independence?' "

He then says to me, "Tecumseh was criticizing those who didn't have the courage to continue to fight the good fight, no matter the outcome. To Tecumseh, it didn't matter if you lost—what mattered was that you acted on your beliefs, and were willing to sacrifice yourself for them."

Cheryle, who is in traditional Sioux dress, says to me, "When I think about courage, I think about the English word *to*. I think of: courage to care, courage to persevere, courage to resist. For instance, even though our tribe is very poor, we've resisted offers of huge amounts of money in exchange for our sacred lands. Our legendary chief Crazy Horse said, 'You cannot sell the sacred land the people walk on.' White people would jump on the money offer, because to them money is everything. But to us, our identity is everything, and the sacred land gives us that. We have the courage still to care about things that are worth really caring for: our land, our identity and culture."

The U.S. Supreme Court has ordered the federal government to pay the Sioux Nation tens of millions of dollars for land illegally taken from them in the nineteenth century, because it was believed to have large gold deposits, but the Sioux have refused to accept it. They want back the land, called the Black Hills, or *Paha Sapa*—"the heart of everything that is"—which to them is sacred; it was where the tribe originated and where all their creation stories spring from.

After a long pause—one that's so long that I think the participants have had their say and are ready for the dialogue to wind up—an elderly Navajo woman says, "Yes, I agree with this idea of 'courage *to*.' Because courage is always shown by an action. For instance, it can take courage to leave the reservation, to leave your nest and go out into the world, and still be who you are."

Then she says, "I think of all the Native Americans who went to serve their country. They were harassed by other U.S. soldiers, in spite of their heroics, just for being who they were. But many Native American soldiers still did their spiritual sings and their dances, though they were taunted, and though they were way over on the other side of the world."

She does not see it—she is looking straight at me as she talks—but a few of the older veterans nod in silent agreement. She goes on: "Not only that, but some of our veterans here who volunteered to fight in wars for the U.S. were ridiculed by some people on their own reservation. They thought that the whites should be left to fight their own wars, and that we shouldn't have anything to do with it. But our veterans, in fighting for the U.S, were not in any way selling out. They see themselves as members of Native American tribes, and also as U.S. citizens."

Another pause ensues, and then a Navajo woman named Frannie says, "I agree that courage can best be shown when you've left your security behind. I encouraged my granddaughter to go to a college outside the Navajo reservation, so she could learn about other people and places, and make friends in the greater world, and so they could learn about her and her people. My granddaughter was afraid at first, and she missed home very badly. She overcame her fears, though she always missed home.

"She ended up loving her experience of going to college in California. Every year while at college, she organized a protest during the Columbus Day holiday, so people could know that for the indigenous in the U.S., we don't see that as a day fit for celebration.

"Many people taunted her, but some she won over. She had the courage to face them, and to be proud of who she was. She was more of a true Dineh than ever when she went to the outside world and stood up for who she was."

## COURAGE SAMURAI-STYLE

I'm in an elementary school, and am with a group of nineteen seemingly docile Japanese fifth-graders and their martinet teacher. I've almost reached the end of my tether in terms of trying to hold a meaningful dialogue.

Just a short time earlier, Japan had changed the school week from the traditional six days per week to five. This teacher was none too happy about it. "Children complained to their parents that they didn't have enough free time," she told me as we walked to her classroom, and speaking in a way that made it clear her views were not to be gainsaid. "So then their parents complained to the government, which gave in and gave parents what their children wanted. Parents no longer have the courage to stand up to their children and make decisions that are best for them, and society. Instead they spoil them rotten."

Perhaps it was this statement on her part that inspired me to ask her charges, "What is courage?"

The students seem so cowed by the teacher, they only respond with answers they think she wants to hear. So far, their comments have been of this variety: "Courage—*yuuki* in Japanese—is doing your home-work, even when your friends try to pressure you to go out and play."

And I would ask, "Who agrees with this?" All hands would shoot up at once. Universal agreement. The teacher would look on, beaming. The students simply would not stray into any territory they thought would incur her ire.

I'm about to call it a day when, against all odds, the teacher is called away to the principal's office, and I am left alone with the students and our interpreter.

As soon as they're sure their teacher is out of sight and earshot, the students come to life. One of them, Hiroshi, now says to me, "Courage is Samurai Jack!"

This comment, like all earlier ones, meets with near-universal approval, but this time, it is because of their enthusiasm rather than some sort of desultory sense of obligation.

The popular American-produced cartoon series *Samurai Jack* is a huge hit in the United States, but I hadn't realized it was popular here too. The series' main character, a samurai warrior, hails from an ancient era in Japan when samurai warriors were considered the most noble of citizens. Jack's nemesis Aku, who has shape-shifting and time-traveling powers, exiles Jack far into an apocalyptic future. In each episode, Jack tries to return to his era. At least for the two years the show has been on the air, Samurai Jack has failed to find a way to return to his own time and place. But as he continues trying to get home, in each episode he risks his life to take on evildoers in the futuristic era in which he finds himself thrust.

Hiroshi goes on, "Like, there's this one episode where these people are trying to build a spaceship so they can escape the evil tyrant Aku. But Aku has the entire planet sealed off by a huge blockade. Jack fights off the entire blockade himself, so they can escape and live in freedom."

Emi, sitting in front of him, says, "Jack is a true samurai warrior. He's always willing to risk his life against impossible odds to help out others in trouble. He *is* courage."

"Jack is all alone in an alien world," she then instructs me, "but he is still a warrior, and he still follows the Bushido code. *Bushido* means 'way of the warrior.' And *samurai* means 'one who serves.' Only a select few in twelfth-century Japan ever were chosen to be samurais. Their code of *bushi no ichi gon*, or 'word of the samurai,' demands complete loyalty to their warlord, or *daimyo*, and their fellow samurai—even above their own family. All samurai believe in self-sacrifice for their kingdom. You can't be a samurai like Samurai Jack without the greatest courage."

All the children seem to agree wholeheartedly. But then Seiren shyly raises her hand. "I'm not sure Samurai Jack is so courageous," she says softly. The other students are aghast that someone doesn't share their unadulterated adoration of their cartoon hero.

"Why?" I ask.

"Well," she says, trying to look just at me and avoid the angry glares that are coming at her from all other angles, "take that episode when Samurai Jack helps those people escape the tyrant on the spaceship.

He only does it because, in return, they promise to help him find a way back to his own time. A person with courage is someone who helps out people in distress without asking for anything in return."

Hiroshi, no longer able to contain himself, now springs to Samurai Jack's defense: "I think he *did* have a lot of courage. He took on all the planet's bad guys on his own."

I ask, "Would he have been even *more* courageous if he hadn't expected any sort of favor in return?"

First, Hiroshi grudgingly says, "Yeah, I guess so." But then he says, "What's wrong with expecting a favor in return? Why shouldn't you be rewarded for your courage?"

"I'm not saying you shouldn't be rewarded," Seiren, the Samurai Jack critic, replies softly but firmly. I admire her courage for standing her ground in the face of nearly universal opprobrium from her classmates. "I'm just saying you shouldn't *expect* to be rewarded, or *ask* to be rewarded, in return for your courage. Especially a samurai warrior shouldn't expect this. He is courageous out of duty, nothing else."

In her book *Samurai from Outer Space*, author Antonia Levy, a scholar of Japanese culture, writes of the long-popular tradition of Japanese animation, called *anime*, and of the typically heroic bent of its protagonists, whose samurai-based code of loyalty and self-sacrifice holds such appeal to young viewers today. "Losing and therefore gaining nothing confirms the hero's altruism and renders his or her sacrifice all the more tragic," she writes.

"I bet Samurai Jack still would've helped them, even if they couldn't help him," says Hidecki, in a bit of a huff. "Because in almost all the other episodes, he helps people without ever asking for any sort of favor. Like, how about that episode where Samurai Jack helped a Scotsman rescue his wife, who was kidnapped by an evil lord? He agreed at once to help. He rescued the Scotsman's wife, he got no favor in return."

Hidecki then says to Seiren, who dared cast aspersions on Samurai Jack's image, "And besides, it's not like Samurai Jack succeeded in getting back home in that episode you're talking about. Even when he realized they wouldn't be able to help him, he never regretted coming to their aid."

"So is it enough to risk your life, in order for something to be courage, or do you have to risk your life for the cause of good?" I ask.

"I'm not sure," says Yukiku. "Lots of people risk their lives for others, like the *yakuza*, the Japanese Mafia. And they definitely aren't good."

*Yakuza*, or the Mafia, still exist in Japan, though in attenuated form. They spring out of the samurai and ninja tradition, but did not come to the fore until the seventeenth century, just as the samurai and ninja were dying out (except as movie and literary figures).

"Nobody has loyalty to one another like the *yakuza*," says Hasuiki. "Did you see the movie *Black Rain*, with Michael Douglas as the good-guy policeman? This one *yakuza* guy, whom Michael Douglas is trying to catch, cut off his finger to show his loyalty to his fellow *yakuza*."

"And this is courage?" I ask him.

He thinks about this awhile. "Well, I don't think it's something most people would ever have the guts to do."

"Or the stupidity," interjects Seiren almost inaudibly.

"What if they rescued one of their fellow bad guys?" I ask. "Would that be courage?"

"Well, they're bad guys," says Seiren. "So if they risk their lives to rescue a fellow bad guy, it can't be courage. Courage has to be in the cause of good."

"I think it *is* courage," says Hasuiki, " but for a bad cause. So it's not the best form of courage, because it's not a form, like the form Samurai Jack practices, that makes the world a better place."

Another student, Kaoru, now says, "Samurais are cooler than the *yakuza*. But they're nothing compared to ninjas. They're *really* courageous."

"My friends and I play ninja video games for hours after school," he then says. "There's this really cool one called *Ninja Ryukenden*, or *Shadow Warriors*. It's got this ninja whose mission is to fight it out with assassins and terrorist squads in all these big cities. He knows all these cool moves—the flying neck throw, the hang kick, the Phoenix black flip. See, in the video game, you actually get to play the ninja yourself and do all these amazing moves. The game ends when you fight your way through all the goon squads and then defeat the big boss. Then the ninja gets to go back home to Japan. Nobody puts it on the line like the ninjas."

Like the samurai, the ninja also originated in the twelfth century; they were employed to undertake clandestine espionage work on behalf of feudal lords against enemy forces.

"I don't like the ninja so much," says another, "because they did everything undercover. They disguised their real identity, lying about who they were and what they were trying to do. If you're really courageous, you don't hide who you are. So the samurai are much cooler."

"I don't like *any* of these people," says Seiren. "None of them are courageous. You can't be courageous without fear, and these people are trained to be fearless. So they have no fear to overcome. How can you have courage if you have no fear?"

Hiroshi, who up till now has been her staunch nemesis in this dialogue, now says, "Even if you have fear, it's not enough to have to overcome it. Bad people can overcome fear when they do an armored car heist. That would be bad courage. Good courage is when you overcome fears so you can do good things."

Then he shrugs and says, "I guess I have to agree with you." The other students stare at him in wide-eyed amazement over his courage to side with his antagonist when he feels she is in the right. "None of the real samurai and *yakuza* and ninja had that kind of courage," he says, "because they were fearless."

Laszlo Versenyi notes in *Socratic Humanism* that, for Socrates, "courage comes not from fearlessness but from wise fear, the fear of the loss of a greater good. . . . A man who exposes himself to danger for no reason at all"—or just because, as with the samurai of old, his master tells him to—"is foolhardy rather than courageous, stupid and unreliable rather than wise and good." For Socrates, "cowardice is not lack of bravery, but lack of wisdom."

In Plato's dialogue *Laches*, Socrates says to the character Nicias that "courage is knowledge of future good and evil." Since humans are not omniscient, one can never know for sure, until one acts, whether one's actions have the consequences intended. This statement by Socrates has been widely misinterpreted to indicate that he didn't think there could be any such thing as courage, because of our inability to predict infallibly whether our actions would result in good or evil. But what Socrates is saying is that while we are not endowed with perfect foresight, we still can have foresight of a sort, by reckoning, based on past experience, whether the likely outcome of a present course of action will lead to good or evil.

Now Seiren, encouraged that Hiroshi is at least somewhat her ally, says, "All of these types—samurai, ninja, *yakuza*—believe in duty and loyalty above everything else, but in a bad way, because they don't put country or family first. None of them question what they do. Sure, they believe in honor and duty and loyalty, but to whom? If you don't ever question how you're being loyal, or to whom you should owe your allegiance or your duty, how can that be courage? Like, our Kamikaze pilots in World War Two. They were courageous, I guess, for risking their lives, but it was for a bad cause that they didn't question."

In *Divine Thunder: The Life and Death of the Kamikazes*, Bernard

Millot writes that the World War II kamikaze pilots operated on the same "principle of deliberate self-sacrifice" as the samurai of old. The kamikaze pilots emulated the Bushido code of the samurai, which stressed "honor, courage, loyalty, the ability to endure pain in silence, self-sacrifice, reverence for the emperor, and contempt for death"— and never to question the orders of their superiors, or their belief in *Hakko Ichiu*, "according to which the Japanese were divinely predestined to dominate the world."

Then Seiren says, "There *is* one samurai I admire. I admire Sano, the samurai warrior in Laura Joh Rowland's books."

All the students seem familiar with what Seiren is referring to, and for once, they nod in agreement with her. Rowland's historically precise novels, set in ancient Japan, all feature Samurai Sano.

"Is it ever courageous to follow someone out of blind loyalty?" I ask.

"I don't think so," she says. "Sano believed in honor and loyalty and sacrifice, just like all samurai. But he didn't believe in them blindly, and that made him different than all the rest."

In one of her books, Rowland writes that "a samurai's sole purpose" traditionally was "to give his life to his lord's service. Duty, loyalty, and courage were its highest virtues, and together formed the foundation of a samurai's honor." Yet her novels' samurai protagonist, Samurai Sano, does not unquestioningly adhere to this tradition. Rather, Sano also has cultivated a "personal concept of Bushido," which is "encompassed in a fourth cornerstone, as important to his honor as the others: the pursuit of truth and justice," which spurred him on to an "exhilarating quest for knowledge."

"Sano's kind of courage often got him in hot water," Seiren goes on. "In fact, in every tale, he always comes close to losing his life, because he refuses to give up his principles. Sano never accepts corruption or dishonesty or evil, not even from his warlord. He has a higher code. I think to have courage, you have to have this higher code."

Now fully comfortable on her soapbox, Seiren seems on the verge of saying something else. But just then, her teacher walks back in the room. She and all the other students immediately clam up, their new-found courage to speak their minds put on temporary hold.

## THE WAY OF THE WARRIOR

In the *Seven Samurai,* a movie by the internationally acclaimed Japanese filmmaker Akira Kurosawa, set during the sixteenth-century civil war, soldiers and warriors and peasants form a rare alliance to defeat a group of bandits trying to loot their rice fields. Risking their lives "to make the village defensible," Stephen Prince says in *The Warrior's Camera* that their actions reflect Kurosawa's own "insistence that true human action must carry a socially beneficial aim," and genuine courage and heroism are "measured by the rectification of social oppression."

By this conception, an act of courage can never be undertaken by just one individual, and can never serve solely individual ends. Rather, it must benefit an "entire community" and inspire it to become "morally transformed." This societal conception of an act of courage and heroism—or heroic courage—in which it is considered shameful for any individual to stand out, would seem to gainsay the notion that a hero must be someone extraordinary, and must necessarily stand out. It offers an alternative conception of heroism, one based on a type of courageous action that can only occur on a communal or societal scale, in which everyone stands out together, and in which there must be a "socially beneficial aim."

Stephen Prince notes that some considered Akira Kurosawa "the last of the samurai," and that the actions of his movie heroes "are generated and informed by the ideals of the samurai warrior" that inspired Kurosawa's own conduct. These ideals, set forth in the Bushido code, emphasized "courage, integrity, fortitude, and fealty." To Kurosawa, all these qualities go together. There is no such thing as an act of courage if it is not done with integrity, fortitude, and fealty. But courage itself has many facets, all of which must be intertwined. For instance, there cannot be moral courage without physical and spiritual courage. In Kurosawa's films, "the hero is always as strong as the ideal samurai. This strength may be physical, as in the samurai heroes of *Seven Samurai, Yojimbo* and *Sanjuro.*" But it also must be moral and spiritual, and have a specific end in mind, namely an "abiding commitment to securing the basic needs of other human beings." Consequently, Kurosawa transforms the traditional obligation of the samurai, specifically "to serve his lord," and sublimates it into an "obligation to serve humanity." He makes it their goal "to humanize a corrupted world."

Kurosawa, born in 1910, lived through the last part of the Meiji period, during the waning of the samurai tradition. Prince notes that Kurosawa witnessed during "the era of interwar social protest, the war years of intense nationalism and anti-Westernism, and Japan's postwar period of rapid economic growth" the erosion of the samurai qualities of courage, integrity, fealty, and fortitude which had largely defined Japanese society. The heroes portrayed in Kurosawa's body of work—which often calls into question the destructive direction he saw his society taking, and so put him at odds with authorities—seem to reflect his own virtues. His film heroes were working toward the same ends as he was, namely, "to humanize a corrupted world."

In *Bushido: The Soul of Japan,* Inazo Nitobe, who like Kurozawa also lived at the tail end of the samurai era, says that for a samurai, "courage was scarcely deemed worthy to be counted among the virtues, unless it was exercised in the cause of righteousness," in "doing what is right." This mirrors Kirosawa's philosophy of courage.

So, if you act in a rash way, without considering whether your act is or isn't a "right" one—even if you face numerous hazards, and even jeopardize your life—then your act isn't courageous. Rather, it would be what Shakespeare called "valor misbegot," and so would be, in Nitobe's words, "unjustly applauded." As he puts it, "death unworthy of a cause worth dying for" is not a courageous death, but a foolhardy one, a "dog's death." Quoting a prince of Mito, Nitobe writes that "it is true courage to live when it is right to live, and to die only when it is right to die."

Nitobe writes that Socrates' willingness to go to his death was one of supreme courage, if one takes the long view, because Socrates acted out of "love, magnanimity, affection for others, sympathy and pity" for his fellow man; he acted to "humanize a corrupted world." Nitobe writes: "His conscience he followed, alive; his country he served, dying."

The samurai philosopher Yamamoto Tsunetomo (1659–1721) wrote that "men who did well at the time of their death were men of real courage," while those who "are agitated at the time of their death do not have true courage." If this is so, then Socrates had real courage.

How do you know when your act is the "right" one? Can one person's act of courage be another's act of foolhardiness, since people hold such different notions of what is right? A homicidal bomber, for instance, may believe that his is an act of courage based on what he deems the absolute righteousness of his cause. Nitobe asserts that for an act to be right, to say nothing of courageous, a person must have the "supreme virtues" of "love, magnanimity, affection for others, sympathy and pity" for all one's fellow humans. A homicidal bomber convinced that he must obliterate a race or an ethnic group or society to achieve his ends does not have such a set of virtues. He does not act to humanize a corrupted world, but acts out of a corrupted view of what is right.

# A DIFFERENT KIND OF COURAGE

"Courage is getting out of bed each morning and facing the day."

I have just asked the question "What is courage?" to a group of ten at a facility for the mentally ill. I was given half an hour to hold a Socratic dialogue here, and had been forewarned that those seated with me around an oak table, where we drink herbal tea as we engage in dialogue, tend not to be very communicative except in very directive and controlled settings. But my experience with the mentally ill has been that they have a remarkable openness and focus and clarity when philosophizing in a setting in which everyone is on equal footing.

I look intently at the participant Patricia, whose first response has started off our dialogue. "How so?" I ask her as I see others nod at her insight.

"My mom used to say that every time you step out the front door of your home, something can happen, good or bad. If you know this, and still step out the front door, it's courageous, because you're facing the unknown. But I think that it's not even when you step out the front door that courage kicks in. I think it's when you wake up and climb out of bed. I wish sometimes I could stay in bed and never have to deal with the pain inside. But that would be giving up and giving in. So far, everyday I've managed to get up and face the day, face myself. That is courage."

"Would you call yourself courageous?" I ask.

"I'm not sure I'd go that far," she replies after careful consideration. "I think the fact that I get up each day is a courageous *act*, but I don't think one act makes a person courageous. I think it would be up to others who know me to decide if I'm courageous."

"I think everyone who has problems, but stills get out of bed each day to face up to them, is courageous," says Laura, sitting beside her. "And everyone I know has problems. So I think everyone who faces them, or tries to face them, is courageous. I would call this 'everyday courage.' In its way, it's no less courageous than rescuing a baby from a burning building or saving someone from drowning."

"I came here to this place to save me from myself, to rescue me," says Arthur. "I'd never thought of that as courageous before."

"Your personal rescue has to come first," says Carlos. "Because as you rescue yourself, you gain greater wisdom about these types of problems, and this gives you more empathy with others. So then you can be more helpful to others. Courage has to begin with saving yourself, so you can reach out to others crying out for help."

"The people here tell me that I'm the only one who can really help me, that all they can do is help me to help myself," says Bronson. "I think what they do is help me find my own reservoir of courage."

"The best healers and helpers make you feel like they're just like you," says Cary, who is sitting somewhat far back from the table, and who did not seem inclined to take part.

"What do you mean?" I ask.

"They have the courage to let you know that they aren't above you, that just like you, they have highs and lows. The only difference is, they've gained the wisdom to learn to deal with these problems—and now they want us to gain our own wisdom. Their courage has a foundation of love and compassion."

Jocelyn says now, "I've been thinking of what Henry David Thoreau said: 'The mass of men lead lives of quiet desperation and go to the grave with the song still in them.'"

She is silent for a moment and bows her head. Then, looking back up at us, she says, "Those who love me try to help bring the song out in me. All of us have a song that's uniquely ours. But sometimes it can be more painful to bring it out than to leave it buried inside. Most people never discover their song. I've finally discovered a few notes of mine, because of the love and compassion of those here who've helped me discover the courage to face and overcome my darker dispositions. Now I want to discover the whole symphony!"

## COURAGE TO BE—OR NOT TO BE

The renowned philosopher and theologian Paul Tillich (1886–1965)—who began teaching at Harvard after he was released in 1933 from his academic position in Germany, because of his opposition to Nazism—says that the "courage to be is the ethical act in which man affirms his own being in spite of those elements of his existence which conflict with his essential self-affirmation." According to Tillich, the courage to continue living, in the face of those elements of our nature that seduce us into thinking it'd be easier, or better, if we put an end to this thing called our life, is a reflection of our ethical values.

But as with all truisms of this sort, it doesn't always hold true. Throughout human history, many have lived in circumstances in which they have had no control over their existence, in which having the opportunity to value their lives, or to find value in life, did not enter into the equation. Such circumstances seem as prevalent today in many parts of the globe as they've ever been. It isn't only a matter of individuals having elements within themselves that might prompt them to question whether they should go on living. Instead, there are elements from without who make it clear to them day in and day out that their lives are worthless except in how they can serve those who oppress them.

There are significant numbers of people around the globe today who can and do treat others as if their existence has no intrinsic or inherent worth. Until and unless such people, through some miraculous "conversion," are inspired to realize that every human has the right to live in dignity, and to have a significant degree of control over her existence, Tillich's limited insights seem largely inapplicable.

In *The Courage to Be*, Tillich calls courage "the act of the individual self in taking the anxiety of nonbeing upon itself by affirming itself either as part of an embracing whole or in individual selfhood." By recognizing that "not being" is an option, and by not giving in to it, you affirm how alive you are, and that you are alive by choice.

But can suicide ever be an act of courage?

On July 2000, the *Washington Post* reported that Dr. René Favaloro "walked into the bathroom of his Buenos Aires home and shot himself through the heart." Favaloro was an internationally renowned and pioneering surgeon who had invented a procedure that had "saved countless lives." He seemed to have every reason to live.

But he was also a champion of universal health coverage for Argentines. Even though he could have practiced at the most prestigious hospitals in the world, he returned to Argentina to promote this cause. Favaloro, whose guiding dictum was that "all patients are equal . . . paying or not," had, according to the article, "grown distraught" that universal health coverage would never come to pass. He was increasingly distraught that "only the affluent were enjoying . . . 'the right to live.' " Ultimately, he took his life, after "a failed struggle by one of the greatest minds in medicine to save the heart foundation here that he had built into a symbol of altruistic health care in the developing world."

Favaloro's suicide, according to the article, "has deeply affected Argentina. It has caused soul-searching about the rise in poverty and the collapse of social services . . . His death also has reverberated internationally, underscoring one of the biggest challenges of globalization: providing quality health care in developing countries." As a fellow surgeon at Favaloro's foundation put it, "Because of who he was, what he had accomplished, he felt he could do more with his death than he could alive."

Perhaps not only by choosing to live do we always take the most courageous route. The reasons Favaloro ended his life—to heighten awareness of the plight of the marginalized, with the long-term aim of creating a more egalitarian and compassionate society—were every bit as excellent as those he aimed for while he lived.

WHAT IS PIETY?

# DISHONOR THY FATHER

"Piety is a blend of reverence, obedience, loyalty, and duty," I'm promptly told by a man named Chung, a retired executive of an accounting firm, after I pose the question "What is piety?"

He's one of eighteen, ranging from adolescents to seniors, with whom I'm gathered in a low-slung, single-story tearoom situated in a historic enclave in Seoul, South Korea. The wood-and-clay structure has just a few oval windows and one entryway. All of us are seated in the sparsely furnished room on thick mats set over the traditional *ondal* floor (*ondal* means "warm stone"), made of granite blocks kept warm by flue gases of a fire under the floor.

"But we normally don't discuss piety in itself," Chung then says. "For Koreans, all piety centers on filial piety. We're still a strong Confucian society, and at the center of the Confucian ethic is filial piety."

Like schoolchildren reciting a lesson from a textbook, a number of older male participants take spirited turns relating to me that virtually all social relations, for all those who still adhere to Confucian values, revolve around filial piety, or *Hyo*.

Says one, "In Book 1 of *Analects*—the recorded sayings of Confucius—Confucius said that filial piety is 'at the root' of all benevolent actions. In chapter 6, he goes on to say that 'young men' first learn to 'be filial' when they are at home. This means their parents teach them to live by the qualities of piety that Chung listed. As they grow older, Confucius says it will be second nature for the young to extend this code of being 'respectful to their elders when away from home,' and to learn to 'love all extensively and to be intimate with all humanity.' So love and intimacy are also qualities of piety, along with reverence, obedience, loyalty, and duty."

"To Confucius," another tells me, "filial piety is based on five primary relationships—ruler and subject, father and son, husband and wife, elder brother and younger brother, friend and friend. All of these, except friend to friend, are hierarchical relationships."

Says still another, "The ruler is set over the subject, the father over the son, husband over the wife, elder brother over younger brother. But these hierarchies are established in a way that people are inspired to live within their framework. For instance, a father will naturally inspire the piety of his eldest son, his wife, his other children—just as a ruler would that of his subjects—by his wisdom and kindness and his own upright behavior."

Chung now says to me, "None of these roles is more important than that between a father and son. The father's foremost duty is to his son, and vice versa. But their duties aren't equal. The father is the authority, and the son's devotion to him must be complete. If the son shows reverence, obedience, loyalty and duty to his father, then when he's an adult, he'll show the same piety to authority figures in society. By doing so, he'll contribute to society's overall harmony.

"Even in modern society, filial piety still applies widely in Korea. No one is more loyal to a father than his eldest son. Not even his wife."

This comment prompts a woman named Hae to say with a sigh, "He's right. And it's why I refuse to marry a man who's the oldest son in his family. Because he refuses to let go of this outmoded way of practicing piety." The striking, demure woman's remark seems to jar many of the others, who up till now had nodded approvingly at the litany of encomiums to filial piety.

"Why?" I ask, as everyone looks on in a way that makes me think they are both anxious and afraid to hear what she has to say.

"Because," Hae says, "the form of filial piety that exists here is patriarchal, chauvinist, and sexist. For women, it's also what you would call a Catch Twenty-two. The men with traditional values are the best catches, because they work the hardest, are the most ambitious and well-connected, and have the most integrity. But nothing can break the bond between them and their fathers. All the others with whom they have relationships, particularly their wives, are second-class citizens."

Hae goes on: "I've resorted to matchmaking services to try to find a husband. I want to marry someone who will practice a modern type of filial piety, that puts his wife and children first. But it seems, in this country, that you either meet men who have forsaken the old ways, and virtues like piety, or you meet those who hold on to them in an orthodox way and refuse to let them breathe new air and change with the times."

The woman beside her now says, "I also believe in the spirit of filial piety, but like her, I believe the strongest bond should be between a husband and his wife." She sighs. "I just want to live with my husband, in a cozy apartment, in the city. When we have children, I want to live farther out, in a comfortable house. I want it to be just for our family. But if I marry an eldest son, he'll insist on taking care of his father and mother in their old age. Why? Because that's the way it always has been, and to them, not to continue with this tradition would be impious."

Then she says, "Why does it have to be that way? Can't filial piety apply above all else to wife and husband, as she said? Because husbands and wives *choose* to marry one another and form a family, while eldest sons don't choose to be born and have all this responsibility dumped on them."

The man whose remark prompted her heartfelt comments now says, "I couldn't disagree with you more." While his face is red, and he appears angry, he speaks in a low voice: "I would have given anything to be able to care for my father. He commanded obedience, because he deserved it. My nine brothers and sisters never lacked for anything. He made many sacrifices for us and for our mother, and our country. When North Korea invaded us on June 25, 1950, even though my father had retired as an army commander, he immediately volunteered to resume his duties. He took to heart what Confucius's pupil Zizhang said in the *Analects*, that a public servant, when facing danger, should be 'ready to give his life.' "

Then he says, "My father was killed in the fighting, in the area that is now the demilitarized zone. He didn't hesitate to put his life on the line for country and family."

What is officially called the "Korean Conflict" ended on July 27, 1953, when the two Koreas signed a cease-fire. By war's end, approximately 228,000 South Korean soldiers were killed in action, and an untold number of civilians. Nearly 34,000 U.S. soldiers also were killed in action.

His voice breaking, he goes on, "I only have a vague memory of what my father looked like. I was very young. But I revere him. Because of people like him, because of their piety to their homeland, I was inspired to devote my life to the reunification efforts between the north and south. Even though often it seems like reunification might never come to pass, I press on, because I know it's what my father would want. It is what he deserves from me, for the sacrifices he made."

"So sacrifice is an important quality of piety?" I ask.

"It is," he says. Eventually he adds, "I just came back home here to Seoul from visiting my father's grave in Jinju and honoring him for his sacrifices." For the first time, I notice that he is fingering a piece of hemp cloth, which signifies both his mourning and his reverence for his father.

His father's childhood hometown of Jinju is revered by Koreans as a place where one of the ultimate acts of piety for their country took place. In 1592, after Jinju Fortress was conquered by Japanese forces, Non-gae, a noted twenty-year-old *Giseng*, or entertainer, whose husband was killed in a battle with Japanese forces, lured a Japanese general to a rock known as Uiam rock, which stood on a steep precipice overlooking a swift-moving river. Non-gae grabbed the general and jumped into the river, killing both herself and the general. Her act, which crushed the morale of Japanese forces, was considered pivotal in turning the tide of the war. A frequently visited shrine is now built at the rock she leaped from, to honor her pious sacrifice of her life, on behalf of the long-term good of her nation.

Another man, speaking for the first time, now directs his gaze at Hae and says to her, "I don't think you have to worry so much about the young men of today being overly pious to their parents. My oldest son and daughter fight over me. They fight over who *won't* have to take care of me and my wife when we're too old to care for ourselves. Neither wants the responsibility."

He nods toward the serious-looking young man in a three-piece suit seated beside him. "Only my youngest son joined me here today." His son does not seem comfortable in the limelight. "He's the only one of my children who believes still in the old ways. He likes to eat what I eat, read what I read, learn what I've learned. Even though he's a very busy executive, he accompanies me to Suwon every Children's Day, no matter how many other obligations he has. We join the thousands of other families who travel there from around the country, and we climb to the summit of Mount Paldalsan in the outskirts of Suwon and toll the Bell of Filial Piety."

A city forty-six kilometers from Seoul, Suwon is the Republic of Korea's first planned city. Suwon was built by the subjects of King Jeongjo, during the Joseon Dynasty of the eighteenth century, out of the king's longing to relocate his royal court from Seoul to Suwon, so he could live in closer proximity to the tomb where his father was buried. The king, like most Koreans of his era (and many to this day), felt his debt to his parents did not end with their death, and in fact increased. Hence the still-strong rites of ancestor worship that are practiced here.

He now says, "I must admit that I agree with this woman, that we must adapt filial piety to our times today. My youngest son, not my eldest, is the one who has shown me piety, and so deserves my piety."

An elderly man now shakes his head and says firmly, "But people aren't supposed to practice piety out of expectation or hope of any reward. It should be practiced with no strings attached. If we expect reciprocity, it's not piety. You love and honor and obey your parents because you want to be pious towards them, period, not because you have to or because you anticipate a reward down the road."

I ask him if this is how his own children practice piety toward him. He is silent for some time. At last he says, "I haven't seen my children in months. They say they're too busy to visit. Kids are self-centered these days. I live by myself in a retirement home." He looks at the elderly man at his side. "Only my friends, people my age, come to spend time with me, and make sure I get out some." His face is a blend of bewilderment and gloom. "Even a generation ago, there was hardly such a thing as a retirement home for old people. But all that has changed. Children today don't want their parents to be seen or heard."

An editorial in the major daily newspaper in Seoul, the *Korean Times*, says that filial piety has long been considered "the source of all virtue" in Korea. But, it says, this is no longer so prevalently the case. "Filial devotion is increasingly fading," laments the editorial. While many children "remain devoted to their aged parents and elders, even under difficult circumstances," it says that "weakening filial piety amid the spreading egoistic trend of young people in this society accounts for the poor treatment of elderly citizens, whose number is ever-increasing." This is so, according to the editorial, even though it was due to the sacrifices of the nation's elderly that South Korea is currently enjoying economic boom times. "(F)ar from benefiting from the economic growth and abundance admired by the world," it says Korea's elderly "now suffer difficulties due to the lack of welfare policies and the indifference of society." The editorial goes on to say that, more than anything, seniors long for "someone with whom they can have heart-to-heart talks, as they are increasingly alienated from society and their families in the rough waves of globalization, industrialization, and Westernization." In its call for a resuscitation of filial piety in this nation of nearly fifty million, whose age sixty-five-and-over population now numbers more than four million, the editorial says that the "problems of senior citizens are problems for all of us."

The elderly man now says to us, "My children will come to see me later today, only because it's Parents' Day. They'll stay for an hour or so, give me a flower in accordance with custom, and then I won't see them again for months. What kind of piety is that?"

"It's disgraceful," says Byung, a serious, bespectacled young man with a neatly trimmed beard. He turns to the elderly man and says, "I feel very bad for how your children are treating you. I know we don't know each other . . . but would you mind if I visit you? For me, it would be an honor to spend time with you and learn from you."

The elderly man is visibly touched. "No, I wouldn't mind that at all." Then he says to Byung, "Your parents, I'm sure, believe you to be *Hyo-Ja*, a good boy with a deep filial piety toward them."

After a pause, Jae, a thoughtful teenager who stands out in the crowd of conservatively dressed people in her hip-hugging, navel-revealing jeans and array of skin-piercing jewelry, says, "Everyone says I should show piety to my father and grandfather and older brother because 'they're older and wiser.' But I don't think wisdom is based on how old you are. I know people way younger than they are who are way wiser, because they've had more experiences, and learned from their experiences. My older brother and father and grandfather are like petrified rock. They never grow or change."

Keong, the youth sitting beside her, who appears to be her boyfriend, says with more than a touch of disdain, "I don't think most Koreans practice any sort of filial piety anymore. I don't think most people my age respect the old just because they're older than we are. They have to earn our respect if they're going to get it."

"And vice versa?" I ask.

He hesitates. "Yeah, I guess so."

Jae chimes back in: "This Confucian piety is too cultish for me— and too impious. This filial piety has no regard for human life, at least, for female human life. To this day, many Korean couples have an abortion if their fetus is female."

An article from the *New York Times* News Service says that while worldwide, about 105 boys are born for every 100 girls, in South Korea, 116 boys are born for every 100 girls, "one of the highest such ratios of any country in the world." In Korea, it says, "30,000 fewer girls are born each year than would be the case if there were no such abortions," in which women secretly abort their female fetuses, because they "feel an age-old obligation to bear sons." The data in the article suggest that "about one female fetus in 12 is aborted" in South Korea "because of its sex," even though "(e)xcept in rare cases, abortions are illegal," and even though "disclosing the sex of a fetus is also against the law."

There is a considerable silence. No one seems inclined to respond to mordant criticism of Korean piety.

Eventually, Jae's boyfriend says, "In our country's entire history, we've only had a democracy for just over the last fifteen years, because we've been brought up to be blindly obedient and loyal. I don' t think these qualities are part of genuine piety. I think commitment, with your eyes wide open, to an open society, is the best piety we can have in Korea."

I ask, "So a certain type of commitment is another quality of piety?"

"I think it's the main quality, this open-eyed commitment," he says. "You have to be committed to something, to make a difference in life.

But you should examine your commitment from time to time, to make sure it's for the good of everyone in society. The commitment our prodemocracy activists had to toppling the dictatorship is the best kind. The blind commitment to the dictatorship that our elders had is the worst kind. Any sort of blind commitment—including the type eldest sons have for their fathers, and vice versa—is the opposite of piety."

Hashem Aghajari, a university professor in Tehran, Iran, shares a view similar to Jae's. In the fall of 2002, he exhorted young people in Iran never to follow blindly their religious or political leaders. To him, piety must derive from what Jae called "open-eyed commitment" based on autonomous thinking. However, Aghajari's statement was considered so impious by Iran's leading clerics that at one point he was sentenced to death (that sentence has since been commuted).

Jin, a retired factory worker, now says, "I don't disagree with what Jae says. But today's young aren't all so pure. I wish today's young people had an open-eyed commitment to integrity. Just look, for instance, at the children of our president, and the shame they've brought to us all."

Shortly before this dialogue took place, thirty-nine-year-old Kim Hong-gul, the youngest son of Kim Dae Jung, the president of the Republic of Korea—who won the Nobel Peace Prize two years earlier for his attempts to reunify the two Koreas—was arrested for taking bribes. Moreover, the second of President Kim's three sons is also under a cloud of suspicion over accepting bribes, though at the time of this dialogue no formal charges have been filed against him. The president is quoted by the Associated Press as saying that the scandal surrounding his two sons is "more than just disappointment. It is the biggest misfortune of my life."

"I think the actions of President Kim's sons epitomize the breakdown of piety in our society," Jin then says. "Our president has brought so much pride and esteem to our nation. He captured the presidency on an anticorruption platform. Yet his moral authority now is called into question. His reputation will always be tarnished, because of the actions of his sons. The president has apologized repeatedly for what they did, but he can't force them to live like him. All he can do is try to model a way of being an upright person."

Says an elderly woman: "His children committed *Bul-Hyo*, impiety to their parents and to society. They had no loyalty, no *chung*, to filial piety. Confucius said that we must 'promote the upright,' and 'place them above the crooked,' and that this is piety at work. I admire our president for seeing to it that even his own children, if guilty, are punished. This makes me even more faithful to his rule, and I hope it has the same effect on everyone else."

Seung, who with his father runs a family-owned car dealership, interjects, "But what you're suggesting contradicts Confucianism. Confucius asked, If a man can't control how his family members behave—if they are not loyal and obedient and dutiful to the virtues he instilled in them—then how can he govern the nation's affairs?"

Choon, the woman beside him, replies, "I think if a father and mother do all that's possible to raise their children to be upright citizens, then they shouldn't be blamed for their children's mistakes. We all have free will. The president's children decided on their own to go against their upbringing and commit impiety."

Cho, the young man in the three-piece suit who has come to this dialogue with his father, mulls this over and says, "Confucius taught that the main way to instill filial piety in your children is by example. He said that if the adult leads an exemplary life, so will his children. But if our president's children cannot follow this great man's example, how can other young people who had less fortunate upbringings ever be expected to be pious?"

"In book fifteen chapter eight of *Analects*," he continues, "Confucius says that a 'resolute scholar and person of virtue'—a person of piety, in other words—would 'rather sacrifice his life' than 'seek to live at the expense of injuring humanity.' Yet the president's children, who were raised by a 'person of virtue,' *did* seek to 'live at the expense of injuring humanity.' "

Byung replies to him, "But it's not the president's fault that his sons turned out this way." He then says, "We've just been singling out the president's children in these corruption scandals. But there were many others involved, too, and I'm sure most of them also were children of upright families. Yet they still went down the wrong path. Just as in the times of Confucius, these corrupt people felt that the traditional piety was obsolete and beneath them. In that respect, I think our times are very similar to those Confucius faced. And what we need to do, as suggested earlier, is to take the best of what piety stands for and apply it in new ways."

He turns to me and says, "We have a traditional proverb: 'Father Tiger has a Puppy Son.' It relates that many of the most esteemed people throughout history have had children who are impious to the values they were brought up on. The president and his children are an example. So was the son of Confucius himself! In both cases, the father did the best he could. But if Confucius's own son turned out to be so impious, how can we blame our president, or any parent, if theirs don't turn out any better?"

## ALL PIETY TO THE PEOPLE

Confucius (551–479 B.C.)—who was fond of saying "I am not wise by nature, but have become wise by hard work"—lived in a time when Chinese society was fragmenting. He witnessed the collapse of the ruling Chou Dynasty, which was characterized by rampant corruption, gluttonous waste, and pervasive moral and political cynicism by rulers and subjects alike. As fierce factionalism, and a concomitant rise in violence, began to take hold, he became convinced that a dearth of virtue was the reason for his society's demise. Confucius believed that if society ever was to be redeemed, it had to rediscover traditional moral teachings.

Like his fellow inveterate conversationalist Socrates, Confucius lived in a time when the Golden Age of his society was on a rapid downward slide. Socrates believed that virtue was not to be unearthed primarily from past teaching, but rather was something that always could be more fully discovered; and that one of the best ways to go about doing this was to hold dialogues with one's peers. Confucius, on the other hand, believed that virtue could only be discovered from past teachings. To this end, he delved deeply into the lore of China's so-called Golden Age, or Great Age of Harmony, which flourished in the early years of the Chou Dynasty. Ultimately, Confucius concluded from these teachings that only by cultivating a very specific way of being in the world, with piety at its core, could society hold hope of attaining another Golden Age.

Confucius traveled far and wide throughout war-torn China, holding conversations with people and proselytizing. As he roamed from place to place, Confucius touched a chord with virtually everyone, winning them over to his notion that lasting social harmony could only come about by practicing filial piety. As D. Howard Smith notes in *Confucius*, "In stressing filial piety and brotherly affection, Confucius was emphasizing that the closest of human relationships are those within the family, and in those close and intimate relationships the highest qualities of personality may find their development." These "highest qualities" of piety included loyalty, duty, commitment, and integrity and were meant to be cultivated in a way that would elevate everyone in society.

Less than a century after his death, the slender *Hsiao Ching*, or *Book of Filial Piety*, was published, which features recorded dialogues that purportedly took place between Confucius and his disciple Tseng-tzu.

Rather than using these dialogues to advance Confucius's humanistic piety, rulers throughout Asia for their own ends, defined piety, Smith writes, as that virtue in which the ruler "is everywhere regarded as the parent of his people, who form a huge family," and in which the ruler "exercises benevolence and justice toward all his subjects, while they . . . render obedience and dutiful service." This authoritarian slant to filial piety, which was counter to Confucius's own outlook, subsequently set the stage and justification for authoritarian rule, in government and family alike, in male-dominated China and then Korea, as well as other Asian nations, for centuries to come.

Those who took part in this dialogue on piety seemed to agree that the notion of Confucian piety in Korean society needs to be fine-tuned and updated. But perhaps the genuine notion of piety, as set forth by Confucius, and elaborated by some of his followers, needs to be rediscovered and practiced.

While Confucianism did not originate in Korea, a great deal of original Confucian thinking did; Korea was home to several iconoclastic thinkers whose work was later called Neo-Confucian. They were largely ignored, until this recent democratic era, because their notions of piety did not jibe with those of Korea's authoritarian rulers. They seem to point to a type of piety that could chart a course for a more open and egalitarian society in modern Korea.

Take Yi Yulgok (1536–84), a philosopher who lived during a period of highly authoritarian and paternalistic rule in Korea. In spite of the enormous personal and professional risks involved in taking a stand that differed from that of his rulers, Yulgok actively promoted a type of humanistic piety that conceived of members of his nation as a family of equals. Yulgok tried to advance the heretical notion that a government's rule and legitimacy "depended on the people," and that "the people" should not be expected to be blindly subservient toward their ruler. If anything, the people were more deserving of a ruler's piety than the other way around, while the ruler must strive above all else to ensure that all his subjects have the freedom and the resources to lead fruitful and meaningful lives. Yulgok asserted that such an enlightened view of Confucianism was much more in keeping with the beliefs of Confucius himself, and that the authoritarian and oppressive type that had won the day was not at all genuinely Confucian in spirit or intent.

Julia Ching, professor of religious studies at the University of Toronto, writes that Yulgok believed that "(t)he desires for virtuous behavior—for humanity, righteousness, propriety, . . . loyalty, faithfulness, filial piety" could only "result from the moral mind." But this mind could only be cultivated on a broad scale, Yulgok felt, if one first lived in a nurturing and liberating society; and that did not exist.

―

The most striking feature of the Korean city of Suwon, where many Koreans go to this day to celebrate filial piety, is Hwaseong Fortress, built by King Jeongjo in reverence to his father. The fortress was designed by the neo-Confucian philosopher Jeong Yak-yong (1762–1836), a leading scholar of the so-called Sirhak—or Practical Learning—school, which shunned lofty and abstract thinking in favor of learning that could be experimented with and applied in the real world. This philosophical school advanced a type of Confucian-based piety that was similar to that of Yulgok. Even in constructing this tower for the king, Yak-yong, a radical thinker and revolutionary reformer, used this project as an opportunity to advocate for improved working conditions for common laborers. As scholar Han Yong-U notes, Jeong Yak-yong and his fellow philosophers were "reform-minded Confucianists" with a "modern consciousness." Their piety toward humanitarian pursuits—at a time when their rulers demanded absolute obedience and reverence—was exemplified by their demand for "civil rights and equality of all people both in economy and in social standing." Yak-yong believed that there was no innate difference between rich and poor, except that the rich were born with the means to attain whatever they needed. One way he tried to implement a more level playing field was by his call for radical land reform.

Yak-yong's attempts to advance a more humanistic form of Confucian piety met with tremendous resistance from so-called traditional Confucian thinkers, who propped up the ruler's authoritarian version of piety. They claimed that morality comes to us *a priori*, as something "given" in the nature of things, and that the duty of the king, as absolute authority, is to tell his subjects what this *a priori* morality is. Of course, it always was of a type that benefited the king at the expense of almost everyone else. Yak-yong, however, rejected the premise that ethical or moral norms come to us in this fashion; rather, he believed that we develop and cultivate such norms ourselves. He wrote that piety was composed of "benevolence, righteousness, civility, and wisdom," and held the iconoclastic view that humans can only develop these qualities "after corresponding conduct."

For instance, Yak-yong asserted that "benevolence can be achieved only when one first loves others." He said that until "this act of love" is demonstrated, "benevolence cannot be said to exist." Likewise, he held that "one can recognize righteousness" only "(a)fter one does a good act." Until a person acts in a righteous way, "righteousness does not exist. . . ." So, to Yak-yong, conduct comes first; it must be demonstrated in one's works and deeds, and only then can one determine whether one's conduct is pious.

Yak-yong asked, "How can anyone claim that benevolence, righteousness, civility, and wisdom"—the ingredients of piety—"are inherent in the human mind, like seeds in an apricot?" His answer: They can't. Consequently, rather than accept unquestioningly that one's ruler is the most pious of all the people, Yak-yong maintained that one can only discover whether this is the case by looking at his conduct—namely, how he treats his fellow citizens, and what type of society he is trying to develop.

—

Neither Yulgok nor Yak-yong ever questioned the validity or sanctity of Confucianism itself. Instead, they contended that the version of Confucian piety they were setting forth was the most faithful to the original intent of Confucius. In the name of Confucianism, they tried to advance and elevate the conditions of all members of society, while those in power strove just as mightily to maintain the status quo, in which the few "haves" lived in unbridled luxury at the expense of, and without the slightest concern for the welfare of, the overwhelming majority of "have-nots."

The enlightened views of Yak-yong and Yulgok were deemed threatening and heretical to those who had a vested interest in perpetuating the belief in "the innate superiority of the feudal ruling class and the inferiority of the ruled," Yong-U writes. But today, the philosophy of Confucian piety espoused by Yulgok and Yak-yong is ripe for rediscovery.

## HEROIC PIETY

I'm with a group of students at a public junior high school in central Athens. I'd already been there for over a half an hour, and I'm beginning to fret that we're never going to have the chance to engage in a dialogue. Before the school principal allowed me in the classroom, he grilled me on various subjects in ancient philosophy, to make sure I was well versed.

As he accompanied me to the classroom, he lamented that the current ministry of education in Greece was trying to cut out education in the classics, in order to put more emphasis on "practical education." I commiserated with him that there seemed to be a skewed idea of the meaning of "practical education" among some educational administrators today. I said I wondered whether students who are divorced from the classics—from their historical and cultural roots—could make as lasting and meaningful a "practical" contribution to society as those who are not. He agreed. But we parted company on how a traditional education in the classics should best be applied. For him, rote learning was the way to go. I believe, on the other hand, that children learn best about and appreciate the classics not solely by rote learning, but by building a bridge between the classics and the modern world, and that they should not just study classical works passed down to us, but engage in classical endeavors, like Socratic inquiry.

Now in the classroom, every time I try to steer away from the lecture format and ask a question—which immediately jolts the sixth-graders into an animated state—the principal cuts me off and begins to lecture on some arcane piece of philosophical history.

Finally, he returns to his office. The students, who learn to read and write classic Greek, had been reciting to me what they'd been studying about the Greek gods. One of the students had just remarked, "No one had piety like the Greeks of old had for their gods."

Which prompts me now to ask, "What *is* piety?"

The students come to life, and almost every hand in the class goes up. The first to speak is Yiannis. "Piety is usually defined as reverence, but I don't think that's sufficient. Because you still have to ask: reverence to what? I think for piety to be piety, it has to be reverence to something greater than yourself. I don't think 'something greater' *has* to be to a god or higher power. They can serve as a reason or excuse for your piety, but what I mean is reverence to a cause, a purpose in life that's greater than any individual's more selfish interests."

"I agree," says Kalliope, who like the rest of her classmates speaks flawless English. "We've just finished reading *Antigone*, by the fifth-century playwright Sophocles. I think Antigone, the heroine of the play, is a great example of the piety Yiannis is talking about."

She goes on to say, "Antigone was willing to defy even her king, the king of Thebes, because of her reverence for her brother Polynices, and her reverence to the rituals commanded by the gods—in this case, following their injunction that her brother be properly buried. Antigone felt that the traditions of the gods, which all Greeks back then lived by, should never be severed, certainly not by a mortal—not even by the king, who forbade the burial, because Polynices had invaded the kingdom to try to overthrow his corrupt rule."

It was Antigone's duty, as Polynices's only kin, to see to it that he was buried properly. But if she did so, the king threatened to put her to death. Antigone, however, felt that her first piety was to the gods, and she buried her brother according to their strictures. True to his word, Creon then sealed her in a cave, and left her to die. The king's son Haemon, in love with Antigone and engaged to marry her, told his father that the people supported and admired her piety to the gods, and that he was the one in the wrong for punishing her. Creon eventually gave in to his son's protest. He tried to take back what he did, but when he unsealed the cave, Antigone was found dead. His son then killed himself, as did his mother. The only one who was impious toward the gods, Creon himself was the sole survivor of these tragic events.

"But what is the 'higher cause' in what she did?" I ask.

"Giving up her life in the name of her beliefs," says Alexandros. "Antigone felt that remaining faithful to these beliefs was greater than any individual life, because it was these beliefs that made their society glorious."

Then Maria says, "I think piety, for it to *be* piety, has to be heroic, like Antigone's was. Socrates is another example. No one had a piety for questions like he did."

"What is it about his piety for questions that makes it heroic?" I ask.

"He asked questions about the virtues, and about virtue itself, because he wanted to build a better society," she replies. "He felt that individuals in a society couldn't become better, and discover higher ideals, unless they explored certain questions, and then put their answers into practice. They tried to put these ideals into action, and even were willing to sacrifice themselves, to keep doing so."

"I think this quality of sacrifice—the Greek word for sacrifice is *ipervaci*—is the key ingredient of piety," says Zoe. "To be pious, to a belief or an idea or a cause, you have to be willing to make great sacrifices, maybe even give your life."

"Socrates preferred to be put to death than quit his investigations into the nature of virtue," says Kosta. "He refused the choice of going into exile and questioning elsewhere. I think he felt that if he couldn't question in Athens, the best civilization anywhere, then what was the use of going elsewhere, where he'd probably meet the same fate even more quickly."

He then says, "I think Socrates had a piety—a reverence and loyalty—for place. I think he revered Athens as a sacred place inhabited by the gods. I think Socrates felt that there was no sacrifice worth leaving Athens and its gods, who'd inspired him to 'know thyself.' He felt if he was to die for his piety, he should die there. And the tragedy is, by not leaving Athens, he had to sacrifice his life."

After a pause, Nikos says, "I think Antigone was more heroic than Socrates, because she gave up her life in the flower of youth, with her whole life ahead of her. Socrates gave his up probably not long before he would've died anyway. What's heroic about that?

"Besides that, he isn't the first Greek philosopher to pay the price for practicing 'impious piety,' though he gets all the notoriety. Anaxagoras was put in a dungeon as punishment for his beliefs that the gods were human inventions. His piety, like Socrates', was for the truth. I'm sure Socrates was greatly influenced by him."

The pre-Socratic philosopher Anaxagoras (500–428 B.C.) was condemned for his belief that the gods were just myths and metaphors, mere human constructs, that served to make "transcendent" the virtues that the Greeks had invented themselves, but wanted to attribute to a "higher power."

"Is heroic piety the only type of piety?" I ask.

"Absolutely," says Spiro.

"If heroism is actually a quality of piety, rather than piety itself, then is the word *heroic* superfluous in describing piety?" I ask.

"All piety is heroic, but not all heroism is pious," he says after further thought. "Like, if I'm a bad guy, and I put my life on the line to save a member of my gang from getting shot by the police during a bank holdup, that's heroic but not pious, because their goal is awful. The heroism I'm talking about that's part of piety is based on putting the welfare of others, of your society, above yourself. You can practice this virtue in the name of your gods, or whatever, but you're still doing it mostly in the name of a greater good, and willing to sacrifice yourself in the process."

He looks out the window, where the Parthenon can be seen in the remote distance. "I think Maonolis Glezos and Apostolis Santas are examples of people who practiced this piety," he then says. "They're the ones who tore down the Nazi flag that had been draped over the Parthenon at the peak of the Nazi occupation in 1941. They were members of the Greek resistance, and were the spark that inspired Greeks to stand up to the Nazis. They weren't worried about sacrificing their lives; they thought their lives were puny in comparison to the greater good of having a free society. They weren't thinking about reward or glory or honors, just doing the right thing."

Now Philip says, "We've been studying in class about Athena, the goddess of wisdom. She was the only goddess born out of Zeus's head. Athena taught that a wise person knows that piety is a choice. To be pious, you do have to have *agiotita*, reverence, and you have to be *pistos*, loyal. But you also have to be wise, so you can choose what and whom you should revere, and when and where and to whom you should be loyal."

"Like the students of the 1973 uprising," says Katrina. "They were pious to democracy, pious to its principles, and so they had the wisdom Philip is talking about—they knew what to revere. Many of those students lost their lives because of their piety. I think they are like the Greeks during the Golden Age, because like them, they believed that an open society was the only kind worth having. They felt like, what's the good of being alive if you aren't free?"

On November 17, 1973, thousands of students at Athens Polytechnic University protested the military dictatorship which had ruled Greece since 1967. The students demanded a return to democracy. But the military intervened and crushed their protest. Hundreds of the unarmed students were wounded, and at least twenty-three died. Many more were arrested and tortured. While their protest was quelled, their movement for democracy wasn't, and served as the catalyst that finally brought down the junta a year later.

"There's now a terrorist group in Greece that's named itself 'November Seventeen,' after the student uprising," says Voula. "They dishonor what the students of nineteen seventy-three did. The students thirty years ago protested out in the open, and their aim was to restore democracy. But the November Seventeen terrorists only want to bring about chaos through random violence. They are pious to a cause, like the students at Polytechnic in nineteen seventy-three, but unlike those students, theirs is a dishonorable cause. So I think their type of piety is a bad piety. Any fanatic who's willing and eager to kill innocent people, who doesn't think for himself and who doesn't value humanity, is impious."

"My uncle took part in the nineteen seventy-three protests," says Nikos. "He was badly wounded, but recovered after a long convalescence. Every year, there's a ceremony to commemorate the uprising, and I go with him and place a wreath at the place where the students were killed."

He then says, "Antigone wasn't real, and I don't know for sure if Socrates was, though I'm pretty sure he was. But I think a lot of these protesters in nineteen seventy-three were inspired by their example. I know my uncle was."

"Starting next year," he goes on, "teachers may have to quit teaching us about the classics—about people like Antigone and Socrates. If we don't learn about them, how can we learn to be pious like them?"

## IN THE NAME OF THE FATHER

"What is piety?"

We are in a coffeehouse across the street from the urban American Catholic church this group of seventeen Socrates Café participants attend. I'd been invited to facilitate this dialogue after the national child sexual abuse scandal involving scores of Catholic priests hit. In the past months, the scandal had dominated newspaper headlines around the world; the media coverage had continued for months, with no signs of abating.

"*Catholic* piety, I think, means to obey certain injunctions set down by Church canon" is the first response out of the starting gate, from Edward, who is sitting, as we all are, in rather uncomfortable straight-back chairs. "This piety is one of the seven gifts of our catechism, or instruction, which is the statement of our Church's faith and its doctrine. Our catechism says that the 'seven gifts of the Holy Spirit are wisdom, understanding, counsel, fortitude, knowledge, piety, and fear of the Lord. . . .' It says that these gifts 'complete and perfect the virtues of those who receive them.' It doesn't say that any one of these gifts is more important than the others. But I think that without piety, the rest are meaningless. Because without piety—which I define not just as faith in God, but faithfulness to cultivating the gifts with which the Holy Spirit endows us—you'd never understand the nature or source of these gifts, and so wouldn't have any reason to develop them."

"I agree," says Patricia, who is sitting farthest from me in the circle. "I think the central ingredient or component, if you will, of piety, isn't so much faith as it is *faithfulness*, or fidelity—fidelity to the ideals of your belief system. It doesn't always mean you live up to those ideals, but it does mean you make a lasting commitment to *try* to live up to them. I think this fidelity is important among all the Catholic faithful, but especially so with our priests and bishops, who give vows before God of their fidelity to Him, to Catholic doctrine, and to their sacred duties."

She goes on, "Church canon three seventy-eight says that for a person to be a candidate for the priesthood, he must be an example of 'piety . . . wisdom, prudence, and human virtues and endowed with the other talents which make him fit to fulfill the office in question.' But I don't think any priest is ever able to uphold completely this canon, and so can never be completely pious, because human beings are fallible. But when a priest willfully stumbles, intentionally betrays his faithfulness, then he's impious to an unthinkable degree, because all his actions are expressly in the name of God. There's no separation, for a priest, between a public or private life; their entire life is carried out in the name of, and under the eyes of, God."

"I'd especially characterize Cardinal Law, Boston's archbishop, as impious in an unthinkable way," says Andrew, who converted to Catholicism when he was eighteen. "He's known for years of many of the priests who are pedophiles, and he did everything he could not just to cover up what they did, but to protect them. But besides Cardinal Law, every priest who abused a child, every priest who knowingly allowed this abuse to continue, and to spread, for years on end, is beyond impious. He's the worst form of hypocrite to all that the Catholic faith represents."

The National Book Award–winning writer James Carroll, a devout Catholic, writes in *Toward a New Catholic Church* that "children abused by priests. . . . were typically abused twice: once by the physical assaults, and then by the deflection and denial tied to the holy powers of the priesthood and the needs of the clerical culture around it. Priests raped children, and their bishops protected the priests, allowing rape to happen again. And much of these occurred in the name of God."

Frank, who'd invited me to hold the dialogue, says, "I was stunned to read in a newspaper article that the Church has been trying to get laws passed that would immunize them, or limit their culpability, in sexual abuse cases—as if they're somehow above the law, or at least less culpable than other adults who commit pedophilia. But they should be *more* culpable than most."

"Should they be more culpable than a parent or any other adult who commits child sexual abuse?" I ask.

"I think so, because of their vows of piety," he replies.

"But," I press, "isn't any person who becomes a parent or spouse also making a type of vow of piety, to live their lives as parents or spouses in service to their family, to make sure that they're never harmed because of any intentional action they may commit? Isn't anyone who's put in a position of responsibility or authority over others who are more vulnerable promising to be pious to certain standards of conduct? Should any of them be more, or less, culpable than any other when they act in an impious way?"

He doesn't reply right away this time. Eventually he says, "I was thinking that a priest is a type of parent, a type of authority figure— we call a priest 'Father.' And yes, I think anyone who gives a vow to take on certain responsibilities has to accept the consequences when you intentionally don't live up to what's expected of you—because you yourself vow to live up to those expectations, to those standards of conduct. When you don't, you're accepting responsibility for your failure, and have to accept the consequences.

"Piety is about making a commitment," he then says, "and being faithful to that commitment to the best of your ability."

Another participant now says, "Our parish priest is such a good and completely pious person. He's never done anything that hints or smacks of taint or scandal. But because of what so many other priests have done, I find myself even wondering about him. It's terrible to have such thoughts."

"When you speak of Catholic piety," I say to the group, "it seems you identify it primarily with priests. But doesn't it apply to all members of the Church?"

"A priest is the human embodiment of divine piety," says a woman sitting just to my left. "He's an example to all of us of how to be pious in the name of God. It's his life's work. That's why it cuts us to the core, what has happened."

The man beside her says, "I was thinking that what distinguishes our Church's piety from that of other faiths is that the ways Catholics have for demonstrating their piety are supposed to be unchanging and immutable—our obedience to the Church dogma, to its rituals, to its everlasting truths, and to our priests, as the voice and embodiment of Church authority. But now, with what's happened, I think this needs changing. We should never again look to priests as authority figures."

"If you change this form of piety, which is supposed to be 'unchanging and immutable,' is it still piety?" I ask.

"I see what you're getting at," says Frank. "I think the fact that some priests have made the most grievous errors shouldn't make us change the way we demonstrate piety. This is the greatest test right now. Of course, we shouldn't just accept blindly however priests act. But we should still look at what the priesthood itself is meant to stand for in the same way we always have, even if, or especially if, individual priests fall terribly short of what the priesthood symbolizes. What we really need to do is become *more* pious than ever to what Catholic piety, ideally, represents."

His wife, Lucia, who is from El Salvador, now says, "Just before communion, when the priest is about to present the blood and body of Christ, the priest says, 'Lord, have mercy on us all.' But in Spanish, the priest, instead of saying 'have mercy,' says '*ten piedad*,' or 'have piety.' So I think part of piety is to show mercy, or forgiveness."

Then she says, "If we can no longer turn to priests with confidence that they're the embodiment of the Catholic ideals of piety, then we should turn to ourselves. I think we, the parishioners, have to set an example for others of what piety really means."

She turns to me and says, "We can punish priests and still forgive them. They must be removed from the Church as priests, but they shouldn't leave the Church. We shouldn't abandon them, even as they go to prison. They've failed the canon, and us, but we shouldn't fail them. We should serve as examples of piety to them. If I gave up my belief in how to be a pious Catholic, if I quit practicing charity, humility, forgiveness, and mercy, then I would be impious myself."

There's a silence before Edward says, "I think Catholic piety is to never give up on people, no matter how low they've sunk. It's to be faithful to their capacity to change for the better. I think our piety is put to the greatest test when the failings of those we trusted and revered the most are revealed to us."

## A NEW KIND OF PIETY

In his call for a "new Catholic church," it seems that author James Carroll, a former priest, is calling for a new kind of piety, in which priests' faithfulness is no longer taken for granted, but instead their conduct is constantly scrutinized and critiqued by the faithful. It is done so via "checks and balances, due process, open procedures, elections, a fully educated community, freedom of conscience, the right of dissent, authority as service instead of as domination, moral leadership by rational explanation instead of by assertion."

While Carroll says that "all of this must come into the Church," all indications are that the Church hierarchy is resistant to any fundamental changes, to say nothing of the radical ones that he insists are necessary. For instance, on October 13, 2002, then-Cardinal Law, according to the Associated Press, announced that he refused to allow any new chapters of Voice of the Faithful, an international reform group created in the wake of the sexual abuse scandal, to meet on Church grounds, even though the group seems dedicated expressly to fulfilling the types of piety spelled out in Church canon. Founded initially by twenty-five members of the Catholic church in Wellesley, Massachusetts, the group now claims more than twenty-five thousand members worldwide. One of the founding members, Peggie Thorpe, says on the group's Web site that its members share "outrage, pain, deep love of Church, and commitment to act." Its mission statement, she notes, calls for "structural change" that marks "the end of 'pay, pray, and obey,' " and "the beginning of what Catholic priest and author Henri Nouwen noted of lives lived in hope—they are lives of 'prayer, community, and resistance.' "

The group's mission seems in line with James Carroll's call for "moral leadership by rational explanation instead of by assertion," and for "freedom of conscience." This would mean that priests would need to start engaging regularly in thoughtful and honest dialogue, on an equal footing, with their parishioners. Can "immutable and unchangeable" forms of piety be reconciled with "prayer, community, and resistance"? Or is it that prayer, community, and resistance are precisely those elements of the Church that should be immutable and unchangeable, in terms of piety?

The Vatican itself seems to be engaged in a different kind of prayer, community, and resistance—a closed kind. On October 19, 2002, the Vatican issued a long-awaited and surprisingly terse response regarding the sexual abuse scandal. According to the *New York Times*, "far from providing a conclusive resolution to the sexual abuse crisis," the Vatican "only called for yet another committee to consider it further." If the Vatican itself is so intransigent in coming to grips with this pervasive scandal, and in fact seems to be engaging in institutional denial and stonewalling, one can't help but ask: To whom is it pious? Where is its faithfulness and fidelity directed?

George Weigel, a modern Catholic theologian, echoes in his own way Carroll's call for a new form of piety, which he seems to equate with fidelity. He writes in *The Courage to Be Catholic* that the " 'answer' to the scandal of clerical sexual abuse is fidelity—a deeper conversion of American priests to Christ. No set of revised clergy personnel policies can induce a revolution of fidelity and deepened conversion among priests." Such a revolution in fidelity and accompanying deeper conversion, he stresses, would apply only to priests who have not committed unconscionable acts. "A priest who sexually abuses the young," he asserts, "has so disfigured himself as an icon of the eternal priesthood that he cannot function any longer as a priest. Period."

Rather than the "deeper conversion . . . to Christ" that Weigel calls for, perhaps what is needed is a deeper conversion of character. Clearly, some who make vows to God (or to anyone, for that matter) do so with the idea that the vow itself obviates the necessity of confronting one's darker impulses or baser inclinations, that somehow the vow itself will put an end to such impulses or sublimate them and bring about a conversion in character. But for most humans, this rarely happens or lasts for long. What is needed is honest confrontation of one's character, then visualization and articulation of the character one would like to forge and become—and then making an unflagging commitment to this conversion. This is not a matter of naked confession, simply admitting one's failings—as if such a purging is in itself all that's necessary to bring about a deeper conversion—but of confronting, perhaps with others, or perhaps alone, one's failings and fears, with the intent of then determining how to face up to and overcome them. This is very different from an approach in which one is first faithful to the expectations of others, without ever having taken the opportunity to learn what one's own expectations are, much less how to be faithful to them. A deeper conversion among priests likely will stand greater chance of success if, contrary to what Weigel asserts, priests are no longer placed on impossible pedestals as "icons," but instead are seen as no more or less human than anyone else. Only then can any sort of "revolution of fidelity" take place.

Shakespeare's Hamlet says, "This above all: To thine own self be true," and then says, "And it must follow, as the night the day, thou canst not be false to any man." Might this "being true" be an integral part of any piety? Can you ever be true to others if you first aren't true to yourself?

—

For true "conversion in character," one can hardly find a better example than St. Francis of Assisi (1182–1226). According to the *Dictionary of Saints*, St. Francis "spent his youth in extravagant living and pleasure-seeking." But in 1206, he underwent a dramatic character overhaul that inspired him to give up his huge family inheritance and donate it to the poor. He consequently "devoted himself to a life of poverty and care of the sick and poor," and gave himself over completely to "his life's work of poverty and preaching." St. Francis never became an ordained priest, much less rose through the Catholic hierarchy; he had no desire for such trappings. And yet "probably no saint has affected so many in so many different ways." St. Francis often went without food and shelter, and at times he was treated worse than the poor to whom he reached out; but by all accounts he was a very contented and fulfilled person.

While the Church was embroiled in scandal in the thirteenth century, St. Francis wrote a discourse on how Christian virtues—"compassion, kindness, humility, gentleness, patience, and love"—enabled one to overcome the most deadly of vices or sins. In a sense, he was offering a prescription for those in the corrupt Church hierarchy who committed knowingly the "Seven Deadly Sins," spelled out in the Roman Catechism: Pride, Anger, Envy, Laziness or Sloth, Avarice or Covetousness, Gluttony, and Lechery, which Chaucer considered "the general root of all evils."

"Whoever possesses one [of the virtues] . . . possesses all," wrote St. Francis. "And whoever offends one [of the virtues] does not possess any of them, and offends them all." This seems to imply that it is impossible to have one of the virtues without having all of them, and is much in line with Socrates' own thinking on the subject.

St. Francis's selfless and Spartan approach to leading a Christian life inspired the founding of several religious orders, but even though he is widely considered one of the Church's eminent reformers, he rarely if ever spoke out directly about reform. Rather, like Socrates, he seemed to feel that the best way to inspire reform in others was by personal example.

St. Francis set a lifelong example of a type of piety that is as rare as it is admirable. He lived in ascetic simplicity, and was by all accounts a person of unparalleled compassion for the down-and-out and ostracized. For St. Francis, to be pious didn't just mean to live according to Church strictures, or to attend Mass as required. Rather, it meant to "live the gospel life," to inspire others to do the same, and to show compassion and charity and love for all God's creatures.

## NEIGHBORLY PIETY

It is the night before Ramadan, an important Islamic holy event that takes place in the ninth month of the Muslim calendar. Many non-Muslims know mainly that during the month of Ramadan, people of the Muslim faith fast during the day; but its primary purpose is for worship and reflection, and to strengthen community ties.

I'm gathered with about fifteen Islamic men, women, and children in a café in a large midwestern city. We're clustered by a large picture window near the café entrance. Several seem somewhat jittery whenever someone outside walks by and stops to peer inside at us. Almost to a person, those here say that this is one of the few times they've been to a public place after work hours since September 11, 2001.

This gathering was arranged hastily. Just the night before, at a book signing for *Socrates Café*, Ghaleb, a soft-spoken man originally from Iran, his little boy at his side, waited until I'd finished signing books and talking with everyone else, then approached me. He told me that

since the tragic events of September 11, a little over two months earlier, the Islamic community in the city had met with increasing suspicion, and even hostility, from other local denizens. He said that recent
immigrants in the area, from countries like Somalia and Yemen and
Iraq and Iran, were feeling increasingly isolated and fearful.

He asked me if I might hold a dialogue with them, saying that it
might be beneficial and even inspiring to them in a number of
respects. He said it would give them a chance to reflect. Most of all, he
said those taking part would find it gratifying that someone from the
United States would genuinely like to get to know them and learn
more about their values and beliefs, which in his opinion, had been
distorted by the media.

I told him I'd be delighted to take part in a dialogue, but that I was
only in town for one more night. He quickly set about arranging for
us to gather at a local independent café the following evening.

—

Try as I might, the people with whom I am set to hold a dialogue are
not comfortable picking one of the six questions themselves. They
insist that I ask them a question—that I, as their guest, should have
the honor of choosing the question.

I finally settle on "What is piety?"

"Piety—or as it is called in Arabic, taqwa—means right conduct in
the service of God," replies Hammad, who immigrated here with his
family from Iran four years earlier.

"What do you mean by 'right conduct'?" I ask.

"Conduct that would please God. Conduct that would further
God's ends. The name of our religion, Islam, means to 'give ourselves
up to the will of God,' and God's will is that we only do those things
that please him."

Ghaleb, my host, says, "Muslims believe in khilafa, that we are stewards or caretakers of this world, because Allah, or God, commands us to tend to the world's needs, because this is what is righteous. The Quran, which is the word of God, says in chapter forty-nine, verse thirteen, 'The most honored of you in the sight of God is the most righteous among you.'"

Then he says to me, "This righteousness *is* piety, because it is righteousness in the service of God. There can be no piety if you are not acting on God's behalf."

"Why can't you act rightly without doing so on God's behalf?" I ask.

"Because it is God who instructs you how to act rightly," says Abdul, who is Palestinian, and is a construction foreman. "It is God who instructs Muslims that piety is the cardinal virtue, made up of many other virtues, like love, respect, reverence, a sense of duty and commitment to God, and to one's fellow humans."

"Can a person who doesn't believe in God be pious?" I ask.

"Well, they may say they don't believe in God, but if they act rightly, then they are serving God's ends, even if they don't acknowledge it."

He then says, "When a person isn't pious, he's in conflict with himself, and he creates conflict with others—and with God. Muslims believe in a harmonious and peaceful universe based on *tawhid*, which is the unity of God and his creations."

"Can someone give me an example of 'piety in action,' as a type of service, in the name of God, that creates more harmony?" I ask.

Syed, dressed in a typical Western suit, sitting between his wife and young daughter, both of whom are wearing ankle-length robes and partial veils, says, "A big part of right conduct in service to God is reaching out to your neighbor."

"How so?"

"After September eleventh, whenever neighbors saw me, they'd close their doors immediately," Syed tells me. "They'd never been really friendly, but they'd never been overly cold toward us. All that changed after September eleventh. They wished we'd just go away. This was very hard for us. We'd lived in refugee camps for two years before coming here from the African continent, escaping the civil war in my homeland of Somalia. We thought we'd left hostility behind. I have a good job at a printing press, my child is getting a good education, my wife has been happy to be resettled here. After September eleventh, once again we felt like we would never be able to live in peace and safety, in a welcoming environment."

He goes on: "We didn't go away, but we tried to be as invisible as possible, because we were even more afraid of our neighbors than they were of us. A number of mosques in the area have been vandalized. And some people who'd recently arrived here from Muslim countries were taken into custody, after they didn't have their immigration papers on hand. A lot of us here have been approached by the police since nine-eleven." Several nod. "This made us fearful even to go outdoors. And many of our children were teased at school. Their classmates call them 'terrorists.' "

He falls silent, visibly upset. His wife, Afaf, puts her arm around him. Eventually, Syed continues, "I asked myself, 'Why do our neighbors hate us? What have we ever done to them?' I thought they should be glad we're here. We start businesses, we live in homes and apartments that sometimes had been vacant for years. We work at least six days a week, and live honest, decent lives. I thought, 'What's their problem?'

"My wife said to me one day, 'What have we done to be good neighbors?' I was shocked. I looked at her and said, 'What haven't we done? We work hard, play by the rules, never cause trouble. What more could anyone want?' "

Afaf now says, "I told him, 'There's more to being a good neighbor than that. Being a good neighbor is . . . being neighborly. It's reaching out to others, especially in difficult times.' I said to my husband, 'What have we done to show them that we care about them, and put at ease their fears about us?' "

Her husband says to me, "At first, I wouldn't accept what she said. But then I began to wonder: Have I conducted myself piously, as God would want, toward my neighbors—in a way that would build love and trust rather than fear and suspicion?' Because they shouldn't think that a handful of terrorists represent in any way the one-point-seven billion Muslims around the world.

"My wife was right. I hadn't been a good neighbor. The core of Islamic piety is to revere God by showing compassion to others. But I'd been so caught up in self-pity, it hadn't occurred to me, until my talk with my wife, that I needed to begin putting others' concerns first. That changed my entire approach to the 'problem.'

"We all have a piece of God within us, and our highest service is bringing out this piece of God, this pure goodness, of others. When we do that, we further reveal the goodness within ourselves. So I began to think, how can I practice compassion?"

Sherwa, the man beside him, an Ethiopian immigrant who lives two doors down from him, now says to me, "Syed's brainstorm was to hold a cookout. At first, I thought he was nuts. But when he told me about his conversation with his wife, he won me over, and I agreed to help. We put a sign in our yards announcing the cookout. And every time we saw neighbors on the sidewalk, we'd approach them. Sometimes they'd stop, like they were frozen in fear. But most of their frowns turned into smiles when we told them what we wanted to do."

As he caresses his twin children, one perched on each knee, Sherwa says, "It was a big success. About thirty people came. Our children played together. Adults engaged in a lot of small talk, though once in a while mention of nine-eleven would come up. Some seemed surprised—maybe relieved—to see how angry and upset we were about it. And even those who didn't come found out about the cookout from those who did."

"Since then," he says, "most people in our neighborhood have been much friendlier. Now we're planning a 'friendship walk' to our mosque.

"It all started with reaching out to our neighbors. If we hadn't done this act of piety, Osama Bin Laden and his fanatics would really have won. But we didn't let this happen. We obeyed the Quran, where it says in chapter three, verse one hundred that Muslims must 'take part in the good and forbid the wrong.' This is a type of piety we can practice in our everyday lives, by having cookouts and friendship walks, and so building good while preventing wrong."

"Islamic piety," says Omar, the owner of a small variety store, "is a reverential respect for others, based on a belief in the sanctity of human life. There are people everywhere who claim to do acts in the name of God, who claim to hold life sacred, but who pervert piety. Those here in the U.S. who commit hate crimes are of that sort, and of course Osama Bin Laden and his followers are. The Quran says that God honors the most righteous, and that 'God has complete knowledge of all things.' So God knows of all our actions, and will judge us accordingly. Bin Laden will have a bad day, the day he stands before God."

Another says, "Osama's followers praise the 'force' of his piety. It's force, yes, but force by torture and terrorism by a bloodthirsty man, not force of sincere belief in the Quran or in Allah."

The longshoreman philosopher Eric Hoffer, in *The True Believer*, wrote that "(t)he proselytizing fanatic strengthens his own faith by converting others. The creed whose legitimacy is most easily challenged is likely to develop the strongest proselytizing impulse." He goes on to say that such movements, "irrespective of the doctrine they preach and project, breed fanaticism . . . hatred, and intolerance." Theirs is a piety with inhumane ends.

Fuad, whose face is severely disfigured, says after a pause, "Charity is the key to piety. The Quran, chapter two verse one hundred seventy-seven, says that piety 'does not mean that you turn your faces towards the east or west,' but that you 'spend your wealth for love of Him, for your kindred, and orphans, and the needy, and the wayfarer in need, for those who ask . . . and practice regular charity.' "

This conception of piety is very similar to that of the Christian theologian and philosopher St. Augustine (354–386 A.D.), who in his work *The City of God* describes piety as "works of charity which arise from the fact that God enjoins the performance of such works, and declares that He is pleased with them . . . "

Fuad then says, "A pious person is charitable to all people, but especially to his loved ones." He is silent for a moment, before continuing: "I was a warrior in Somalia. I fought for democracy. When I was captured, I was tortured. I escaped, and eventually was able to come to America."

"Several here are members of my clan in Somalia," he tells me. "We escaped the civil strife in Mogadishu, the capital of our country, where warlords with perverted piety manipulated clans into fighting one another—even though clans are supposed to be sacred forms of community. When we came here, we left thousands behind who are in our clan. Until last month, we were able to send a portion of our incomes back to them. They live on the brink of starvation. The *hawala*, or money-transfer system, that we had in place here to wire money to our clan members back home, was the difference to them between life and death. It leaves us with less money for our own needs, but we please God by doing this."

Fuad shakes his head and says, "Two weeks ago, the U.S. government closed down all of the *hawalas*. They claim they may be linked to Al-Qaeda, though there is no proof that any of them have anything to do with that. We don't know what to do. Without this money we send them, they will starve. To us, the U.S. government's decision is one of impiety, because we can't be charitable to our loved ones back home.

"The *hawala* system is pious, because it allows us to be charitable. It is a big part of the way we fulfill Allah's commandment to give to those who are in need."

There's an extended silence before Musse, who immigrated from Yemen, says, "Every time I reach out to another person, here or back home, I think I am doing God's work."

He then says, "Imam Ali ibn Abi Talib, our first imam and a cousin of the Prophet, wrote in *Nahjul Balagha*, which translates as *Peak of Eloquence*, that piety is 'the key to honesty and purity and to acquiring merit . . . ' He says piety is 'freedom from the chains of bondage, salvation from the blows of every adversity,' and that it 'puts a man's goals within his grasp, fends off evil . . . and helps him realize his heart's desires.' "

"When the imam said this," Musse tells us, "he was fighting against terrible corruption and oppression. Like then, these are dangerous times, filled with hate and fear and suspicion. Like then, it's up to the pious to overcome this. As the Prophet Muhammad said, 'The only distinction between human beings that God recognizes is spiritual excellence and genuine piety.' "

Karen Armstrong says in her book *Islam* that "the notions of social justice, equality, tolerance and practical compassion" served as "the mainspring of Islamic spirituality." Those taking part in this dialogue seemed intent on staying faithful to these notions, in service to Allah.

## SOCRATIC PIETY

In Plato's dialogue *Euthyphro*, the sophist Euthyphro first says that piety is "saying and doing that which is pleasing to the gods by praying and sacrificing." Socrates rebukes this view, saying that the gods do not need such "commercial exchanges." Because the gods are already are perfect, and their needs already are met, Socrates maintained that they needed no sacrificial offerings from humans. After establishing that all good in our lives comes from the gods—that the gods are incapable of doing or creating evil—Socrates then asks, "What works and deeds do we undertake," as servants to the gods, "that are of service" to them? The most significant aspect of the question is "lost" to Euthyphro, according to the late eminent Socrates scholar Gregory Vlastos, because the groundbreaking notion set forth by Socrates— "that the gods have work to do, work in which human beings could assist them"—is one that until then was "foreign to Greek religion," and so couldn't be readily grasped by most.

Greeks in Socrates' time, Vlastos writes, believed that the gods were capable of a "whole range of divine activity which torments and destroys the innocent no less than the guilty, . . . careless of the moral havoc it creates." But Socrates, Vlastos contends, was setting forth an entirely new notion of the gods, as those who "can only be good, never evil," as those who "can only cause good, can never be the cause of evil to anyone, man or god." To Socrates, the gods "are of their very nature relentlessly beneficent: they want for men nothing but what men would want for themselves if their will were undividedly will for good." Vlastos says, "Heirs of the Hebraic and Christian traditions" would not find this perspective a "bold" one—and, I would add, neither would those of Islamic traditions, and many other religious traditions—but "(f)or those bred on Greek beliefs about the gods it would be shattering."

Vlastos says that Socrates "saw his own work, in summoning all and sundry [people] to perfect their soul, as work he did . . . as his own service to the gods." Socrates, in other words, was defining piety as "doing . . . work the gods want done." In the *Euthyphro* and in *The Apology*, Socrates makes even clearer his philosophy of piety: "Piety is doing the gods' work to benefit human beings."

Socrates believed that by undertaking those works and deeds that best utilize our talents to benefit humanity, we are also doing that which is of most benefit to ourselves—that which makes us happiest.

To Socrates, his talents, in serving the ends of the gods, were best suited to inspiring others to lead the examined life. He showed others how to explore the world in and around them in ways that would best enable them to gain forms of knowledge—what I would call pious knowledge—that led to greater human excellence, and so benefited all human beings.

What is pious knowledge? Edward W. Said, the noted Middle East scholar, offers a good working definition in *Covering Islam*, when he describes it as "something to be won to the service of coexistence and community" rather than "of particular races, nations, classes, or religions." Such knowledge builds bridges of understanding, and further cultivates a type of social conscience that inspires people to create a type of world that enables all to live in dignity. It is a type of knowledge cultivated in the service of humanity.

—

What if we chose to emulate Socrates' notion of service to humanity without harboring a belief in any sort of god or gods? What if we believed that good works are their own reward—were, in a way, "holy," in and of themselves? Would that make us impious?

Gregory Vlastos poses this question: "Would Socrates have given his life to this task" of creating a more excellent society "if his piety" for the gods "had not driven him to it"—particularly in light of the fact that his actions seemed "thankless," given the eventual collapse of Athenian society, and his own execution?

Vlastos insists that Socrates would not have given his life to this task if he had not believed that there were gods. He says that if not for the fact that Socrates received a "divine command," there is "no reason to believe that he would have ever become a street-philosopher . . . forcing himself on people who have neither taste nor talent for philosophy."

Socrates *did* thrust himself on people, in the sense that he held dialogues in places where anyone could join in. In doing so, he inspired those who may otherwise never have had a chance to know the joys of philosophical inquiry to experience it firsthand. While he may have derived his ideas of virtue, and virtuous conduct, from then-contemporary beliefs of the gods, this doesn't necessarily mean that if he dispensed with his belief in the gods, he would not have acted this way. For instance, the great human-rights activist Mohandas Gandhi, as V. S. Naipaul wrote in *Beyond Belief*, "got his social ideas from Christianity," though Gandhi was never Christian. In a similar vein, while Socrates initially "got his social ideas" from the gods of his day, this is by no means to say that he had to be a "true believer" in order to devote himself to his chosen life's work.

―

I think Socrates would have lived precisely as he had lived, with the same sense of mission, even if he came to the conclusion that there were no gods. Moreover, his unique notion of service, and his "will to do good," for the benefit of humanity, likely informed his views of the gods every bit as much as the other way around.

It's also important to note that Socrates did not preach and proselytize as typical "believers" do. His iconoclastic form of proselytizing was to set an example of how a certain way of living and questioning is its own reward. Those whom he "converted" were not subject to any hard sell, but were inspired to follow the example he set of personal autonomy and integrity.

The classical Greek historian Xenophon writes in his *Memorabilia* that he, for one, is "amazed that Athenians were convinced that Socrates . . . did anything that constituted impiety toward the gods." On the contrary, says Xenophon, Socrates "prevented many [Athenians from being impious], and instilled in them a desire for virtue, giving them hope that if they cultivated themselves, they would be good and noble." As Xenophon put it, "by being the type of person he was, he inspired those with whom he passed time to hope that by emulating him, they could become such a person, too. . . . How could such a man corrupt the youth, unless concern for virtue is corruptive?"

There, of course, was the rub: Those corrupt people in power believed his "concern for virtue" was indeed "corruptive"—corruptive to *them*, in the sense that if too many people came to emulate Socrates, the corrupt would be removed from power.

IS
EXCELLENCE
STILL POSSIBLE?

# STRIVING FOR EXCELLENCE TODAY

In the popular movie *Gladiator*, released in 2000, after caressing for a moment a sculpture of Socrates, Comitus learns from his father, Caesar, that he will not be the next king, for "Rome is to be a republic again."

Comitus, deeply upset over these tidings, says to his father, "You wrote to me once, listing four chief virtues: wisdom, justice, fortitude, and temperance." Comitus then says, "As I read the list, I knew that I had none of them."

Then, with great emotion, Comitus says, "But I have other virtues, Father."

He ticks them off: "Ambition—that can be a virtue when it drives us to excel. Resourcefulness. Courage—perhaps not on the battlefield, but there are other forms of courage. Devotion—to my family and to you." Then he laments, "But none of my virtues are on your list."

The virtues Comitus possessed drove him to kill his father, destroy the gladiator Maximus, and derail society. Caesar had planned to hand over the reins of power to Maximus, because he possessed the virtues on his list—virtues that were determined by Maximus's interest foremost in the long-term excellence of his people. Comitus's set of virtues, conversely, represented an extremely self-aggrandizing type, which were determined by his interest, above all else, in his personal gain and glory, and his willingness to commit any act, no matter how base, to elevate himself at the expense of everyone else.

—

Socrates believed that once each person gained sufficient knowledge, he would become committed to excellence, because to do so was part of our "ultimate" nature. I don't believe, though, that we have any such ultimate nature, any more than we have, as some philosophers contend, dual natures of good and evil. Rather, I suspect we have dueling natures, all of which are competing with one another, jostling and jousting to come out on top. But instead of discovering this nature within by some sort of self-absorbed introspection, we discover it through our works and deeds in the world.

Ultimately, even if we each aspired to what most would consider the most excellent ends, no one set of virtues would serve in every circumstance. To achieve certain ends, every situation may demand different virtues, and different degrees of certain virtues. And of course, our ends themselves, no matter how oriented they are toward excellence, are never absolute. Even if we all agreed that we should aspire to create a society where everyone can live in dignity and can realize his or her potential, we would have competing ideas of dignity, of potential, of the type or types of potential and dignity we should strive for. And, of course, we all have different talents and unique ways of making a contribution to reach these ends. But what distinguishes an excellent society from others is that its members can constantly test out their ideas, compare them with others', and create and experiment with new ones, as they all the while remain committed to the end of advancing humanity.

———

There are no tidy formulas—no single set of virtues, no cardinal ones, no civic ones, that will infallibly or inevitably lead to excellent ends, which themselves change as one experiments and cultivates a greater intellectual, social, and imaginative vision. Sometimes patience can be a great virtue, sometimes utter impatience, sometimes both. Sometimes love, but sometimes hate—hatred of intolerance, of poverty, of oppression—born of love. There may be occasions when blunt honesty is called for; others in which someone must unflinchingly tell a falsehood; still others in which the truth must be revealed, but in small and palatable doses.

This does not in any way mean that morals are relative—only that they are *relational* to specific moral contexts. A person who agonizes over what to do in each situation that demands an ethical response may still operate from "universal premises." You may be someone who respects the rights and well-being of others, and indeed believe that you can realize your fullest potential only if you act so that others are enabled to do the same. But you may also recognize that there can be exceptions to any ethical rule. You may operate from dictums of "honesty is the best policy," of "do no harm," and yet recognize that in rare cases there are warrantable and necessary exceptions. You may recognize that there are some forms of harm that you *do* want to do to others. As I hold dialogues around the globe, participants sometimes do wonderfully violent harm to my worldview, as they expose me to alternative perspectives. Obviously, even this "code" of self-scrutiny, self-improvement, and striving for the long-term good that I'm suggesting here should be subject to continual scrutiny; it is not set in stone. As you act more in the world and gain more experiences, and learn more about other peoples and cultures, your idea of what an excellent person is, and what an excellent society is, may and probably will change over time. But over time, the commitment you have to becoming a more excellent person, and to helping create a more excellent society on a local and global scale, may become more steadfast than ever.

—

Still, it does seem that some virtues or qualities do play a more prominent and "universal" role than others. A sense of social justice, a degree of courage, a decided piety toward humanity, an element of love or empathy for others seem to be imbued in the ethos of the most memorable people over the eras who have worked for positive social change.

Patience may be a virtue, but it may also be a horrible vice, depending on one's ends. Osama Bin Laden's horribly well-executed attack on the United States, meticulously planned over several years, is a too-familiar example of patience as the worst vice, since it served inhumane ends. He convinced those who carried out the plot he hatched that their ends were excellent; but in truth his ends are to create a closed and oppressive society with vindictive and arbitrary "justice" at its core. His ends are the furthest thing from excellent, and would in no way address or ameliorate the social dilemmas in society about which he has sporadically professed concern.

Sometimes a combination of patience and impatience may be called for in achieving excellent ends. I may be impatient to do what I can to create a more open and egalitarian society, and yet work with deliberate patience tempered by persistence to achieve these ends, recognizing that in my practical efforts, impatience born of exasperation may be detrimental to achieving my long-term goals.

I think an excellent individual and an excellent civilization do share certain attributes: They are forward-looking. They are cognizant of how their actions impact others, not just today, but in coming generations, and strive to act in ways that will enhance the lives of individuals and societies not just of today, but also of the future—and not just the next one or two or five generations, but the next hundred and thousand and ten thousand generations.

To this end, at minimum, they forever strive to diminish, rather than increase, those types of human suffering born of a lack of food, shelter, clothing, education, and self-determination, not just within its national bounds, but, as much as possible, globally as well. They not only seek to liberate people from death and terror and oppression, but they also go the next step, and aim to give everyone the opportunity to discover and develop their unique intellectual and physical, spiritual and moral, aesthetic and cultural potentials.

# EXCELLENCE IN CIVILIZATIONS PAST

Do all civilizations committed to becoming more virtuous have a certain shelf life? Is it part of their makeup that they are doomed to fall after they've risen awhile? Or is it possible, if we learn from past mistakes and patterns, to chart a course that will enable individual societies, and perhaps society on a global scale, to continue on an ever-onward-and-upward course toward excellence, without ever peaking once and for all?

Jean Yarbrough writes that Thomas Jefferson "argued strongly against relying too heavily on the wisdom of the past" in seeking to become a more excellent society. Still, Jefferson did believe that we "must study well the vices that corrupted earlier republics," if modern society is to achieve higher and more sustaining levels of excellence than those in the past. "If they fail to heed these melancholy lessons, America will degenerate, just as surely as Greece and Rome before her."

What are these "melancholy lessons"?

Let's take two ostensibly polar-opposite civilizations whose ethical landscapes more than compensated for deficiencies in their *terra firma*. These civilizations were situated on far-flung parts of the globe. One was brought down by outsiders, while one brought itself down. For a time, they were unrivaled paradigms of excellence.

First, let's look at the Aztecs, who the French archaeologist Jacques Soustelle said had "one of the few cultures of which mankind can be proud." Ultimately, the Aztecs were decimated by invading Spaniards, who considered it their "manifest destiny" to use their guns, germs, and steel to appropriate the Aztec land, and either to enslave or destroy the indigenous "heathens." The Spaniards believed that in doing so, they were realizing the will of their god, and putting themselves well on the road to immortality. They believed they were indisputably both more human and more divine than those they encountered—in fact, it's doubtful that they viewed those they conquered as human at all—and that it was their god-given right and duty to obliterate anyone who stood in the way of fulfilling their destiny.

Is this a complex worldview, much less a profound value system that reflects an excellent society? I think not. Rather, their values and ends bring into stark relief the contradiction between societies that are technologically advanced, and yet have a simplistically barbaric ethic. Since these tend to be the types of societies that survive and thrive throughout human history, they serve as exemplary cautionary tales when we examine today where we're going, and when we speculate about the prospects of sustaining human excellence over the long term.

Michael D. Coe, professor emeritus of anthropology and curator emeritus at the Peabody Museum of Natural History at Yale University, writes that the Aztecs, unlike the Spanish *conquistadores*, believed that they dwelt in a tempestuous and hostile universe presided over by capricious deities." Coe says it was this clear-eyed outlook that for centuries enabled and inspired the Aztecs "not only to survive misfortunes, disasters, privations which would have broken others, but also to create one of the most advanced political states ever seen in Mexico"—or elsewhere, I would add.

The Aztecs, who were brought up "in the most stern fashion in their homes and schools, trained to withstand cold and hunger . . . embodied ideals which would have done credit to an 'old Roman.' " These primary ideals, or virtues, Coe writes, were "self-restraint and humility," and they were "expected even of those whose fortunes soared, including the emperors themselves." These virtues are reflected in this Aztec codex:

The mature man:
A heart as firm as stone,
A wise countenance,

The owner of a face, a heart,
Capable of understanding.

Coe points out that such a view is the polar opposite of "the mega-lomaniac self-esteem and lust for riches exhibited . . . by the Spaniards." He also stresses that the widely held, and errant, "image of the Aztec people as bloodthirsty savages bent only on rapine and mur-der" was one originated and "carefully fostered by the *conquistadores*" themselves—and sadly is perpetuated by many today, even though it "is belied by the great compendium" of extant works of Aztec art and poetry and philosophy and architecture.[1]

To whom did the Aztecs owe such an excellent worldview? Their philosophers, the *Tlamantinime*. Though to this day unheralded, the *Tlamantinime*, in their way, were every bit as astute and worthy of note as the philosophers of ancient Greece. Mexican anthropologist Miguel León-Portilla, in *Aztec Thought and Culture*, notes that the *Tlamantinime*—which means "knowers of things"—created and developed for their people "the cultural standards to be transmitted from generation to generation through . . . a well-defined moral code, history, and art." They succeeded in engendering "an authentically creative movement of immediate social significance." They were, first and foremost, "interested in the assimilation of individuals into the life and highest ideals of the community," and so "focused on what is most elevated and significant about man, his person, 'his good heart, human and stout.' "

---

1. None of this is to gainsay or gloss over the violent nature of Aztec rites. But if one puts it in context, as does scholar Philip P. Arnold, one cannot overlook or ignore the fact that "throughout the Americas, Europeans killed or were directly involved in the deaths of mil-lions more human beings than the Aztecs." What is more, "while the Aztecs fully understood the violent nature of human existence and articulated it in their rituals, Europeans, while professing a peace-ful yet millenarian-utopian dream, were unable" — or, more aptly, unwilling — "to reconcile those dreams with the brutality of colonialism."

To support his view, León-Portilla cites a translation of one of the *Tlamantinime* codexes:

Even if he were poor or lowly,
... only his way of life mattered ...
The purity of his heart,
His good and humane heart
His stout heart. . . .

This codex, says León-Portilla, is representative of a society that held "the highest humanistic ideal." Another ancient Aztec document that has been discovered shows that Aztec children were taught, beginning at a young age, "how they should live, how they should respect others, how they were to dedicate themselves to what was good and righteous; how they were to avoid evil, fleeing unrighteousness with strength, refraining from perversion and greed."

The Franciscan friar Bernardino de Sahagun (1500–90), the first to take an abiding interesting in studying the Aztec value system, says that the *Tlamantinime* "taught ... from experience that in order to live morally and virtuously, it was necessary to have rigorous discipline, austerity, and continuous work in things beneficial to the state." Moreover, the Aztecs' continual effort at developing a more "meaningful moral code was not at all related to a desire for reward in the afterlife," writes León-Portilla, but simply due to their goal of becoming of more " true face and heart," and their "quest for self-completeness and sincere social approbation."

What enabled the Spanish *conquistadores* to obliterate this excellent civilization in such short order? Michael Coe notes that the Aztecs believed that when one fought, one should do so in a virtuous way, in which combatants were equally and fairly matched. But this concept of a " 'level playing field' meant nothing to the Spaniards, whom the Aztec warriors perceived as cowards—they shot their weapons at a distance, avoided hand-to-hand combat with native braves, and took refuge behind their cannons." Coe says that to the Aztecs, "the Spanish policy of wholesale terror, so well exemplified by the act of Cortes [the leader of the *conquistadores*] in cutting off the hands of over fifty . . . [Aztec] emissaries admitted in peace into the Spanish camp . . . ," was "equally incomprehensible." The *conquistadores* believed that winning at all costs, no matter how amoral the methods they used, was all that mattered. To the Aztecs, victory without virtue was worthless.

—

Do today's most technologically advanced societies have an ethic at least as equally excellent as the Aztecs', or are they bogged down in the same type of worldview that enabled the Spaniards of old to conquer without feeling the slightest twinge of conscience?

Victor Davis Hanson, professor of classics at California State University, writes in *Carnage and Culture* that, if anything, the Western powers today are more entrenched and smitten than ever by the approach perfected by the *conquistadores*: "The Western way of war is lethal precisely because it is so amoral—shackled rarely by concerns of ritual, tradition, religion, or ethics, by anything other than military necessity."

What happened to the Aztecs, then, leads to this question: Is a virtuous civilization doomed to end precisely because of its belief that certain ideals are so precious that they must be nurtured and adhered to, even at the cost of its very survival?

—

What about a society that, by almost anyone's standards, was dedicated to excellence—only to abandon it suddenly, with no prompting or prodding from an outside aggressor? Let's look at "unjust, imperfect, reflective, disputatious, democratic Greece," where, as Earl Shorris put it, "the glory . . . was not the answers but the questions." The Greek scholar H. D. F. Kitto writes that the Athenians of old had developed "a totally new conception of what human life was for," which catalyzed an unprecedented flourishing of creativity and experimentation.

In his bestseller *Guns, Germs, and Steel: The Fates of Human Societies*, Pulitzer Prize–winning author Jared Diamond, professor of physiology at the UCLA School of Medicine, contends that throughout human history, "real estate" determines whether a given society flourishes, and so whether a people progresses or declines. Diamond maintains that the advantages accrued by living on land rich with natural resources and tributaries, and ideal for the development of complex agricultural systems enabled some societies to become incomparably more advanced and complex technologically than others.

In developing his "historical science," Diamond conveniently overlooks how ancient Athens excelled over other societies on the continent (or anywhere else), despite the fact that its real estate—which Diamond claims is *the* determinant in whether a society flourishes—was a quintessential hindrance, rather than a help, in enabling it to attain excellence. As Victor David Hanson writes, "Few ancient societies . . . were situated in a more *disadvantageous* position than Greece." At the time, Athens was "neighbor to a hostile . . . empire, . . . with less than half its land arable, without a single large navigable river, cursed with almost no abundance of natural resources . . . , its tiny and vulnerable island polities closer to Asia than Europe." Yet it excelled anyway, like no other.

Why?

In large measure, it was its system of government—self-government and collective government—that the Greeks constructed on top of their *terra firma*. The Greek polis, or city-state, H. D. F. Kitto wrote, "was made for the amateur. Its ideal was that every citizen . . . should play his part in all of its many activities . . . It implies a respect for wholeness or the oneness of life, and a consequent dislike of specialization. . . . [In] democratic Athens . . . a man owed it to himself, as well as to the polis, to be everything in turn." Each individual owed it to the rest of society to be as excellent as he could be.

The social and political philosopher Karl Popper (1902–94) includes in his book *The Open Society and Its Enemies* the funeral speech of Pericles, as transcribed by the classic Greek historian Thucydides, in which the Athenian leader said this about ancient Athens's democracy:

> . . . We do not copy our neighbors, but try to be an example. Our administration favors the many instead of the few: this is why it is called a democracy. The laws afford equal justice to all alike . . . but we do not ignore the claims of excellence. When a citizen distinguishes himself, . . . he will be called to serve the state . . . , not as a matter of privilege, but as a reward of merit . . . The freedom we enjoy extends . . . to ordinary life . . . Our city is thrown open to the world; we never expel a foreigner . . . We are free to live exactly as we please, and yet, we are always ready to face any danger. . . . We love beauty without indulging in fancies, and although we try to improve our intellect this does not weaken our will . . . We consider a man who takes no interest in the state not as harmless, but as useless . . . We do not look upon discussion as a stumbling block in the way of political action, but as an indispensable preliminary to acting wisely . . .

The depth and breadth of freedom, or range of freedoms, that the

Greeks of Pericles' era enjoyed flourished to an unrivaled extent. In Hellenistic Greece, as the classics scholar E. R. Dodds notes, "it mattered little where a man had been born or what his ancestry was." For centuries, the city's institutions "stood exposed to rational criticism; its traditional ways of life were increasingly penetrated and modified by a cosmopolitan culture." Just as important, in addition to a "leveling out of local determinants," there was "a new freedom for the mind to travel backwards in time and choose at will from the past experience of men those elements which it could best assimilate and exploit." Even more important, I think, is that the mind had the freedom to travel *forward*, to imagine and experiment with completely new possibilities of being in the world. So it was not just, as Dodds put it, that "(t)he individual began consciously to use the tradition, instead of being used by it," but that the individual began consciously to envision and experiment with altogether new traditions.

This experiment in excellence, however, didn't last. Kitto writes that the fall of ancient Athens represented a "sudden collapse of a whole . . . system."

What happened?

Kitto says that the collective pursuit of excellence was replaced with "political lethargy, almost . . . indifference." Suddenly, "men were interested in other things than the polis." By the time they realized they were sealing their own doom, it was "too late" to change course. This unraveling wasn't merely due to the fact that Athens was "exhausted by the long Peloponnesian War," maintains Kitto, because history shows that "(f)rom such exhaustion, communities recover," as the United States did after the Vietnam War. What happened, rather, was "a permanent change in the temper of the people" and "the emergence of a different attitude of life."

There was a wholesale upheaval in the set of virtues by which the citizenry guided itself: "For generations Greek morality . . . had remained severely traditional, based on the cardinal virtues of Justice, Courage, Self-restraint [moderation] and Wisdom. Poet after poet had preached . . . the beauty of Justice, the dangers of Ambition, the folly of Violence." This created "the foundation, simple and strong, on which a common life could be built." But by the fifth century, this had altered dramatically. Citizens no longer harbored any collective sense that they were working toward shared ends, with the paramount goal of becoming more excellent. Kitto concludes that there was an "intimate connection" between the rampant rise of individualism—in which there was an obsessive concern "with individual traits, with passing moods, instead of trying to express," much less discover, "the ideal or universal"—and the dissolution of the Athenian *polis*. Athens crumbled from within, needing no outside aggressor with the advantages wrought by superior real estate to bring it down.

Socrates did not enter the scene front and center in ancient Athens until it was already in a state of irreversible decline. Before then, Athenians were too caught up in living the excellent life to take pause and inquire about it. It seems that throughout history, people begin to gather and examine moral questions in earnest only after they recognize that their society has, perhaps irretrievably, lost its moral compass, and is far removed from excellence.

In the Golden Age of Greece, Athenians had attained a type of collective freedom, Rex Warner writes, that was "not so much limited as reinforced by self-discipline and patriotism." When the Golden Age unraveled, and rampant individualism ascended, the Athenians' "chosen and disciplined freedom . . . passed through a process of indiscipline and self-seeking, to a lack of confidence, a failure of nerve . . ." — and ended in "disaster."

—

Jean Yarbrough writes that Thomas Jefferson constantly pondered this question: "What is the connection between the virtues relating to the independence and competency of the individual, and the more admirable moral obligations we owe to others?"

To Jefferson, the answer was that "moral excellence and civic virtue begin with the government of the self. Before we can fulfill our obligations to others we must first achieve independence and learn to exercise responsibility, moderation, patience and self-control." But I think that one of the ways we learn to govern ourselves is first to recognize our responsibility toward others, and realize that the greatest individual excellence can only be had when one's society strives for collective excellence.

The ideals Jefferson embraced for the newly created United States were remarkably similar to those investigated and espoused by Socrates, who examined them intensively for the very reason that they had for so long been held dear by almost all Athenians. And yet, in the historical blink of an eye, they were abandoned wholesale by his people.

Are these same patterns of decline repeating themselves in the United States and other nations today?

Thomas Jefferson, writes Jean Yarbrough, believed that excellent societies depend not on statesmen, "no matter how 'great and virtuous,' " but, in Jefferson's words, on " 'enlightened, peaceable and really free' people"—free in the "disciplined" sense that Rex Warner described. In such societies, excellence necessarily "flows from the bottom up."

Is that the case in today's open societies?

# FUTURE PROSPECTS FOR HUMAN EXCELLENCE

Though what André Gide wrote in *The Immoralist* was for a different context, the significance of his words are no less compelling: "What is man still capable of? . . . Is what man has said up to now all he is able to say? . . . Is repeating old things all that's left for him?"

Can we sink to new depths—or rise to new heights?

While small-mindedness seems to have won the day for now, does it have to stay this way, and can it stay this way, if human civilization is to thrive and become more excellent?

While human history seems to show that, as a species, we're frighteningly adept at perpetrating evil in the world, maybe we're still in the dark ages in terms of our ability to understand what human excellence is or can be. Maybe we can come up with very sophisticated and nuanced definitions of virtue, and yet still have but the vaguest notions of how best to put virtue into action on behalf of realizing lasting forms of human excellence.

The writer and social critic H. G. Wells, in his futuristic novel *The Time Machine*, believes that our ideas still are "vague and tentative, and our knowledge is very limited," though he speculates hopefully that perhaps "some day the whole world will be intelligent, educated, and cooperating . . ."

But traveling far into the future, the Time Traveler of Wells's novel found that civilization "had committed suicide. It had set itself steadfastly towards" a certain set of shared virtues—of "comfort and ease . . . with security and permanency as its watchword"—virtues that led to "languor and decay." In reaching a point of absolute comfort and ease, security and permanency, the Time Traveler discovered that civilization had reached a point of intellectual and moral and physical stasis, and then utter regression. "What," he asked, "unless biological science is a mass of errors, is the cause of human intelligence and vigor?

Hardship and freedom: . . . conditions that put a premium" upon such virtues as "the loyal alliance of capable men, upon self-restraint, patience, and decision."

According to the narrator, the Time Traveler of Wells's novel "thought but cheerlessly of the Advancement of Mankind, and saw in the growing pile of civilization only a foolish heaping that must inevitably fall back upon and destroy its makers in the end. But, he concludes, if that is so, it remains for us to live as though it were not so."

## EXCELLENCE AND AUTONOMY

While all indications may point to a downward spiral for civilization today, I think it behooves us all to act "as though it were not so." This in no way means we should bury our heads in the sand. On the contrary, more than ever we should strive to conduct ourselves in such a way that a tragic outcome is far from inevitable. This has to be done on a societal scale, and a global scale. But it begins with individuals.

Aristotle said famously that what separates man from all other species is our ability to reason. But more often than not, we've used this ability throughout human history to rationalize barbarous acts, to rationalize inhumanity. So I would add that humans are that species that is capable, on rare occasions, of using its ability to reason in excellently noble ways. Such autonomous individuals as José Vasconcelos and Thich Nhat Hanh, Martin Buber and Nishida Kitaro, Yi Yulgok and Sari Nusseibeh, Rigoberta Menchu and Simone de Beauvoir all are paradigms of individuals who employed their reasoning powers for the most excellent ends. They lived, and inspired countless others to live, as though a tragic outcome for humanity "were not so."

The ends you decide to commit to in life may be largely influenced and determined by the role models you choose. The aforementioned people are among mine. Not long before finishing this book, I was invited to hold a Socrates Café at a private school. One of the philosophy instructors there, who was not keen about my visit, and kept referring to my dialogues as a "show," asked me, "To whom do you think you're accountable?" I replied, "I think I'm accountable to myself, mostly, to letting my conscience be my guide. And my conscience dictates that I should feel accountable to all those who came before me and risked it all so that humanity had a chance to inch forward."

He did not find this answer agreeable. Eventually he said to me, "Don't you think it's dangerous what you're doing, giving young people the license to question everything?"

"Yes," I said, to his surprise. "Wonderfully dangerous. And I think it's even more dangerous—terribly so—if we don't give them license, along with the tools, to think for themselves. It seems to me that we adults have made a pretty good mess of things. Maybe young people, if imbued early on with a social conscience, can show us the way out of it."

—

Socrates' pursuit of the virtuous life was one based on accountability, and on faith in young people to accomplish over the long haul what he couldn't over the short term. Rather than preach and proselytize, he modeled an example of a way a human could live. Rather than saying "Follow me," he inspired the young people he encountered to create and chart their own course of excellence. Rather than looking at Socrates as a guru or guide, they saw him as an autonomous person who set an example of a radically alternative way of living and acting in the world, in which his acute social and intellectual conscience was his guide.

One of my favorite philosophizers, Bono of the Irish rock band U2, said in a magazine interview, "In the end, you've got to become the change you want to see in the world." Bono, who has a nonprofit group devoted to convincing wealthy nations to erase the Third World's crushing financial debt to them, so they can devote these resources to housing and education and health care, clearly was inspired by Mohandas Gandhi. The human-rights activist, who practiced nonviolent resistance and advocated religious tolerance, and was assassinated in India for siding with the poor and oppressed, had once said: "We must be the change in the world that we want."

Socrates never articulated this outlook in so many words. But as far as we know, he did articulate it by his deeds.

# ACKNOWLEDGMENTS

My cherished friend the late Alex Haley was fond of saying that if you see a turtle on a fence post, you know he had help getting up there. I have been blessed with a great deal of help from people I cherish in getting where I am. My wife, Cecilia, the most excellent human being I have ever known, is my guiding light in all endeavors. If not for her wisdom and insight and encouragement (in fact, insistence) that I continue to take sublime risks, I never would have come close to realizing so many of my higher aspirations. My association with Alane Mason, my editor at Norton, has been a wonderful boon. My mom, Margaret Ann P. Phillips, is one of the rare adults during my upbringing who keenly recognized that if you expect young people to live lives of conscience and integrity, then you have to serve as an abiding example. Twelve-year-old Veruch, a Tzotzil indigenous child in Chiapas, Mexico, who spends her days selling beautiful handmade goods in the plaza of San Cristobal, is a dear friend of mine and my wife; her profound ways of world-viewing and world-making have enriched our lives. My great friend and kindred spirit John Esterle has gone way out of his way, again and again, to see to it that I can continue moving in the direction in my dreams; I don't think it's possible to convey adequately how grateful I am to this exceptional human being. I'd also like to thank deeply these dear people: Kathy Glyer, director of Curriculum, Instruction, and Assessment at the New Mexico School for the Deaf, is one of the most innovative and dedicated educators I've ever had the privilege to know; Shelley Gabriel, an amazing human being; Sheldon Kelly, writer extraordinaire, who paved the way for my first big break as a writer; Ron Stern, superintendent of the New Mexico School for the Deaf; Jake Baer, best of freinds; José Pedro Espada; Anthony Johnston; Elaine Rioux; Steve Marchetti; writer Clay Morgan; Pat, Tom, and Sean McGee; Marlene Carter; Alessandra Bastagli; Virginie Vandaele; Bruno, Merel, and Myrte Tange; Larry Parker; Sam Sadler, vice president of Student Affairs at the College of William and Mary; Lauren Burger; Bill Hayes, my buddy from Toms River; Andrew Burton; Clarisa Toledo; Bill Schulz; Lowry Bowman, the incomparable essayist and newspaperman; Mark Haag; Steve and Pam Hornsby; Nick and Norma DeMatt; Curtis Boschert; Pat Davidson; Evan Sinclair; Scott McCord; Laura Norin; Mizgon Zahir; Rebecca Nassif; Patti Roumel; Olga Vidalis; George Tsironis; Hisa and Takako Hara; Yoko Nishiyama; Mariola Lopez Albertos; Jin-Whan Park; Juani Sanchez Cerda; Min-Kyu Park; Joane Deadman; Joong-Seo Park; Julia Fournier; Evora Jordan; Dora Deadmore; Mary Canonico; Aida Montiel-Jaramillo; Dr. Carla Narrett, dean of the Graduate School at Montclair State University; Dennis Dienst; Nicole Geiger; Bill Schulz; Bill Hayes, professor of Biology at Delta State University; Dr. Shirley Strum Kenny, president of the State University of New York at Stony Brook; Josie Hays; Auntie Bubbles Beloff; Omar Jamal; Nick Szczesniak; Jackie Chee; Elaina Vann; Armando and Lucrecia Chapa; Bob Davison; Maria Murakami; Kazu Mahoroba; Len Wheeler; Dan Wolf; Andrew Stuart; Carol McGorry; Mary Weeks; Jim McStay; Felicia Eth; Rebecca Nassif; the staff at the *Bridgton News*, where I began my writing life many moons ago; Alex Phillips, my dad; Mike Phillips, my brother; Robert Coles, James Agee Professor of Social Ethics and professor of psychiatry and medical humanities at Harvard University; James Phillips, my late uncle who sparked my interest in my Greek heritage; Angelo Cali; Leigh Haber; and as always, my cherished friend; Mat Lipman, founder of the Institute for the Advancement of Philosophy for Children, who has lived a life of unsurpassed excellence.

I'd also like to thank the many volunteer coordinators and facilitators of Socrates Café and other philosophical dialogue groups around the globe who share my passion for a certain type of philosophical inquiry. And I want to thank the thousands of people from across the globe with whom I have engaged in philosophical dialogue; their insights have nudged me further forward on the road to becoming a better person.

# FURTHER READING

In addition to the many books and authors I mention throughout the text of *Six Questions of Socrates*, here are some other works that may be of interest to anyone who wants to learn more about some excellent philosophical thinkers, who in some instances also were activists of social and intellectual conscience, from across the ages around the world: Nishida Kitaro's *An Inquiry into the Good* (New Haven: Yale University Press, 1992) is widely considered his landmark work, in which the Japanese philosopher elucidates his notion of "pure experience" as the foundation for morality, metaphysics, and reality itself. José Vasconcelos' *Mexican Ulysses: An Autobiography* (Bloomington: Indiana University Press, 1963) places the singular social and political philosophy of one of Mexico's most revered thinkers within the context of the turbulent times in which he lived. Antonio Caso, in *El Concepto de la Historia Universal y La Filosofía de Los Valores* (Mexico City: Ediciones Botas, 1933), covers considerable philosophical terrain, from axiology to phenomenology to logic to the impact of national ideology on Mexican morals, and his *La Persona Humana y El Estado Totalitario* (Mexico City: Ediciones de la Universidad Nacional Autónoma, 1941) is a provocative work that examines how and whether we can build a world in which each person lives with greater dignity, via the inculcation of shared, human-elevating values, and counter the trend toward growing depersonalization. Rigoberta Menchú's *I, Rigoberta Menchú: An Indian Woman in Guatemala* (New York: Verso Books, 1987) is a gripping account not just of one indigenous person's tribulations and ability to surmount nearly impossible obstacles to become one of the world's most prominent human rights activists, but also is a celebration of a rich indigenous culture and heritage that has survived and endured despite endemic poverty and systematic oppression; Menchú's *Crossing Borders: An Autobiography* (New York: Verso Books, 1998) is a less compelling work, but develops in more depth her political outlook. Thich Nhat Hanh's *Our*

*Appointment with Life: The Buddha's Teaching on Living in the Present* (Berkeley: Parallax Press, 1990) offers a uniquely illuminating explication of one of the earliest teachings of the Buddha, as set forth in the Sutra "Knowing the Better Way to Live Alone"; his *Peace Is Every Step: The Path of Mindfulness in Everyday Life* (New York: Bantam Books, 1992) explores how to convert potentially negative or destructive predicaments into positive, life-affirming experiences. Nelson Mandela's *Long Walk to Freedom* (London: Abacus, 1995) is a quintessential story of the triumph of the human spirit over all attempts to subjugate and dehumanize, and also elaborates Mandela's paradigmatic moral and political philosophies. Kim Dae Jung's *A New Beginning* (Los Angeles: Center for Multiethnic and Transnational Studies, 1996) is a somewhat scholarly account of the former president of Korea's views on how and why democracy can be reconciled with traditional Asian values. In *Israelis and the Jewish Tradition* (New Haven: Yale University Press, 2000), philosopher David Hartman unflinchingly addresses many of the most pressing and divisive issues among Israelis, and offers provocative prescriptive suggestions for how to build a more inclusive modern society without rejecting Jewish tradition. Walter Kaufmann's *Man's Lot: A Trilogy* (New York: Reader's Digest Press, 1978) is a beautifully written, lamentably unheralded, and movingly personal work, and is one of the few books from a modern Western philosopher that examines and embraces an array of existential philosophies from across the globe, with a particular focus on the philosophical traditions of the developing world that have been neglected by the West. *In the Language of Kings: An Anthology of Mesoamerican Literature: Pre-Columbian to the Present* (New York: W. W. Norton, 2001), Miguel León-Portilla and Earl and Sylvia S. Shorris, editors, is a marvel of a collection of literature that is an invaluable resource to anyone interested in the breadth and depth of thought of Mesoamerica's indigenous peoples. Louis Althusser's

*Lenin and Philosophy and Other Essays* (Monthly Review Press, 2001) is considered by many to be a seminal work that offers a defense of Marxist thought that at the same time serves to elaborate Althusser's rather singular Marxist political philosophy. Roger Arnaldez's *Averroes: A Rationalist in Islam* (Notre Dame: University of Notre Dame Press, 2001) is a fine account of the renowned medieval philosopher that details how Averroes reconciled his iconoclastic rationalist philosophical thinking with his Islamic faith. I also recommend: Eli Wiesel, *All Rivers Run to the Sea* (New York: Knopf, 1995); Voltaire, *The Portable Voltaire*, edited by Ben Ray Redman (New York: The Viking Press, 1949); Sidney Hook, *The Hero in History: A Study in Limitation and Possibility* (London: Secker & Warburg, 1945); Gary MacEoin, *The People's Church: Bishop Samuel Ruiz and Why He Matters* (New York: Crossroad, 1996); John Sugden, *Tecumseh: A Life* (New York, St. Martin's Press, 1998); *Teachings from the American Earth: Indian Religion and Philosophy*, edited by Dennis and Barbara Tedlock (New York: Liveright, 1975); Paul Ricoeur, *Political and Social Essays*, edited by David Stewart and Joseph Bien (Athens, Ohio: Ohio University Press, 1976); Gregory Vlastos, *Studies in Greek Philosophy*, in two volumes (Princeton: Princeton University Press, 1995); Laszlo Versenyi, *Man's Measure: A Study of the Greek Image of Man from Homer to Sophocles* (Albany: State University Press of New York, 1974); Octavio Paz, *The Labyrinth of Solitude: Life and Thought in Mexico* (London: Allen Lane, 1967); *Itinerary: An Intellectual Journey* (New York: Harcourt, 2000); and Elena Poniatowska, *Massacre in Mexico* (New York: Viking Press, 1975).

# INDEX